URBAN SHELTER
AND
SERVICES

URBAN SHELTER AND SERVICES

Public Policies and Management Approaches

G. SHABBIR CHEEMA

New York
Westport, Connecticut
London

Library of Congress Cataloging-in-Publication Data

Cheema, G. Shabbir.
  Urban shelter and services.

  Bibliography: p.
  1. Poor—Housing—Government policy—Developing
countries. I. Title.
HD7287.96.D44C47   1987   363.5'8   87–6982
ISBN 0–275–92653–2 (alk. paper)

Library of Congress Catalog Card Number: 87–6982
ISBN: 0–275–92653–2

First published in 1987

Praeger Publishers, One Madison Avenue, New York, NY 10010
A division of Greenwood Press, Inc.

Printed in the United States of America

The paper used in this book complies with the
Permanent Paper Standard issued by the National
Information Standards Organization (Z39.48–1984).

10 9 8 7 6 5 4 3 2 1

To
Sherry, Yasmeen and Zacky

CONTENTS

Preface   ix

1 Urban Shelter and Services   1

2 The Urban Poor   15

3 Evolution of Policies and Programs   33

4 Capabilities of Implementing Agencies   57

5 Community Participation   79

6 Financing, Cost Recovery, and Affordability   109

7 Land for the Urban Poor   133

8 Policy and Program Impacts   157

9 Factors Influencing Implementation   175

10 Conclusions and Implications for Action   193

Bibliography   203

Index   213

About the Author   221

PREFACE

During the past three decades, governments in the developing countries of Asia, Africa, and Latin America have been attempting to formulate and implement several types of policies and programs aimed at providing shelter and basic services to the urban poor. In the process of implementing these policies, programs, and projects, however, a number of critical policy issues have emerged. These include access to land for shelter, mobilization of resources, affordability and cost recovery of the government-initiated programs, and the role of the informal service sector. Other issues are community participation in settlement-upgrading programs, the integration of the social and infrastructural improvements in slums and squatter settlements, and the capability of the implementing agencies to work effectively with poor urban communities. This study attempts to examine these policy issues, using as a base, experiences developing countries have had in planning and implementing projects to improve the living environment in poor urban settlements.

The research design for this study was prepared in 1979 while I was teaching courses on urban development policy and administration at the University of Science in Malaysia. Three factors encouraged me to undertake this work. These were: the paucity of comparative urban studies based on the situation in developing countries; the increasing emphasis of development planners and practitioners on the need for urban policy analysis to identify alternative mechanisms to provide shelter and basic urban services in poor urban settlements; and lack of an adequate focus in most studies on administrative and institutional dimensions of low-income housing and basic urban services.

I am grateful to Dennis A. Rondinelli, Clarence Shubert, John D. Montgomery, and Mohammad A. Nawawi for their valuable suggestions during various stages in the evolution of this book. I have also greatly benefited from my discussions with Ved Prakash, Serj Domicelj, In-Joung Whang, Luciano Minerbi, Viqar Ahmed, Shafaruddin Hashim, and Paulina Makinwa-Adebusoye. The interpretation of data presented and the views expressed in the book, however, are entirely mine.

My family, to whom the book is dedicated, has been constantly encouraging me to write. I am grateful for their patience and support.

1

URBAN SHELTER AND SERVICES

During the past three decades, rapid growth in the urban populations of Asia, Africa, and Latin America has occurred as a result of large-scale rural-to-urban migration and natural urban population growth. Rapid urbanization has had notable consequences: First, there has been an alarming increase in the number of urban poor, most of whom reside in slums and squatter settlements and lack adequate education or skills and, thus, are forced to work for low wages to meet even part of their basic needs; second, the provision of urban shelter and services has not kept pace with increasing demand. There are acute shortages in low-income housing, transport facilities, water supplies, and public health and sanitation services. To varying degrees, governments have played an important role in the attempts to provide basic shelter and services but, because of financial, institutional, and political constraints, have not been able to meet the deficiencies.

The residents of slums and squatter settlements have been affected most negatively by urban service deficiencies. The quality and coverage of urban services tend to be most inadequate in the poorest neighborhoods. Most slums and squatter settlements lack such basic urban services as water, sewerage, roads, garbage disposal, and health services. Even where adequate services and facilities are available, squatters and slum dwellers may not have adequate access to them. Because of their low incomes, the urban poor cannot afford to pay for basic services. They may not qualify because they usually do not have legal tenancy to the land they occupy. They have very little influence because they are usually not effectively organized and are only indirectly, if at all, involved in the identification of community priorities, the formulation of local projects, and the implementation of development activities.

The increasing number of squatters and slum dwellers in cities of the developing world indicates the growing incidence of urban poverty and the magnitude of the difficulty of providing shelter and urban basic services in low-income settlements. The situation is likely to become even more serious in the future, for World Bank Studies show that by the end of the 1990s more than half of the absolute poor will be concentrated in urban areas.[1]

Since the 1960s governments in the developing world have tried several types of policies, programs, and projects aimed at improving low-income settlements. The scope and the focus of these have varied among the countries and have even changed within the same country. Typically, the first response of most governments is to demolish and clear squatter settlements. This stage is generally followed by a gradual recognition of the need to improve social and economic conditions in slums and squatter settlements. This recognition often leads to the initiation of urban projects oriented toward poverty alleviation and designed to provide basic urban services and an infrastructure.

POLICY ISSUES

During the process of formulating and implementing policies and programs aimed at providing shelter and basic urban services for the poor, a number of issues emerge. What actions government elects to take at the national, the regional, and the local levels regarding these issues often determine the success or failure of attempts to upgrade low-income settlements and to provide sites and services for self-help housing. The relative significance of any of these issues may vary for each country, depending upon its socioeconomic and political structures and the circumstances of each poor urban settlement. It may be helpful to look at some of the significant issues that seem to be crucial in these situations and that, therefore, require appropriate policy responses from governments.

First, in order to encourage meaningful self-help, the urban poor need to be provided with adequate access to land. Such access would involve the granting of legally recognized land occupation and/or tenure to the residents of squatter settlements or the acquiring of a title to the land for sites-and-services schemes. With increased security, the risk to these residents in low-income settlements is greatly reduced, and they become more likely to invest their own resources in improving their housing and community facilities. The acquisition of land should be a necessary first step toward upgrading slums and providing sites and services. Not surprisingly, however, the land issue in developing countries is highly complex. Government intervention in the urban land market is constrained by the vested interests of powerful groups in the society—the hereditary landowners, real estate speculators, private developers, the local politicians and governmental officials—who by blood or financial ties are related to each other; by a lack of cooperation and coordination among the concerned implementing agencies; and by fear on the part of the government agencies that any assistance to the poor might only legitimatize and encourage more squatting. Several pertinent questions could be raised on this issue: What is the legal status of the land and of the current occupation and tenure in these low-income settlements? What public intervention efforts have been attempted to increase the access of the urban poor to land for shelter? What alternative mechanisms are available to increase the supply of land for the urban poor?

Second, any new provision of shelter and services draws from already strained financial coffers and requires the mobilization of additional resources. The allocation of public funds for improvement in low-income settlements is necessary because the poor lack (by definition) the resources to meet their own service needs. However, governments have their own financial constraints, and in most cases they cannot adequately provide basic services to the ever-increasing number of slum dwellers or squatters. It seems that an effective partnership is needed to share the cost of services between government and the community concerned. Some of the questions with regard to resource mobilization are: How can family savings and resources by mobilized for housing improvements and the provision of community facilities? What mechanisms exist to increase the access of poor urban communities to credit for shelter by linking them with financial institutions in the country?

Third, affordability and cost recovery are critical, interrelated issues. The cost of providing shelter and services far exceeds the capacity of the poor to pay. This may be partly attributable to rigid construction standards and building codes or to the involvement of private developers motivated by profit. It is obvious that if affordability levels are too high, the urban poor will not have access to shelter; yet some minimum health and safety standards have to be maintained. Also, while the recovery of costs is always desirable, it is extremely difficult to accomplish in actual practice. Greater subsidies, on the other hand, would limit the ability of governments to replicate programs and projects. Several questions could be raised concerning affordability and cost recovery. Should the provision of basic urban services especially to the poor be considered a social welfare burden, or should the government investment be fully or partly recovered? What are appropriate mechanisms for cost recovery? What has been the cost-recovery record of past upgrading projects? To what extent have the existing sites-and-services projects or squatter improvement programs reached the poor?

Fourth, the informal service sector may need to be strengthened and encouraged as a way of creating more employment opportunities within the low-income settlements and of providing some of the needed services at lower costs. The government could provide support to the informal sector in several ways. Credit facilities and technical assistance could be provided to small-scale enterprises in slums or squatter settlements. Cooperatives could be established among the workers and family enterprises involved in informal sector activities to facilitate their access to raw material and to market their products. Some of the questions that could be raised here are: What services can be provided more effectively by the informal service sector? What has been the impact of the government's low-income housing policies on the informal service sector?

Fifth, some policy actions or changes may be needed to eliminate any political bias or bureaucratic constraints that are limiting the access of the urban poor to government-sponsored services and facilities and to create appropriate governmental or nongovernmental structures capable of responding effectively to needs and priorities of the urban poor. The delivery systems of municipal governments and semiautonomous development authorities are typically characterized by a lack of adequate responsiveness in the formulation and implementation of development projects. The urban poor usually are not effectively organized, and, therefore, they are unable to assert enough collective pressure upon the government functionaries who are responsible for implementing poverty-oriented urban projects. Several interrelated questions concerning appropriate structures and procedures for increasing the access of the urban poor to services need to be examined: What types of organizational skills are needed by urban planners, engineers, or other related professionals to enable them to work more effectively with residents of slums and squatter settlements? What structures and mechanisms are most effective in facilitating interagency coordination? How should responsibilities between the various levels of administration be divided?

Sixth, physical and infrastructural improvements in slums and squatter settlements need to be integrated with government programs for the provision of social services. Such an integrated approach would seem to facilitate the identification of the community with the government-initiated program, the mobilization of community resources, and the compatibility of actions by different government agencies. The implementation of such an integrated approach on a large scale requires simultaneously increasing the government funds for the two classes of program as well as providing the effective mechanisms of interagency coordination.

Finally, community participation is one of the most important issues in the formulation and implementation of urban shelter policies. In the literature, several arguments have been presented in favor of community participation in the process of providing urban shelter and services.[2] The implementation of participatory urban programs, however, is often discouraged by factors such as factionalism in the community, absence of innovative leadership, inegalitarian power structure, or lack of effective organizations. Slum or squatter community participation might also be constrained by the reluctance of national governments to tolerate greater politicization and conflict at the grass roots; by the paternalistic attitude of bureaucracy; or by the inability of government officials to organize and motivate these communities for such participation. In this regard several questions suggest themselves as being pertinent: How can a viable community organization be established? What conditions are conducive to community participation? In what ways can communities be involved in the acquisition of land, selection of project beneficiaries, mobilization of community resources, maintenance of urban services and facilities, or other tasks involved in upgrading settlements of the urban poor?

INSTITUTIONAL ARRANGEMENTS AND MANAGEMENT APPROACHES

Governments in developing countries have utilized several institutional arrangements to upgrade the settlements of the urban poor. Local urban governments are usually the providers of most civic amenities, and many of the functions related to social welfare and infrastructural development will typically be administered by central government ministries or departments. With the rapid growth of large cities, semiautonomous public enterprises have assumed an important role in providing such specific services as water, transport, and housing. In recent years, policymakers have shown an increasing concern for planning and management at the metropolitan level, and thus, several organizational forms of metropolitan management have emerged.[3]

The increase in the demand for urban shelter and services and the attempts to solve the related problems of urban poverty, unemployment, and environmental degradation have led to the proliferation of government, semigovernment, and voluntary organizations in urban areas. As the tasks of urban development management became wider in scope and more technically complex, new specialized agencies were created to deal with such tasks. Some of the management problems resulting from the proliferation of government agencies are those dealing with interorganizational relationships and linkages; those concerning capabilities and resources of implementing agencies; and those related to beneficiary organization and participation.[4]

Management approaches utilized in urban areas of the developing world to provide sites for self-help housing, improve squatter settlements, and upgrade slums include:

1. approaches that seek to upgrade low-income settlements through the community's own initiative and self-reliance without any direct assistance from outside governmental and nongovernmental agencies;

2. approaches that are aimed at promoting community upgrading activities through

financial and technical assistance from government agencies and/or voluntary organizations;

3. approaches focused on planning and managing upgrading schemes by government and/or nongovernmental agencies with the support and participation of the beneficiary community;

4. approaches that assign the tasks of upgrading to a single government agency that is authorized to plan, coordinate, implement, and monitor poverty-alleviating projects in low-income settlements;

5. approaches that are aimed at experimenting with and perfecting procedure through accumulated experience in pilot projects and then upgrading various areas through systemic replication; and

6. approaches that use governmental agencies to regulate, control, and monitor the growth of settlements of the urban poor with a view to discouraging growth of poverty enclaves in the future.

Effective implementation of upgrading projects through self-help or other low-income housing policies requires reforming some of the existing structures and processes through which poor urban communities' priorities are identified, project choices concerning location of services and beneficiaries are made, development activities are carried out, and community resources are mobilized. Chapters 4 and 5 examine the appropriateness of structures for carrying out policies and projects.

ANALYZING THE IMPLEMENTATION OF URBAN SHELTER POLICIES

The Study of Policy Implementation

Policy provides guidance for action. Public policies are usually presented through government statements on specific issues and are incorporated in public documents such as long- and medium-term development plans or annual budgets. The scope of public policies can range from broad statements of intended objectives and guiding principles to more specific schemes of achieving them. Real and meaningful public policies are not what a government intends to do but what it actually does. In this volume, therefore, public policy is defined as a set of government actions concerning an issue.

A program or a project is a collection of related activities designed to harmonize and integrate actions by government agencies and other organizations to achieve policy objectives. A project is, thus, a component of a policy, and a government's policies concerning urban shelter and services would be reflected in its slum-improvement projects, sites-and-services schemes, or other specific projects or activities for the urban poor. Policy statements by governments in developing countries are usually presented in an idealized form without adequate consideration of financial limitiations.

Projects, on the other hand, are the revelation of what a government is actually doing to achieve its real policy objectives. Therefore, "the study of the process of policy implementation almost necessarily involves investigation and analysis of concrete action programmes that have been designed as a means of achieving broader policy goals."[5] The analysis of such projects should thus be an effective way to understand the content, context, execution, and the impact of the government's shelter policies.

Experience shows that in the developing world, projects are the main instrument for achieving policy goals. According to Dennis Rondinelli, one of the main reasons is that "as identifiable, bounded and organized sets of activities focused on specific goals and purposes that must be completed within a given period of time and budget, projects are one of the most effective ways of disaggregating broader development plans and policies."[6] National governments, donor agencies, and international organizations are, therefore, increasingly channeling development funds through specific projects to local areas. Indeed, development projects are indicative of government policies in practice.

Implementation has been defined as a "process of interaction between the setting of goals and actions geared to achieving them."[7] The literature on implementation identifies two competing views of the process: the "compliance" approach and the political approach.[8] The first assumes that implementation is a technical and routine process of carrying out predetermined plans and projects. The second views implementation as an integral part of the policy and project planning process in which projects are refined, reformulated or even abandoned in the process of implementing them.

The focus of studies on policy administration has shifted progressively away from the compliance approach. Pressman and Wildavsky argued in 1973 that implementation should be considered independent of the design of policy.[9] Since then studies have placed an increasing emphasis on the implementers as the critical actors in the policy process.[10]

The study of the process of policy implementation is crucial for our understanding of socioeconomic and political change in developing countries in which people's participation and representation of interests, to a large extent, take place in the process of implementing public policies.[11] Political institutions (such as political parties or interest groups) tend to be weak in the developing world and are, thus, unable to represent the collective views and aspirations of various groups in the process of policy formulation. In some countries, highly centralized planning and technocratic approaches also limit the participation of nongovernmental groups in formulating policies. As a result, when government policies are to be carried out, tensions and conflicts are created because these affect groups with different interests that have not been taken into account and because the policy design is in some cases vague. At this stage, concerned individuals and groups make demands, using their formal and informal channels of communication with administrators and policymakers. The implementation process may, thus, be "the major arena in which individuals and groups are able to pursue conflicting interests and compete for access to scarce resources."[12]

FACTORS INFLUENCING IMPLEMENTATION

The factors that influence policy and project implementation have not been given adequate attention in developing countries. It is often assumed that once policies are formulated and projects are planned, they will be implemented by subordinate administrators and that the intended results will be achieved in a nonpolitical and technically competent way. However, experiences with urban policies and projects discussed in this book indicate that implementation is a dynamic and somewhat unpredictable process of political interaction. Several factors determine the extent to which policies and projects are implemented in the manner they were intended and the degree to which they achieve their formally stated goals.

Figure 1.1 portrays the relationship between five sets of factors that seem to influence the implementation of urban development policies designed to provide shelter and services to the poor. Discussed in greater details in the chapters that follow, they are: environmental aspects, government policies for urban development, interorganizational relationships, beneficiary organization and participation, and capabilities and resources of implementing agencies.

Interorganizational Relationships

Successful implementation of policies and programs for the urban poor depends upon the complementarity of actions taken by local, regional, and national agencies. A program might be formulated, supervised, and evaluated by a central agency; it might be funded and monitored by a subnational/ state government agency; and it may actually be implemented by an agency at the municipal or metropolitan level. Therefore, successfully linking the implementing agencies with others to form coordinated, supportive structures is a prerequisite to achieving common objectives.

The effectiveness of interorganizational relationships in implementing urban policies and projects seems to depend on (1) the clarity and consistency of objectives; (2) the appropriate allocation of functions among agencies; (3) the standardization of procedures for planning, budgeting, and implementation; (4) the accuracy, quality, and consistency of interorganizational communication; and (5) the delineation of procedures for monitoring and evaluation.

Figure 1.1
Implementing Urban Shelter Policies: A Framework of Analysis

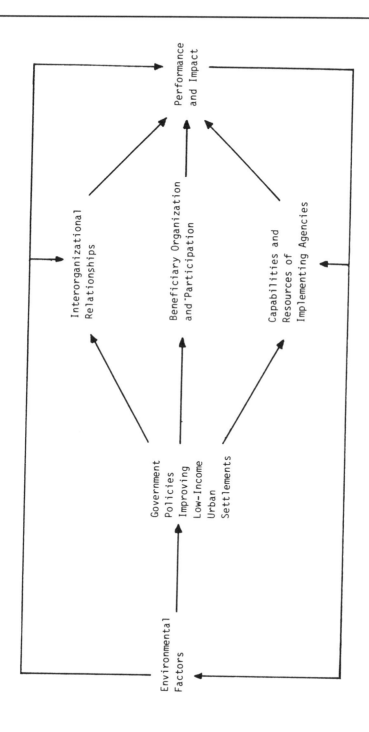

Capabilities and Resources of Implementing Agencies

The technical and managerial capabilities of implementing agencies are significant factors in determining program performance. Rapid urbanization has been accompanied by the need for more technical expertise and skilled manpower. Public sector involvement in activities such as transportation and housing has increased the demand for such professionally qualified personnel as engineers and planners on the planning staff. In several cities, the availability of professionals has not kept pace with expansion in the activities of their government agencies. Furthermore, governmental personnel policies and practices often encourage the more qualified persons to go into positions in national or provincial governments, leaving municipalities unable to attract the required professionals.

The successful implementation of policies and programs of urban development also depends upon the internal communication flows among the implementing agencies, the acceptance and commitment of their staff members to the program objectives, and innovative leadership.

The extent to which the implementing agencies receive sufficient financial administrative and technical support also determines the outcome of policies and projects. The control by agencies over their respectively allocated funds, the adequacy of these budgetary allocations to assigned tasks, and the timely availability of funds are crucial for achieving project objectives.

Beneficiary Organization and Participation

The proliferation of development authorities and government agencies in cities and the establishment of centrally controlled metropolitan entities have weakened the role of urban local governments in providing services. There are several instances in which municipal governments, relegated to minor development roles, have lost their function as meaningful mechanisms for popular participation in local decision-making processes. Nongovernmental, voluntary organizations have also remained weak. Citizen participation in large cities has thus been adversely affected, and the trend is toward a greater degree of control by professional administrators in the managing of urban projects. This may be counterproductive because management requirements for programs for the urban poor are not necessarily the same as those for conventional urban development projects. Squatter upgrading programs, for example, require active community participation, self-help, and partnership between beneficaries and program implementers.[13]

The effective implementation of shelter projects seems to be significantly influenced by community participation in the identification of local needs, the choices of the locations of services or the beneficiaries, the selection of community leaders, the mobilization of community resources, the execution of activities, control over the allocation of project resources, and periodic monitoring and evaluation.

Environmental Factors

Urban policies and projects are formulated and implemented within a complex socioeconomic and political environment that shapes not only the substance of these policies and projects but also the patterns of interorganizational relationships and the characteristics of implementing agencies, and also determines the amounts and types of resources made available for carrying them out. Therefore, an understanding of the social, economic, and political setting of the problem to be addressed is vital for understanding the constraints implementing organizations suffer from, and the opportunities they have in their attempts to translate policies and projects into actions. A nation's political structure, the characteristics of the local power structure in its urban areas, and the social and economic characteristics of groups within urban communities as well as the relative involvement of each of these in procedures for project planning influence the process of implementation of projects designed to provide services to the urban poor.

Performance and Impact

The performance and impact of urban shelter policies and projects for the poor can be indicated by the achievement of the project's stated goals; the impact of the project on specific groups within the society; the effect on the adequacy of service coverage for the poor and for the use of the private and informal sector; and the effects on productivity, income, improvements to dwelling units, and access to government facilities.

SCOPE AND METHODOLOGY

The central concern of this book is to identify policies and programs that represent responses of governments in the developing world to the challenge of providing adequate shelter and services for the urban poor. To this end we shall examine the performance and impact of past policies and projects, analyze factors that have facilitated or impeded policy implementation, and identify alternative approaches and mechanisms for upgrading low-income urban settlements and increasing the access of the urban poor to shelter and basic services.

One of the main sources of the data in the book is a collection of eighteen country papers, ten case studies of upgrading and sites-and-services projects, and nine concept papers on specific themes. These studies were sponsored by the United Nations Centre for Regional Development (UNCRD) as a part of its cross-national research project on managing urban development, which was coordinated by the author. The studies were undertaken by scholars in developing as well as developed countries and were based on a research format and conceptual framework prepared by the author. The duration of the research project was a two-year period beginning in June 1983. As the project coordinator, the author visited the case study locations and had intensive discussions with the concerned development practitioners and case study writers. These studies have been individually cited throughout this book wherever pertinent data of any of them is used to substantiate the arguments. The views expressed and the interpretation of data from the studies are the author's own and not necessarily those of UNCRD.

To provide a broader empirical base for the statements made in the book, reference is made to some of the relevant evaluation studies prepared under the auspices of the World Bank, the United Nations Children's Fund (UN-ICEF), International Development Research Centre (IDRC), United Nations Centre for Human Settlements (UNCHS), the Economic Commission for Asia and the Pacific (ESCAP), and other international institutions. Also consulted were other published materials on settlement upgrading, sites-and-services schemes, and basic housing.

Information and insights from project-level case studies discussed in the book are supplemented by macrolevel studies of shelter policies, concept papers on specific themes and issues, and field visits by the author to eight developing countries where the case studies were undertaken.

The case study method was considered to be more appropriate than a purely statistical and quantitative approach for the purposes of this study. In-depth case studies bring out significant events in the evolution and implementation of policies and projects and facilitate our understanding of the complexities of managing equity-oriented programs. Both successful and unsuccessful shelter projects were chosen for undertaking case studies. A basic assumption of the UNCRD sponsored cross-national project was that the most effective way of discussing the process of policy implementation is by analyzing both successful and unsuccessful cases. Focusing on only one type might lead to a distorted view of reality, and fashioning future learning from failures in providing shelter and services is as important as concentrating on the successes. Furthermore, almost any undertaking has elements of both success and failure, and it is important to find out why some parts of a project's objectives were achieved while others were not.

Chapter 2 examines the incidence of urban poverty, the magnitude of deficiencies in urban services, the typologies of slums and squatter settlements, and the constraints on the access of the poor to urban shelter and services in the developing world. Chapter 3 discusses the evolution of public policies toward poor urban settlements and the main objectives of ten projects that were selected for case studies.

In Chapters 4 to 7, government responses to specific issues are described, and the processes of implementing government-initiated activities are analyzed. The issues discussed are the capabilities of implementing agencies, community participation in settlement upgrading, resource mobilization, cost recovery and replicability, the role of the informal sevice sector, and the access of the poor to land for shelter.

Chapter 8 examines the impact of urban shelter policies and programs. In Chapter 9, critical factors that influence policy implementation and determined policy and program outcomes are examined. Finally, in the last chapter, the main conclusions of the study are presented, directions for improving the implementation of policies and programs are outlined, and alternative actions to increase the access of the poor to shelter and services are suggested.

NOTES

1. World Bank, *World Development Report 1980* (Washington, D.C.: World Bank, 1980).

2. Among others, see Alastair T. White, "Why Community Participation: A Discussion of Arguments," in *Assignment Children 59/60* (Geneva: UNICEF, 1982), pp. 18–19; Caroline Moser, "Evaluating Community Participation Projects" (London: Development Planning Unit Working paper No. 14, 1983).

3. For a comparative overview of these forms, among others, see V. Ramachandran, "Institutional Structure and Capabilities of Local Authorities in Selected Metropolitan Areas in the ESCAP Region" (Report presented at the Regional Congress of Local Authorities for Development of Human Settlements in Asia and the Pacific, Yokohama, 9–16 June 1982); Harvey S. Perloff, "Institution-Building and Finance of Metropolitan Development," and D. L. de Mello, "Metropolitan Institution-Building in the Third World Countries," in H. Sazanami, ed., *Metropolitan Planning and Management* (Tokyo: Japan Society for the Promotion of Science, 1982), pp. 257–273 and pp. 277–98, respectively, and United Nations, *Administrative Aspects of Urbanization* (New York: United Nations, 1970).

4. For a general discussion of this management problem, see Jennifer R. Thornley and J. Brian McLoughlin, *Aspects of Urban Management* (Paris: Organization for Economic Cooperation and Development, 1974); Carlos P. Ramos, "Financial Issues of Metropolitan Planning and Management in the Third World Countries," In Sazanami, *Metropolitan Planning*, pp. 333–359; United Nations, *Administrative Aspects*; Richard Bird, *Intergrovernmental Fiscal Relations in Developing Countries* (Washington, D.C.: World Bank Staff Paper No. 304, October 1978); V. Ramachandran, "Institutional Structure"; and Ved Prakash, "Financing Urban Services in Developing Countries" (Nagoya: UNCRD Working Papers No. 82–06, 1982).

5. Merilee S. Grindle, "Policy Context and Content in Implementation," in Grindle, ed., *Politics and Policy Implementation in the Third World* (Princeton, N.J.: Princeton University Press, 1980), p. 6.

6. Dennis A Rondinelli, "Projects as Instruments for Development Administration: A Qualified Defence and Suggestions for Improvement," *Public Administration and Development* 3:4 (1983), 310.

7. Jeffrey L. Pressman and Aaron Wildavsky, *Implementation* (Berkeley: University of California Press, 1973), p. 8.

8. For a review of the literature, see Marcus D. Ingle, "Implementing Development Programs: A State of the Art Review" (Washington, D.C.: U.S. Agency for International Development, 1979, mimeo).

9. Pressman and Wildavsky, *Implementation*, p. 143.

10. Among these studies are: Donald S. Van Meter and Carl E. Van Horn, "The Policy Implementation Process: A Conceptual Framework," *Administration and Society* 6:4 (February 1975); Thomas B. Smith, "The Policy Implementation Process," *Policy Sciences* 4 (1973); Robert T. Nakamura and Frank Smallwood, *The Politics of Policy Implementation* (New York: St. Martin's Press, 1980); Milbrey McLaughlin, "Implementation as a Mutual Adaptation," in Walter Williams and Richard Elmore, eds., *Social Program Implementation* (New York: Academic Press, 1976); John D. Montgomery, Harold D. Lasswell, and Joel S. Migdal, eds., *Patterns of Policy: Comparative and Longitudinal Studies of Population Events* (New Brunswick, N.J.: Transaction Books, 1979); Peter T. Knight, ed., *Implementing Programmes of Human Development* (Washington, D.C.: World Bank Staff Working Paper No. 403, July 1980); Daniel A. Mazmanian and Paul A. Sabatier, eds., *Effective Policy Implementation* (Lexington, MA: Lexington Books, 1981); Grindle, *Politics and Policy*; and G. Shabbir Cheema and Dennis A Rondinelli, eds., *Decentralization and Development: Policy Implementation in Developing Countries* (Beverly Hills, CA: Sage, 1983).

11. Studies of administration in the developing world have highlighted this issue. Among others, see Fred W. Riggs, *Administration in Developing Countries: The Theory of Prismatic Society* (Boston: Houghton Mifflin, 1964), p. 271; M. Weiner, *The Politics of Scarcity* (Chicago: University of Chicago Press, 1962), p. 217; and J. Abueva, "Administrative Culture and Behavior and Middle Civil Servants in the Philippines," in Edward W. Weidner, ed., *Development Administration in Asia* (Durham, NC: Duke University Press, 1970).

12. Grindle, *Politics and Policy*, p. 19.

13. David Pasteur, *The Management of Squatter Upgrading* (Westmead, England: Saxon House, 1979), pp. 135–57.

2

THE URBAN POOR

The definition of *urban* varies from one country to another, reflecting differences in their socioeconomic structures and historical experiences.[1] In
Brazil, for instance, all administrative centers, regardless of their size, are
counted as urban. In India, an urban settlement is defined as a community
that has more than five thousand people and a population density of more
than one thousand persons per square kilometer, and more than 75 percent
of the population engaged in nonagricultural occupations. In the Philippines,
urban settlements are defined as those that are chartered cities or municipalities and have population densities above one thousand persons per
square kilometer. In order for a settlement to qualify as urban in Colombia,
it must have fifteen hundred people; in Nigeria, twenty thousand; in Mexico,
twenty-five hundred; and in Tanzania, five thousand. In order to facilitate
cross-national comparisons, the United Nations and the World Bank have
defined an *urban settlement* as a community with at least twenty thousand
inhabitants and a "city" as that with more than one hundred thousand
people.

Despite the diversity of the criteria for dividing populations according to
their rural or urban designations, five dimensions of urbanization are discernible in the developing world. First, the rate of urbanization growth has
been extremely high in the past, and it is likely to continue at a similar pace
in the future. Second, rapid urbanization has been accompanied by an alarming increase in the prevalence of urban poverty. Third, several types of
settlements of the urban poor, with their own peculiar features, have
emerged. Fourth, the growth processes of these settlements are not neces-

Table 2.1
Estimates of Urban Population in Less Developed Countries by Size-Groups

| | | | Size-Groups | | | | |
| | Less than 20,000 | | 20,000-100,000 | | 100,000 + | | Total Urban |
Year	Million	% of Total	Million	% of Total	Million	% of Total	Million
1950	75.5	28.2	59.4	22.2	132.7	49.6	267.6 (16.2)
1960	106.1 (40.4)	24.1	96.9 (63.1)	22.1	236.5 (78.2)	53.8	439.4 (21.9)
1970	171.0 (61.3)	26.2	109.1 (12.6)	16.7	371.4 (57.0)	57.0	651.5 (25.8)
1980	246.3 (44.3)	25.4	102.2 (-6.3)	10.5	623.5 (67.9)	64.1	972.4 (30.5)

Source: Adapted from Philip M. Hauser and Robert W. Gardner, "Urban Future: Trends and Prospects," in Documents, the International Conference on Population and the Urban Future, Rome, September 1-4, 1980 (New York: United Nations Fund for Population Activities, 1980), Tables 1-9.

sarily the same as those of middle- and high-income settlements. Finally, there are sharp deficiencies in the availability of infrastructure and basic urban services to residents of these settlements due to biases in the public delivery system. The purpose of this chapter is to examine the implications of the aforementioned dimensions.

THE URBAN GROWTH

Past Trends

The total urban population in developing countries increased from 267.6 million in 1950 to 972.4 million in 1980 while the percentage of this population to total population increased from 16.2 to 30.5 percent. (Table 2.1) World Bank estimates show that between 1960 and 1982, the urban population as a percentage of total population increased from 17 to 21 percent in low-income countries, 33 to 46 percent in middle-income countries, 24 to 34 percent in lower-middle-income countries, 45 to 63 percent in upper-middle-income countries, and 28 to 67 in high-income (oil-exporting) countries (Table 2.2)

In 1950 the urban population of Asia was 15.7 percent of the total population, and by 1980 it had increased to 27.4 percent.[2] The United Nations studies show that in Africa, the urban population increased by

Table 2.2
Urbanization in Developing Countries 1960–1982

Category	Urban Population as Percentage of Total Population*	
	1960	1970
Low Income Economies	17	21
Middle Income Countries	34	46
Lower Middle Income Countries	24	34
Upper Middle Income Countries	44	63
High Income Oil Exporting Countries	28	67

*The growth rates of urban population were calculated from the World Bank's population estimates; the estimates of urban population shares were calculated from the sources cited below. Because the estimates in this table are based on different national definitions of what is "urban," cross-country comparisons should be interpreted with caution. The summary measures for urban population as a percentage of total population are weighted by population.

Source: World Bank, World Development Report 1984, abstracted from Table 22, p. 260. The data on urban population as a percentage of total population are from United Nations, Patterns of Urban and Rural Population Growth (New York: United Nations, 1980), supplemented by data from the World Bank and from various issues of the UN Demographic Yearbook.

more than 4.7 percent per year between 1950 and 1975, and it is likely to grow at more than 4.5 percent annually until the year 2000.[3] These figures indicate the magnitude of urbanization over the past quarter of a century, even when adjustments are made for the low levels of population size at which urban settlements are defined.

A significant feature of urbanization in developing countries is that the rate of growth of large-size cities has been significantly greater than that of small cities. As shown in table 2.1, by 1950 the population of cities of one hundred thousand or more was 49.6 percent of the total urban population, and by 1980, it had increased to 64.1 percent—a significantly greater increase than for other groups. In many developing countries, a significant portion of the urban population is concentrated in the large capital cities. For example, the populations of Bangkok and Colombo are 60 percent of the total urban populations in Thailand and Sri Lanka, respectively. Similarly, 35 percent of the urban population in the Philippines lives in Manila, and 26 percent of the Indonesian urban population is in Jakarta.

The migration of citizens to towns and cities from the rural areas of developing countries has been a major cause of the characteristically rapid pace of urbanization in the developing world. Factors contributing to these large-scale rural-to-urban migrations are widely known and have come to be called "pull" factors; for example, urban areas provide better employment opportunities and have better educational, health, and other social services; wage levels in urban areas are higher; and administrative, financial, and political power is usually concentrated in large cities. In some cases, increased population pressure on scarce agricultural land forces people to migrate to urban areas. This may be referred to as one of the main "push" factors.

Future Growth

Nearly all demographic projections show that the urban population in developing countries will continue to grow rapidly over the next two decades. The United Nations Population Division's projections indicate that from 1975 to the year 2000 the percentage of the population living in urban areas of developing countries will increase from 28 percent to 44 percent.[4] It is estimated that 66 percent of the world's urban population will be living in the developing countries by the year 2000.[5] By the end of the 1990s, it is expected that about 42 percent of the population in Africa, 76 percent in Latin America, and more than 40 percent in Asia will be living in cities. The projections also indicate that the largest cities will continue to expand, and that there will be significant increases in the numbers of large metropolitan areas. Over the next decades, the number of cities with more than one million residents will nearly double from the 118 that existed in 1980 to about 286.[6] Similarly, more than 40 cities in developing countries are expected to have a population of 5 million or more at the end of the same period.

Future urbanization patterns among developing countries, however, are likely to vary. A World Bank study identifies four types of future urbanization pattern.[7] Among the first type are countries in which more than half of the population is already urban, income levels are relatively high, and by the end of the century, most of the population will be in urban areas. Most of the Latin American countries can be included in this category. The second type includes those in which more than half of the population is still rural, income levels are low, and there are population pressures on land. Examples of this type are semi-industrialized countries of Asia (such as Malaysia or the Philippines) and North Africa (such as Algeria or Egypt). By the year 2000, most countries in the second category are likely to have urbanization levels as high as those among the first type of country today.

A third group of countries—which are found in Africa—are still predominantly rural. Though the countries in this grouping are urbanizing rapidly, by the turn of the century these will still be able to maintain their high rates of growth of rural population because their land areas are large and agriculture can continue to absorb more people. Manufacturing and related activities in their cities are characteristically limited and in the early stages of development. Examples of countries in this third category are Senegal, Nigeria, Sudan, and Kenya.

The fourth urbanization pattern category pertains to the larger countries of Asia, that is, China, India, Indonesia, Bangladesh, and Pakistan. Although these countries are predominantly rural, the absolute size of their typical urban populations is very large. Furthermore, these have rapidly growing large cities. In the future, migration from the rural areas and natural urban population growth will result in large-scale growth in cities in these countries.

This trend in the growth of the larger cities of the developing countries is likely to continue in the future. The estimates by the World Bank indicate that by the turn of the century, large metropolitan centres in developing countries will be a much more frequent phenomenon than in developed countries.[8] Furthermore, the growth of urban population mostly occurs in existing urban centers, leading to the further concentration of the urban population.

THE INCIDENCE OF URBAN POVERTY

Rapid urbanization in the developing world has been accompanied by an alarming increase in the incidence of urban poverty.[9] The occupational structure of the urban areas in developing countries is such that it leads to uneven patterns of income distribution. The migration from rural areas of unskilled workers without adequate assets and little opportunity to use their related talents depresses wages of even the poorest groups in the urban areas. The rapid pace of urbanization has increased inequality of income. In India, Sir Lanka, and Bangladesh, pressure on land has resulted in low wages for unskilled migrants from rural areas and hence in further widening income disparities in their cities.

The World Bank estimates show that in 1980, the number of urban poor households in developing countries was 41.1 million (Table 2.3). According to these estimates, by the end of the 1990s, more than half of the absolute poor will be concentrated in urban areas.[10] The number of absolute poor urban dwellers will be 90 percent in Latin America and the Caribbean, 40 percent in Africa, and about 45 percent in Asia. In Eastern and Western Africa, the number of urban poor households is likely to increase from about 2.1 million to 7.9 million by the year 2000. In East Asia and the Pacific, the expected growth of the poor households is 3 million, as is it in the cities of Middle East and North Africa. The number of the poor urban households in South Asia is likely to triple from about 10 million in 1975 to 32.5 million by the turn of the century. In Latin America and the Caribbean the number of poor urban households will increase by more than 6 million. Thus, the number of urban households living in poverty is likely to more than double from 33.5 million in 1975 to about 74.3 million at the end of 1990s.

Large cities in developing countries have a significant percentage of their populations below the poverty line; for instance, the figure is 60 percent in Calcutta, 50 percent in Madras, 45 percent in Bombay, 45 percent in Karachi, and 35 percent in Manila.

Table 2.3
Projected Changes in Number of Poor Households, Rural and Urban, 1975–2000
(thousands of households)

Region	1975	Increase or Decrease	1980	Increase or Decrease	1990	Increase or Decrease	2000
Urban Poor Households							
Eastern Africa	1,039.0	+330.5	1,369.0	+1,175.0	2,544.5	+2,158.5	4,703.0
Western Africa	1,072.0	+333.0	1,405.0	+861.0	2,266.0	+961.0	3,227.0
East Asia and the Pacific	2,664.0	+1,491.0	4,155.0	+956.0	5,111.0	+633.0	5,744.0
South Asia	10,213.0	+3,757.0	13,970.0	+7,285.0	21,255.0	+11,300.0	32,555.0
Europe, the Middle East, and North Africa	5,581.0	+699.0	6,250.0	+1,324.0	7,574.0	+1,169.0	8,743.0
Latin America and the Caribbean	12,945.0	+1,078.0	14,023.0	+2,775.0	16,708.0	+2,530.0	19,328.0
Total	33,514.0	+7,658.5	41,173.0	+14,376.0	55,548.5	18,751.5	74,300.0
Rural Poor Households	83,279.5	-3,738.5	79,441.0	-11,279.0	68,162.0	-11,694.0	56,468.0

Note: Based on estimates of real per capita incomes through the year 2000, using United Nations medium-variant rates of growth of population and World Bank projections of real growth of national income. Poor households in 1975 are here defined as those living in absolute poverty in 1975 in all rural areas except those in El Salvador and Jamaica and in all urban areas in East Asia, Malawi, Zambia, and Egypt. In all other instances the numbers of those in absolute poverty are small in comparison to the numbers of those in relative poverty, which indicates that the relatively poor are the appropriate target group. In determining movements in and out of poverty in the course of time, the thresholds of both absolute and relative poverty are held constant in 1975 dollars. The accuracy of the projected figures is dependent upon a fairly stable distribution of income.

Source: World Bank, Poverty, Shelter, Poverty and Basic Needs Series (Washington: World Bank, 1980), p. 3, abstracted.

The Characteristics of the Urban Poor

The characteristics of the urban poor might vary from one country to another and, therefore, there are limits to the generalizations that can be made about them. Causes of their poverty may also vary. Yet, the urban poor have some common demographic, reproductive, educational, locational, nutritional and health, and political characteristics.[11] They usually have the lowest median age and highest dependency burden within the total national population. Their fertility rates are usually the highest and educational levels the lowest within the urban population. Their access to services and employment is typically more costly because, in most cases, of their inability to legally occupy affordable locations closer to nodes of economic activity within the city. Childhood mortality and diseases linked to malnutrition and unsanitary neighborhoods are more common among the low-income groups. The urban poor are usually not well organized and only marginally represented in urban local councils or political parties. Therefore, they are unable to safeguard their legitimate interests and are usually excluded from most benefits resulting from government-initiated programs and projects. In addition to the above, unlike the rural poor, the urban poor live in almost entirely monetary economies and thus have to pay cash for food, fuel, and other necessities; and they live in slums or squatter settlements that are usually densely populated.

To an extent, each of the above characteristics contributes to the urban poor's low-income levels. The younger workers among low-income groups are likely to have less training, experience, and job security and hence low-paying jobs. At the same time, high fertility levels and dependency rates further limit their accumulation of assets while lack of proximity to nodes of economic activity and the absence of affordable transport have negative effects on their earnings. Diseases linked to malnutrition and unsanitary living conditions often lead to temporary loss of employment and income or to permanent disability. Finally, in the absence of their active participation in the political process, the urban poor are unable to equitably share in the city's resources.

The urban poor are not a homogeneous group, since they are likely to have migrated from different parts of the country to a particular urban area. Their ethnic, religious, and cultural backgrounds might also be different. Some of them might have lived in cities for several generations, while others might be recent migrants. The population densities in low-income settlements might significantly vary.

DEFICIENCIES IN URBAN SERVICES

Due to rapid urbanization, the demand for urban services has substantially increased. In most countries the supply of such services as urban transport, low-income housing, water, public education, and public health has not kept pace with increasing demand.[12]

Urban transport in most cities in the developing world is inadequate to meet the needs of residents and of commercial and industrial sectors. Some areas do not have a public transport system. Privately operated cars, auto rickshaws, and buses are the main means of travel. During the last three decades, governments have initiated several programs to provide public transport within metropolitan areas. Yet, the quality of existing services is low; seating capacity is limited; road capacity is deficient; traffic control is ineffective; privately owned motor vehicles have increased to the extent that the flow of traffic is hindered; and outlying areas have usually not been well connected with the center of the city. Considering the increasing rate of urban growth, future requirements for urban transport will also continue to increase.

Housing shortages are a serious problem in many of the Third World cities. This is particularly the case with low-cost housing for the urban poor. Many dwelling units in these cities are without running water or toilet facilities. Costs of standard housing units have gone up to the extent that the urban poor are unable to buy them. Meeting the future requirements for housing is one of the most critical challenges faced by cities. In this regard, existing shortages have to be overcome, future population growth taken into consideration, and dilapidated areas revitalized.

Another service that is in great demand is adequate water supply. In many cities, a significant percentage of people do not have access to piped water. In some cases, the quality of the available water is low, leading to high disease rates and public health problems. In slums and squatter settlements, this problem is more serious. In view of the rapidly expanding urban population, present facilities need to be considerably expanded to meet future needs.

The facilities for public education in most of these cities are inadequate. Among the relevant typical problems are shortages of qualified teachers, low family incomes, inadequate classroom space, high cost of transport and school supplies, and overcrowded facilities. The children of the urban poor have to compete for limited facilities with those from better-off families and are inevitably in a disadvantaged position. To meet future requirements, the present deficits in educational facilities have to be met and school-age population growth has to be accommodated. This implies a rapid expansion of existing facilities, as well as teacher training and recruitment.

There is tremendous pressure on existing health facilities in urban areas. The urban poor, who are largely dependent on low-cost government facilities, are more negatively affected, since the well-to-do are able to use private facilities. In addition, lack of adequate facilities for sanitation-related services, such as garbage disposal and flood control, are major hazards to public health in slums and shanty dwelling areas.

Situation in Selected Countries

A brief review of urban service deficiencies in selected countries shows the magnitude of the problem, as well as reasons for these deficiencies. In a survey of urban services in Pakistan carried out by Viqar Ahmed, the author noted that the city of Lahore has 272 buses as opposed to an estimated requirement of 1,280 and that only 63 percent of these buses were actually operating in 1981; about 25 percent of the urban population in the country lives in slums; access to clean water is available only to 77 percent of the urban population; only 38 percent of the people in the largest city (i.e., Karachi) have in-house water connections; 48 percent of the total urban population has access to sewage systems; and enrollment in educational institutions in urban areas is available to only 77 percent of children ages five to nine, 52 percent age ten to twelve and 39 percent in the thirteen to fourteen age group.[13] Reasons for deficiencies in urban services include the rapid growth of urban centers, lack of adequate resources, inability to recover cost from users, low-capacity utilization due to maintenance problems, and the rising cost of housing.

The situation regarding the deficiencies in urban services in Indonesia is equally serious.[14] As of 1980, only 26.4 percent of urban households had access to piped water. While the total number of urban households with access to piped water had increased, this percentage had not kept pace with rapid urban growth. It has been estimated that about 300,000 new housing units must be constructed annually in urban areas to meet the demand. This does not include the existing backlog and housing redevelopment demands. According to the 1980 census, only about 45 percent of urban households had private toilets. Drainage systems in most urban areas are inadequate, and flooding in some of the large cities is a serious problem. Garbage collection and disposal is defective. For example, according to the 1971 census, garbage from 24 percent of the urban households was not collected and properly disposed of.

Despite rapid industrialization and growth, housing for the urban poor of Korea also continues to be a serious problem.[15] In 1980, 65 percent of the poor families in Seoul were living in single-room houses and a large number were residing in illegal housing units. In addition, malnutrition among the urban poor still existed.

There are acute urban service deficiencies in Nigeria. Makinwa-Adebusoye reported that in Benin City, Nigeria, about 63 percent of poor households have no independent means of transport. Only 7.8 percent of the poor in neighborhoods surveyed were owner-occupants. Poor households often lacked such basic amenities as piped water and kitchens. Garbage was disposed of by burning (37.9 percent), burying (13.9 percent), moat filling (18.3 percent), road dumping (27.6 percent), and by refuse workers (2.3 percent).[16]

There are significant gaps between the supply and demand of urban services in Fiji. Gunasekera pointed out that housing is a major problem for the urban population, about 16 percent of which was living in "grossly substandard dwellings in 1980."[17] The poor are of course most negatively affected by the housing shortage. The rising cost of housing has led to a situation in which only about 20 percent of the employed urban workers can afford to buy the house being supplied by the Housing Authority. As regards health services, there is over-crowding in government hospitals and urban sewage in small towns is poorly developed.

In Kenya the rapid pace of urbanization has put tremendous pressure on existing urban services.[18] Despite past development-oriented policies and programs, concerned government agencies have not been able to cope with the demand for public health services, primary education, construction and maintenance of the urban road network, water, housing, and similar services. The reasons for these deficiencies are lack of adequate resources, the excessively rapid growth of the urban population, and institutional weaknesses.

A large percentage of the population of cities in the developing world lives in slums or squatter settlements. Table 2.4 shows the proportion of squatters and slum dwellers in selected cities. We find that in Addis Ababa and Casablanca in Africa, the percentage of squatters and people in slums to the city population reaches 70 and 79 percent, respectively. In Bogota and Buenos Aires the percentage is 40 and 60 percent, respectively. In South Asia, we find that Calcutta, Bombay, Delhi, Dacca, and Karachi have a large percentage of their populations living in slums and squatter areas. In Calcutta, for example, slum dwellers and squatters account for 67 percent of the city population. Even in East Asia, the number of those living in slums and squatter areas is significant. As shown in the table, during the 1960s and 1970s, dwellers in squatter areas and slums made up between 30 to 60 percent of the urban population in the developing countries.

CHARACTERISTICS AND TYPOLOGIES OF POOR URBAN SETTLEMENTS

Lower-income urban settlements in the developing world have usually been referred to simply as "slums and squatter settlements." However, other nomenclature has been developed in literature on the subject in attempts to more accurately portray the circumstances and problems faced by the inhabitants of these depressed areas.[19] The designations chosen by the various authors indicate attempts to identify the primary characteristic of a particular grouping, and in that regard often the name is self-explanatory.

Based primarily on Latin America experiences, Leeds proposed several categorizations for the typical lower-income urban settlements.[20] He used the terms *squatter settlements* or *shanty towns* to designate those clusters

Table 2.4
Proportion of Squatters and Slum Dwellers in Selected Cities
(by region in descending order)

Region and City	Year	Slum Dwellers, Squatters (in thousands)	Percentage of Slums and Squatters to City Population
Africa			
Addis Ababa	1981	948	79
Casablanca	1971	1,054	70
Kinshasa	1969	733	60
Nairobi	1970	177	33
Dakar	1969	150	30
Latin America			
Bogota	1969	1,376	60
Buenos Aires	1970	1,486	50
Mexico City	1966	1,500	46
Caracas	1974	1,000	42
Lima	1970	1,148	40
Rio de Janeiro	1970	1,456	30
Santiago	1964	546	25
South Asia			
Calcutta	1971	5,328	67
Bombay	1971	2,475	41
Delhi	1970	1,400	36
Dacca	1973	300	35
Karachi	1971	800	23
East Asia			
Manila	1972	1,540	35
Pusan	1969	527	31
Seoul	1969	1,320	29
Jakarta	1972	1,190	26
Bangkok/Thonburi	1970	600	20
Hong Kong	1969	600	17

Source: Abstracted from John Donohue, "Some Facts and Figures on Urbanization in Developing World," Assignment Children 57/58 (1982), p. 36.

of houses built on land that the occupant/builder does not own or rent. A second type close to this is *government created shack towns* (such as are common in Portugal) where the land is usually owned by the government or large absentee private owners and the occupancy is benignly tolerated by government. These types are characterized obviously by insecure land tenure. Other types Leeds included are: *titled plots without services* (such as one finds in Colombia) where barely developed land is made available (in government land-redistribution programs) to the poor and the housing being built may vary from shanties to solid construction dwellings; *emergency housing*, referring to the kind constructed for temporary shelter pending resettlement of misplaced persons such as political refugees or natural disaster victims; and *inner city slums*, the variety of neglected and dilapidated housing of older settled areas that "occur[s] in the established and legally evolved part of the city."[21]

Turner has identified four types of uncontrolled settlements in terms of their development level and security of tenure.[22] *Tentative settlements* are provisional settlements constructed by squatters who intend to stay on permanently. It is the first stage in establishing a permanent settlement. The next step up, *incipient squatter settlements*, are characterized by the occupants still having insecure tenure, but they have made a significant degree of fixed capital investment. The *advanced semi-squatter settlements* are those of a more developed stage with semilegal and rather secure tenure and with an advanced degree of material investment. The inhabitants in such settlements are from a wide range of social classes. *Provisional* squatter settlements are defined as those in which house builders have illegal but de facto possession and with little or no investment in permanent construction or installations.

In discussing the use of sites-and-services projects for alleviation of urban poor housing problems, Skinner identified four types of schemes indicative of the circumstances of the dwelling arrangements; they were (1) open application schemes; (2) overspill sites for upgraded settlements; (3) relocation sites for eradicated central slums or squatter settlements; and (4) group application schemes.[23]

Yeh has expressed his reservations about the utility of typologies of low-income urban settlements and the regional and global strategies that have been suggested to improve each of these types.[24] Instead, he argued that it would be more useful "to pay greater attention to the component variables associated with common types of low income settlements" and that "by looking at the planning implications of the more important features and some of the ways they interact, we might achieve better understanding and efficiency in improvement design."[25] The suggested variables of community profile level include spatial location, land ownership status, population size, physical characteristics, social and economic services, and community organizations. Some of the variables of the household profile level are tenancy status of the structure, household size and composition, income, assets, savings, and expenditure. Finally, the suggested variables of the individual profile level include demographic characteristics, literacy and education, economic activity, occupation, income, access to employment, and participation in community affairs.

While there may be no agreement on the typologies of lower-income urban settlements, *slums* and *squatter settlements* are more commonly used terms in the literature. Slums are usually characterized by old and poorly maintained buildings, multifamily housing, high levels of population density, and a significant number of rental accommodations. Squatter settlements, on the other hand, are "mainly uncontrolled low-income residential areas with an ambiguous legal status regarding tenancy; they are to a large extent built by the inhabitants themselves using their own means and are usually poorly equipped with public utilities and community services."[26]

The processes of slum and squatter-settlement formation, growth, and change may vary from one city to another. A comparative study by HABITAT, however, shows several common features.[27] Most squatter settlements are formed as a result of the illegal takeover of land. In some cases, the takeover is planned by large groups of households. Lower-income settlements could grow by accretion, developer-sponsored subdivisions, or building of rural villages on the periphery of metropolitan centers. The growth rates of squatter settlements might be higher than those of the surrounding cities due largely to the inability of government and private sectors to provide adequate shelter, infrastructure, and urban basic services. Slums, on the other hand, grow slowly because of their location.

The HABITAT study identified several factors that have affected the formation and growth of lower-income urban settlements in developing countries.[28] These factors are: the increased demand for shelter; increasing industrialization and proximity to employment; historical events such as wars or political upheavals; the inadequacy of existing housing facilities provided through government agencies; the constraints on urban land; and the extent of community organization and the authorities' type of response to community-initiated activities.

CONSTRAINTS ON ACCESS OF THE URBAN POOR

While the governments in the developing world have recognized the urgency of upgrading poor urban settlements, a number of economic, social, administrative, and political factors hinder the access of the urban poor to shelter and basic services. An understanding of these constraints is crucial to the design of appropriate policy and program interventions.[29]

Low Income Level

In cases such as government-initiated low-cost housing, the poor cannot afford to pay for urban services due to their low incomes. Even where some of the services are subsidized or directly provided by government or semi-autonomous agencies, the actual beneficiaries might be the higher-income groups. The structure of price leads to the exclusion of the urban poor from access to basic services. Higher connection charges for the provision of water

or electricity discriminate against poor households that have poor purchasing power and might have to face high borrowing costs.

Illegal Occupation of Land

Residents of squatter settlements (by definition) do not have legal ownership of the land they occupy. This implies that they cannot be forced to
pay user charges for services, and therefore, the concerned government
agencies are reluctant to provide them with such services as water, electricity,
and sewage. Lack of adequate security of land occupation and tenure
impedes the poor's access to institutional credit, subjects them to constant
fear of eviction, and discourages them from improving their dwelling units
and participating in government programs.

Weak Linkages of the People with the Service-Delivery Systems

The delivery systems of municipal governments or semiautonomous development authorities are characterized by a lack of adequate community
participation in identification of the community's priorities and needs, formulation of projects, and implementation of development activities. In the
absence of adequate community participation, the urban poor are unable
to safeguard their legitimate interests. Their access to key decision makers
within government agencics is usually limited, and there is a lack of adequate
dialogue and communication between government officials and the people.
In most developing countries, municipal councils are not directly elected,
thereby denying the urban poor another channel through which some of
their grievances could be communicated to policymakers in the country.
Furthermore, because of the significant gap between the demand for urban
services and the institutional and financial capacity to provide these, some
type of rationing takes place. Those who exercise political and economic
power are thus able to divert investments to services that directly benefit
their vested interests. The poor's access to services and facilities is also
constrained by highly centralized modes of decision making, lack of coordination among the implementing agencies, and inability of government
officials to work effectively with poor urban communities.

Standards for Urban Services

Government standards for urban services are usually very high, leading
to high costs for these services. It is not uncommon, therefore, to find
predominantly middle-income families utilizing some of the services meant
for the urban poor. The establishment of unrealistically high standards leads
to the exclusion of a large portion of the population from access to basic
services. For example, if the standards of low-cost housing are too high, it

would require a large amount of subsidy to make shelter accessible to the vast majority of the urban poor.

Weak Organization of the Urban Poor

The urban poor are usually not organized effectively. The heterogeneity of their social backgrounds and their condition of poverty, among other things, hinder the emergence of viable community-level organizations. While they might have linkages with political parties, they are unable to assert collective pressure from below to ensure adequate access to urban basic services. Even in those cases in which a community is well organized, urban development administrators are usually afraid that the poor may become a threat to political stability.

Lack of Administrative and Political Will

The lack of explicitly stated public policies aimed at providing urban basic services to the poor in an integrated manner also impedes access to them by squatters and slum dwellers. This reflects the lack of adequate political and administrative will on the part of policymakers and planners to allocate adequate resources for providing basic services to the poor. When the public sector is unable to provide adequate urban services to the poor, the private sector might fill the vacuum. However, the economic cost of these services might be higher and the quality lower than those provided by the public sector. In such situations, the poor might be forced to pay more than the rich.

Low Priority for Urban Shelter

In most cases, priority is given to the "productive" sector. While investment in the modern urban-industrial sector is encouraged, planning for shelter and basic urban services in low-income settlements does not receive the priority it deserves. Budget allocations for social services, particularly for those in slums and squatter areas, are not adequate. In the case of squatter settlements, government agencies are usually reluctant to provide services for fear that it might encourage others to illegally occupy land.

NOTES

1. For a discussion of various definitions of the *urban poor* in the developing world, see P. J. Richards and A. M. Thomson, eds., *Basic Needs and the Urban Poor* (London: Croom Helm, 1984); and Jorge E. Hardoy and David Satterthwaite, *Shelter: Need and Response* (Chichester, England: John Wiley, 1981). Quantification of urban poverty is complex. Data are scarce and often unreliable. One needs to

identify the cutoff point for the poverty line. The most common way of doing this is in relation to expenditures for food. Though absolute poverty is viewed within the context of each country, relative poverty has also to be taken into consideration. Thus, poverty measurement could be undertaken on the basis of both an international standard and adjustment to local social norms. However, as an ILO study points out, "when general statements are being made about poverty in the world, or even poverty in a specific country, then it is important to examine the reasons for quantifying poverty and find methods most appropriate for the context" (P. J. Richards and A. M. Thomson, "Urban Poverty Basic Needs: The Role of the Public Sector" in P. J. Richards and A. M. Thomson, eds., *Basic Needs and the Urban Poor*, p. 15).

2. Y. M. Yeung, "Introduction," in Y. M. Yeung, ed., *A Place to Live: More Effective Low-Cost Housing in Asia* (Ottawa: International Development Research Centre, 1983), p. 11.

3. United Nations, Department of International Economic and Social Affairs, *Patterns of Urban and Rural Population Growth* (New York: United Nations, 1980).

4. United Nations Population Division's projections based on 1980 estimates.

5. United Nations, *Patterns*, Table 48.

6. Paul Bairoch, "Employment and Large Cities: Problems and Outlook," *International Labor Review* 121 (1982), 519–533.

7. George Beier, Anthony Churchill, Michael Cohen, and Bertrand Renaud, "The Task Ahead for the Cities of the Developing Countries," *World Development* 4:5 (1976), 363–409.

8. Ibid., p. 376.

9. Ibid., pp. 381–382.

10. World Bank, *Shelter* (Poverty and Basic Needs Series, Washington, DC: World Bank, 1980), p. 3.

11. Beier, "The Task Ahead," p. 383.

12. For discussion of these services in developing countries, see Annemarie H. Walsh, *The Urban Challenge to Government: An International Comparison of Thirteen Cities* (New York: Praeger, 1969); M. Honjo, ed., *Urbanization and Regional Development* (Singapore: Maruzen Asia, 1981); International Bank for Reconstruction and Development, *Urbanization*, Sector Working Papers (Washington, D.C.: World Bank, June 1972); United Nations, Department of Economic and Social Affairs, *Administrative Aspects of Urbanization* (New York: United Nations, 1970); and Alan Turner, ed., *Cities of the Poor* (London: Croom Helm, 1980).

13. Viqar Ahmed, "Managing Urban Development: Focus on Services for the Poor" (Nagoya: UNCRD, 1984, mimeo), pp. 19–22.

14. Mitsuhiko Hosaka, "An Overview on Indonesian Urban Service Management" (Nagoya: UNCRD, 1984, mimeo) pp. 30–35.

15. In-Joung Whang, "Managing Public Services for the Urban Poor in Korea" (Nagoya: UNCRD, 1984, mimeo), pp. 8–15.

16. P. K. Makinwa-Adebusoye, "Urban Poverty in Benin City, Nigeria: Interim Report" (Nagoya: UNCRD, 1984, mimeo).

17. H. M. Gunasekera, "Management of Services for the Poor in the Urban Sector in Fiji" (Nagoya: UNCRD, 1984, mimeo), p. 30.

18. J. O. Kayila, "Managing Urban Development: Kenya's Experience" (Nagoya:UNCRD, 1984, mimeo), p. 18.

19. United Nations Centre for Human Settlements (HABITAT), *The Residential Circumstances of the Urban Poor in Developing Countries* (New York: Praeger, 1981), p. 3.

20. Anthony Leeds, "Lower Income Urban Settlement Types: Processes, Structures, Policies," *The Residential Circumstances of the Urban Poor in Developing Countries*, p. 4.

21. Ibid., p. 41.

22. John F. C. Turner, "Uncontrolled Urban Settlement: Problems and Policies," in Gerald Breese, ed., *The City in the Newly Developing Countries* (Englewood Cliffs, N.J.: Prentice-Hall, 1969), pp. 515–520.

23. R. J. Skinner, "Community Participation: Its Scope and Organization," in R. J. Skinner and M. J. Rodell, eds., *People, Poverty and Shelter: Problems of Self-Help Housing in the Third World* (London: Methuen, 1983), p. 129.

24. Stephen H. K. Yeh, "On Characteristics of Urban Low-Income Settlements and Improvement Strategies: an Asian Perspective," in HABITAT, *The Residential Circumstances*, pp. 191–215.

25. Ibid., p. 193.

26. United Nations Centre for Human Settlements (HABITAT), *Survey of Slums and Squatter Settlements* (Dublin: Tycooly International, 1982), p. 15.

27. Ibid.

28. Ibid.

29. For a discussion of constraints on access of the urban poor to shelter and services, see Riaz Hassan, "Problems of Access to Public Services for the Urban Poor," *Regional Development Dialogue* 6:2 (1985), 42–67; Joan A. Nelson, *Access to Power: Politics and the Urban Poor in Developing Nations* (Princeton: Princeton University Press, 1979); Beier, "The Task Ahead"; and Mary Racelis Hollnsteiner, "People Power: Community Participation in the Planning of Human Settlements," *Assignment Children* 40 (Geneva: UNICEF, 1977), pp. 11–48.

3

EVOLUTION OF POLICIES
AND PROGRAMS

APPROACHES AND STRATEGIES

In the literature, several approaches and policy interventions have been suggested to provide shelter, infrastructure, and basic services to the urban poor. To begin with, Charles Abrams, John Turner, and others who have documented some low-income people's success in building their own dwelling units significantly influenced the opinions of housing experts, planners, and international aid groups.[1] In his book *Housing by People*, for example, Turner argued that each of the three levels of government—local, municipal, and central—offers "different opportunities for participation" in improving the dwelling environments. He contended that it is better for organizations to be responsible only for installing infrastructure and for manufacturing and supplying tools and materials, and that they should not be engaged in building or managing dwelling environments, since in most cases this benefits only the better-off segments of the urban population. Also he asserted that "policy goals must be re-stated in terms that describe the proper matching of people and their environments and of their own contributions with the value of the services that they get."[2] Turner further suggested the imposition of legislative controls for facilitating the supply of land, credit, and technology to low-income groups; the modification of minimum standards and building procedures; the provision for security of tenure to squatters; the clear division of authority in housing activities between local, municipal, and central governments; and the encouragement of informal sector activities. In Turner's view, a "viable" housing policy would be based on the

principle of self-government in housing and the use of small-scale techno-
logical and managerial tools. The principle of self-government implies the
replacement of centrally administrative systems with a "multiplicity of locally self-governing sub-systems."

Burgess has critically examined Turner's conception of the nature of housing, the relationship between popular government and the private sector,
the role of the state and the planner, and his policy recommendations.[3] He
presented the following framework as a means of analyzing the problems
and policies for improving dwelling environment:

The housing problems in the Third World societies can best be understood as the
product of the general conditions of capitalist development rather than the product
of particular technological or organizational systems as theories of the Turner type
would have us believe. These general conditions constitute the structural source of
both the urban and the housing problem: the spread of capitalist relations in the
country side which leads to the expulsion of the peasant to the city; industrial
development of a monopoly character that leads to the destruction of labour-inten-
sive industry; and high levels of dependency on foreign finance capital which among
other things determines levels of interest and the size of urban and housing budgets
and subjects national housing activities to fluctuations in the global economy.[4]

. Using this framework, Burgess argued that, with the exception of a few
token schemes, the self-helping housing policies suggested by Turner are
unlikely to be implemented; that the establishment of the department of
self-help in the government housing agency would not significantly increase
the access of the poor to low-income housing; and that the suggested measures "can be seen as a technical attempt to level out the symptoms of a
structural malaise and to maintain the status quo."[5] He added that even if
policies proposed by Turner were implemented, it would lead to massive
diversion of investments away from the middle class, an increase in prices
of basic building materials, a dramatic effect on land values, and an increased
burden for providing infrastructure.[6]

Legalization and "on-site upgrading" have been recommended as the most
appropriate squatter settlement strategies with several arguments having
been presented in the literature.[7] The main economic arguments are that
legalization conserves the housing stock and the infrastructure investment;
the grant of tenure encourages squatters to use their capital and labor for
housing improvement; on-site upgrading is significantly cheaper than demolition and the construction of new public housing for low-income groups;
and upgrading is conducive to increasing employment opportunities. The
social argument in favor of upgrading is that it facilitates the emergence of
integrated communities, which promotes economic and political stability.
The political arguments are that relocation might lead to social instability
in poor communities, the radicalism of squatters and the hostility of citizens
to the government.

A review of literature on "basic housing" shows that two approaches have been commonly utilized by developing countries—community upgrading, and sites and services.[8] Both approaches are intended to help the urban poor and are focused on land and services rather than shelter. In both approaches the emphasis is on the capacity of the people to help themselves, and the role of the government is perceived to be as supportive, a concept that has come to be known as "aided self-help." In community upgrading, basic services, such as potable water, garbage collection and disposal, electricity, schools, drainage, and community centers, are provided in slum and squatter communities. In the sites-and-services approach, new land is opened up and is subdivided into serviced residential plots. The standard and the range of services provided could vary from one project to another. Most sites-and-services projects are addressed to a fairly large middle stratum of low-income groups.

In their review of different approaches and policy interventions to solve the low-income housing problem, Angel and Benjamin have pointed out several interrelated "myths." [9] They argue that contrary to common belief, high-rise dwellings have not resulted in savings in land and construction; housing built through self-help tends to be better kept and enables the traditional family structure to be maintained; government-sponsored low-cost housing units are often out of the reach of most of the urban poor; most of the Third World housing is built incrementally; and the clearance of squatter settlements in order to implement public housing schemes results in a net loss of houses and money. They add that there is sufficient land in the Third World cities; that the urban poor build their dwellings incrementally and therefore require a different financing system; that squatters usually occupy unused land held by private speculators or by government agencies; and that decisions about land use are made to favor landowning interests that dominate local and national politics. Thus they argue that the middle class and elite values are impediments to squatter-settlement improvement and that without "considerable change" in these values and attitudes, the squatter problem cannot be solved.[10]

The United Nations Conference on Human Settlements held in Vancouver in 1976 made several recommendations concerning the provision of urban shelter, infrastructure, and services that were accepted by the member governments. The conference recommended that (a) "national housing policies must aim at providing adequate shelter and services to the lower income groups, distributing available resources on the basis of greatest need" (Recommendation C–9); (b) "infrastructure policy should be geared to achieve greater equity in the provision of services and utilities, access to places of work and recreational areas" (Recommendation C–11); and (c) "government should concentrate on the provision of services and on the physical and spatial reorganization of spontaneous settlements in ways that encourage community initiative and link 'marginal' groups to the national development process" (Recommendation C–17).[11] Other relevant recommendations were that standards for shelter, infrastructure, and services should be based on the population's felt needs and priorities; that there should be a close contact between planners and the people, especially with regard to the expressed aspirations of the poor; and that communities should be involved in planning, implementing, and managing neighborhood schemes.[12]

The World Bank has played a critical role in identifying alternative approaches to shelter and urban services and has developed the following criteria for evaluating project proposals and assisting borrowers in the shelter sector: (1) government should provide those services that communities cannot provide by themselves; (2) policies and projects should be directed to low- and moderate-income communities; (3) the majority of the investment costs should be both affordable by and recoverable from the beneficiaries; (4) security of tenure should be granted to encourage housing improvements; (5) appropriate responsibilities at various levels of government should be defined; and (6) individual savings and institutional funds should be mobilized for investment in the housing sector.[13]

The Bank's assistance for shelter projects has, therefore, been based on the "Progressive Development Model." This model implies that sites-and-services and squatter upgrading projects will lead to the provision of secure tenure and a range of basic urban services that, in turn, will encourage low-income households to improve their dwellings through self-help financing and construction. Improvements in the living environment would result in increased productivity and income.[14] The World Bank approach has been experimental in nature. As Michael Cohen has pointed out, "It was intended to encourage a high degree of learning by doing, that is to identify solutions or alternative approaches to shelter provision that did not rely heavily on public expenditures, that mobilized private savings, and that at the same time addressed the shelter needs of the city as a whole."[15] In most of the shelter projects, new housing was provided through sites and services and the existing units were upgraded through slum-improvement programs. In the case of sites-and-services projects, appropriate infrastructure standards and costs were developed. The initial shelter unit was to be modest and was to be "progressively improved, depending on the priorities, preference and capacity to invest of the individual households."[16]

UNICEF has advocated the "Urban Basic Services Approach," the principles of which are that communities should be involved in identifying, planning, and implementing community-level actions; services provided should be simple and low-cost; community workers should be selected directly by the community and should be given simple training; and services should "respond to special features of both the low-income urban communities as well as overall urban environment."[17] Five channels have been identified through which urban services are "promoted" and "supported."[18]

In the "long-range comprehensive programmes," social services are extended in partnership with a funding source that finances physical improvements and/or economic activities. The "immediate benefit programmes" are designed to provide basic social services for specific communities, which might involve several levels of governments and non-government organizations (NGOS). "Sectoral Programmes" are designed to facilitate the extention of services into low-income areas. "Local programmes" are undertaken by municipal governments or voluntary organizations with the support of national programs. Finally, "Social service policy and infrastructural development programmes" are aimed at strengthening concerned ministries and institutions for, among others, definition of objectives and policy and the development of institutional mechanisms for the training of officials and the delivery of services.

GOVERNMENT POLICY RESPONSES

Government policies dealing with urban development can be divided into two categories. In the first category are policies and programs that were designed to provide shelter and services. In the second category are included other policies that facilitate the process of urban development within the context of national development strategies and that have significant implications concerning the demand for and the supply of urban services.

The government agencies at the national, regional, metropolitan, and municipal levels in the developing world have implemented plans to improve and expand water supply facilities. Free and compulsory education up to age fourteen has been introduced in several countries; technical training facilities have been expanded; and private schools have been introduced. Transport policies and plans for urban areas have been formulated. Attempts have been made to extend services to outlying areas and to improve the quantity and quality of public transport facilities. Public housing programs have been introduced, with some housing schemes being financed and constructed by public agencies and others implemented through private initiative.

In addition to the above, there are several other policies that governments in the developing world have formulated to facilitate the process of urban development. Attempts have been made to relocate industries from "primate" cities to other industrial centers; to redistribute the government's infrastructure and other investment allocations in favor of secondary cities and economically depressed regions; and to introduce institutional changes to decentralize development planning and management functions to regional and local units. Other urban policies have dealt with private investment; measures to regulate and guide land use; development of small and intermediate size cities; pricing; and tax regulations.

Three types of policies have been implemented in order to provide shelter, infrastructure, and basic services in slum and squatter settlements.[19] "Laissez faire policies" imply the practice of officially ignoring the existence of slum and squatter settlements. "Restrictive policies" aim at reducing the size of low-income areas by, among other things, excluding such areas from urban services, removing and relocating residents in the urban periphery, and evicting residents from their homes to redevelop the area.

Finally, "supportive policies" seek to include slum and squatter settlements in the national development process by improving the existing conditions in these settlements and integrating the residents into surrounding areas. The "supportive policies" seek to legalize tenure of plots on an ownership or leasehold basis, renovate existing structures, provide urban land and housing for low-income settlements by building new units and providing sites and services to low-income groups, and provide assistance for self-help housing.

A review of past policies and programs concerning slums and squatter settlements shows that during initial stages the demolition and clearance of such settlements by the legal owners was a common practice.[20] It was only after the rapid growth of such settlements that planners and policymakers began to seriously think about policy alternatives and that poverty-oriented urban projects were designed to improve dwelling environments in low-income settlements.

Planners and policymakers in developing countries are increasingly recognizing the need to undertake concrete actions to improve the socioeconomic situation of the existing slum and squatter settlements. In Korea, for example, there are three main programs for the urban poor: A public works program has been initiated to increase the income of the urban poor and to provide them with more employment opportunities and vocational training; a public assistance program is aimed at providing subsistence maintenance, medicaid, maternity care, and funeral services to the aged, disabled, and sick; and a squatter housing improvement program is focused on resettlement as well as upgrading existing squatter housing.[21]

In Kenya, policies and programs aimed at assisting low-income urban residents have included slum and squatter improvement programs, sites-and-services projects and low-cost housing schemes.[22] Through these and other programs and projects, the government has attempted to increase the access of the urban poor to mass-produced houses and to provide them with employment opportunities.

Pakistan's Sixth Five Year Plan (1983–88) includes a number of programs to meet increasing demand for urban services and to provide "a safety net to the poor."[23] Public transport facilities are to be doubled; the number of low-income housing units to be constructed by the government is to be substantially increased; and slum-improvement schemes are to be implemented during the plan period. These would benefit about 2 million people and reduce the number of slum dwellers by about one-third. The plan also seeks to improve water supply and sewage systems. The government has already initiated a number of programs and projects to improve employability of the urban poor. Those include the Federal Programme for Skill Development, a training program for skilled and unskilled workers, and the National Vocational Training Project.

In Malaysia the government has utilized several strategies to improve services to the urban poor. These have included resettlement schemes and the upgrading of squatter settlements. Attempts have been made to provide facilities such as drainage, lighting, water, and access roads. In Kuala Lumpur, the Sang Kancil Project has been initiated with the assistance of UNICEF.[24] The project aims at setting up development centers in squatter settlements. Through these centers, preschool education and health facilities are to be provided and income-generating activities for women are to be initiated.

In India, policies and programs for slum clearance and rehousing were initiated in the 1950s. As H. R. Goel has pointed out, "Two basic flaws emerged early: (a) the majority of the poor urban residents could not afford ready-made housing; and (b) low cost housing presented physical shelter improvement but rarely the social, economic, and locational solutions that poor families needed most."[25] In 1972, the government policy shifted from slum relocation to environmental improvement in existing slum settlements. Under the scheme of environmental improvement, the basic services to be provided were water, drainage, community baths, community latrines, widening and paving of existing lanes, and street lighting. By 1983 this scheme was extended to all cities with populations over 300,000. In 1976, the Urban Community Development Project was started in Hyderabad, and since then it has been extended to several other cities. The World Bank has assisted urban development projects in Madras, Calcutta, Kanpur, and Madhya Pradesh. Each of these projects has a component aimed at upgrading slums.

In the Philippines, of several policies and programs that have been initiated to improve lower-income urban settlement, two should be mentioned. The Zonal Improvement Programme (ZIP) aims at upgrading squatter settlements in Manila.[26] This program follows a "total" approach in improving the living conditions of squatters by attempting to improve environmental conditions and to provide social and economic facilities. The program emphasizes site retention, increasing local employment opportunities, and community participation in decision making. Another project, the Bagong Lipunan Sites and Services (BLISS) program, was aimed at putting "model communities of 50 families in every municipality."[27] Each BLISS was to be provided with the minimum requirements for a healthy community life. Government supporting agencies were expected to provide basic social services such as water, power, shelter, health services, sports, and recreation. The Bagong Lipunan Community Association served as a channel through which government services and facilities were delivered. The Kampung Improvement Programme (KIP) in Indonesia is designed to provide services such as access roads, footpaths, piped water, drainage ditches, communal latrines, laundry facilities, and garbage bins. The community is not expected to pay for services except for the use of water. However, it is expected to contribute land, if needed, for the project without compensation. The KIP is primarily an environmental improvement program and does not attempt to directly affect the economic plight of the urban poor.

The Slum Improvement Programme of the National Housing Authority in Thailand divides Bangkok's slums into three categories; those to be improved for permanent low-income settlements, those to be improved temporarily, and those not to be improved because they are likely to be needed by landowners for redevelopment. The slums selected for permanent improvement are those in which government agencies own at least 60 percent of the land; those selected for temporary improvement are provided with minimal public utilities and socioeconomic components. In Colombo, the upgrading program excludes those slums that are located on land evaluated at above a specified amount. Other criteria to be used for selecting slums and shanties for potential benefits are the cost of improvement, the degree of flooding in the area, and whether any alternative use of the land has been planned for.

STAGES IN POLICY EVOLUTION

Generalizations about stages in policy evolution are difficult because some governments, (those in Latin America, for example) were faced with the phenomena of slums and squatter settlements earlier than others and because different levels of government within the same country might have different attitudes to these settlements. In addition, public policies concerning slums and squatter settlements are in some cases not explicitly stated. Yet, patterns of government projects and activities concerning low-income settlements could be assumed to reflect government policies.[28] From a comparative perspective, the following five stages in the evolution of such policies could be identified.

1. *Clearance and forced migration.* At this stage, squatters are evicted from the land that they have illegally occupied. In most cases, they are provided alternative shelter. The assumptions at this stage are that squatter settlements are not a solution to the shelter problems and that such eviction will discourage others from illegally occupying government or private land. In several Asian countries, for example, clearance and forced migration was the common feature during the 1950s and 1960s.

2. *Housing schemes followed by slum clearance.* During this stage, slums are cleared for redevelopment of the area and low-income housing schemes are implemented to resettle those who are dislocated. The provision of alternative sites is necessitated by the fact that those removed from slums

are either legal owners of land or have been staying there over a long period of time. Most developing countries have initiated housing schemes for low-income groups, though these are usually not meant exclusively for the squatter population.

3. *The provision of minimum services for existing slums and squatter settlements.* This reflects a significant shift in the government policy. In response to pressures from the residents and to eliminate hazards to public health, minimum basic urban services are provided. At this stage, the inevitable continuation of such settlements is recognized. Yet, the focus of policies is to provide minimum levels of basic services in order to discourage illegal occupation of land by the squatters in the future.

4. *Extension of tenure security and physical upgrading.* The most significant felt needs of squatters are to have security of tenure and physical upgrading. The assumption at this stage of the policy evolution is that satisfaction of these needs would result in the residents willingness to invest more of their own resources and to improve their houses on a self-help basis. During the 1970s and 1980s, several Asian countries, such as India and Malaysia, have taken steps to provide security of tenure and physical upgrading.

5. *Recognition of the legitimate role of slums and squatter settlements in urban development.* At this stage, squatter settlements are not considered a problem but rather a solution to urban service deficiencies. In addition to physical upgrading, social services are extended to these settlements, standards and procedures are modified to increase the access of low-income groups, institutional credit is made available to the residents to improve their dwelling units, and methods and procedures for partial recovery of cost are streamlined. The World Bank-assisted shelter projects are based on the recognition of the role of slums and squatter settlements in urban development.

RECOGNITION OF THE SIGNIFICANCE OF SHELTER

The significance of shelter and basic urban services has become more recognized by planners and policymakers in developing countries. Indeed, since the 1970s, several efforts have been made at the national, regional, and international levels to meet urban service deficiencies. In the case of Asia, Yeung has identified three major national-level policy trends during the 1970s in providing low-income housing.[29] First, many governments have adopted "a conciliatory and accommodating" approach vis-à-vis squatter settlements. Second, housing is recognized "as a productive sector in its own right and a means to achieve social and economic objectives."[30] Third, the governments have established national housing authorities, among others, to plan and implement low-income housing. At the regional level, na-

Table 3.1
Urban Shelter Projects: Lending and Costs, 1972–81

Fiscal Year	Number of Projects	Amount of Loan*	Total Project Costs*
1972	2	10.3	16.2
1973	1	20.0	26.0
1974	2	18.0	39.3
1975	5	78.0	154.0
1976	2	53.6	108.2
1977	2	65.2	129.3
1978	7	120.3	197.8
1979	3	179.0	431.6
1980	7	192.8	314.4
1981	5	205.0	489.2
Total	36	942.2	1,906.0

*In millions of U.S. dollars.

Source: World Bank, Learning by Doing: World Bank Lending for Urban Development, 1972-82 (Washington, D.C.: 1983), abstracted from Table 1.

tional experiences are being increasingly shared through research networks, conferences, seminars, and study visits.

In Latin America, the potential of community participation in urban areas was recognized by the late 1960s. Alliance for Progress, which was established to encourage reforms, provided funds for greater government intervention in the provision of adequate housing. Attempts were made to provide housing to the poor. In countries such as Venezuela, Colombia, and Brazil, "as part of the development initiative of the Alliance, self-help and community participation became national priorities and governments made more formal commitments to 'community development' programmes than ever before."[31]

At the international level, the assistance for shelter programs has significantly increased. In this regard, the World Bank has played a leading role. For example, by 1982, ninety sites-and-services and community upgrading projects supported by the Bank were in different stages of implementation in fifty developing countries. By 1981, the average amount lent for each of the shelter projects had been U.S. $216 million (Table 3.1).[32] These projects had benefited about 25,000 households per project, providing secure tenure and a range of basic services and emphasizing cost recovery to increase the likelihood of replicability. The propositions on which the projects are based are that the provision of secure tenure and basic services would encourage low-income households to improve their housing through self-help financing and construction and that improved living conditions would lead to growth in productivity and income.[33] As a result of lowered standards in sites-and-improvement projects, a relatively large percentage of the target population has benefited from these projects.

In addition to the World Bank, several other international organizations have provided support for shelter and basic urban services in lower-income settlements. The United States Agency for International Development (USAID), for example, established the Housing Guarantee Loans program in order to provide financing for housing. The Institute of Housing Studies and the Canadian International Development Agency (CIDA) have been providing assistance to train housing administrators. The Asian Development ment Bank established the Urban Development Section and has been assisting shelter projects. The United Nations Children's Fund (UNICEF) has been actively providing support for urban social services in slums and squatter settlements, focusing on the improvement of the socioeconomic situation of women and children. Finally, as mentioned earlier, the United Nations Conference on Human Settlements, which was held in Vancouver in 1976, had a significant impact on recognition of the need to provide shelter, infrastructure, and basic urban services in low-income urban settlements. Delegations representing 124 of the 137 participating governments endorsed a set of recommendations that, among other things, emphasized the need to ensure that the urban poor have adequate access to shelter.

There are reasons why over the past two decades, governments in the developing world have begun to recognize the need for urban shelter and services and, consequently, to project a relatively more positive attitude toward the living environment of squatters and slum dwellers.[34] To begin with, the absolute number of the poor in cities is too large to be ignored by the governments in power. The residents of irregular settlements form large political constituencies for the support of which the ruling elites compete in order to legitimize their power. Government political leaders must appeal to this large segment of the urban population to get their votes and to ensure that they do not participate in antigovernment agitations. Opposition political leaders regard these settlements as centers of poverty and discontentment that could be mobilized against the government.

Conventional approaches to solving the problems related to shelter and services have not yielded the desired results. Thus, some governments recent positive attitudes could be a result of their realization of the inappropriateness of past policies and programs.

The availability of funding for shelter projects from international organizations and bilateral donor agencies has also contributed to the recent change in the attitutdes of governments toward poor urban settlements. As discussed in Chapter 8, the implementation of foreign-assisted projects has, in some cases, brought about changes in government policies.

In some cities (Karachi and Lahore in Pakistan, for example) the availability of public land has enabled national and municipal governments to tolerate illegal ownership of public land while, at the same time, attempting to protect privately owned land. It is obvious that where land is owned by the government, legitimization of irregular settlements is easier than in stituations where land is privately owned.

To an extent, spontaneous settlements support the existing social, political, and economic systems. For example, these settlements provide some of the poor with housing without negatively affecting higher-income groups; provide cheap labor for modern industry and other sectors of the economy; and increase profit opportunities for commercial and industrial enterprises due to large-scale house construction and consolidation. Gilbert has summed up the situation by commenting that "while a spontaneous settlement clearly brings problems for the state, it is generally functional to the maintenance and reproduction of the social and economic order."[35]

THE EVOLUTION OF SELECTED PROJECTS

Since the 1970s, several developing countries have initiated urban projects aimed at providing shelter, services, and infrastructural facilities to low-income groups. The United Nations Center for Regional Development (UNCRD) sponsored case studies of some of these projects in order to identify policy implications for providing basic urban services to the poor. Table 3.2 presents a profile of these projects and Table 3.3 presents their stated objectives.

Nadi Integrated Social Services Project

The Nadi Integrated Social Services Project was initiated in 1979 by the Ministry of Federal Territory in cooperation with UNICEF to improve the dwelling environment in squatter settlements of Kuala Lumpur. It was estimated that the squatter population accounted for about 25 percent of Kuala Lumpur's total population. From 1974 to 1980, this population increased at an annual rate of 9.7 percent. The household incomes for squatters are considerably below the average for the city. Most of the squatters are employed as laborers, drivers, guards, petty traders, and unskilled factory workers. In addition to low-quality housing, the squatters did not have adequate access to amenities such as piped water, electricity, drainage, garbage collection, or waste disposal. In the early 1960s, the government attempted to contain the problem by demolishing some of the squatter settlements and resettling the affected households in low-cost housing. This approach was found to be too expensive and too slow to cope with rapidly increasing number of squatters.

In 1978, the Kuala Lumpur city government organized a seminar on strategies for improving squatter settlements. The seminar, which was attended by representatives of concerned government agencies and those of squatter settlements, recommended the establishment of maternal and child-

Table 3.2
Projects Selected for Case Studies

Country	Project Type	Services Offered	Time Frame	Location	Sources of Funding	Implementing Agencies
Malaysia	Nadi Integrated Social Services Project	Comprehensive health services such as family planning and mother and child health; basic amenities such as water supply, refuse collection, and electricity; community development activities and services	1979-present	Kuala Lumpur	Government UNICEF NGOs	Ministry of Federal Territory Other related agencies
Pakistan	Lahore Walled City Project	Water supply; sewage system; electricity; street lighting; community centers; upgrading schools, loans for house construction	1982-present	Lahore	Government World Bank	Lahore Development Authority Lahore Municipal Corporation Water and Sanitation Agency House Building Finance Corporation
	Katchi Abadis Project	Community centers; sanitation; income generation activities; social services such as health and education, roads and street lights	1981-present	Lahore	Government UNICEF Community	Government UNICEF
Korea	Integrated Social Services Project	Health care; housing improvement; public utilities; income generation activities; donations of food grains and cash grants; child nutrition improvement	1975-present	Seoul	Government UNICEF NGOs	Municipal government NGOs
Sri Lanka	Environmental Health and Community Development Project	Water supply; sanitation and health education; preschool education; community organization	1979-present	Colombo	Government UNICEF	Colombo Municipal Council Urban Development Authority Other agencies when necessary

Table 3.2 *continued*

Country	Project	Activities	Dates	Location		
Kenya	Dandora Community Development Project	Plots for houses; access roads; community development facilities, i.e., school, market, community centers; sewage system; maternal and child health care	1975-80	Nairobi	Government World Bank	Central government agencies Municipality
	Chaani Upgrading and Services Project	Access roads; water supply; sewage system; plots for houses; community facilities, i.e., markets, community centers; electricity	1978-present	Mombasa	Government World Bank	Central government agencies Municipal Council
Nigeria	Oleleya-Iponri Slum Upgrading Project	Improved roads; community clinics; markets; public water supply; sanitary and sewage facilities	1983-present	Lagos	Government UNICEF NGOs	Central ministries/boards Community
Indonesia	Block Grants Project	Sanitation; preschool education; income generation activities; other social services	1979-present	Surabaya	UNICEF Municipality Community	Community Municipality Department of Home Affairs
India	Hyderabad Urban Community Development Project	Environmental sanitation including water; family welfare including immunization, health, and first-aid classes and family planning; recreational and cultural activities; educational activities including vocational training; economic activities including bank loans; housing improvement	1967-present	Hyderabad	Municipality UNICEF Community	Municipality UNICEF Community

Table 3.3
Stated Objectives of the Selected Projects

Project	Stated Objectives
Nadi Project, Kuala Lumpur	1. To provide comprehensive health services such as mother and child health in squatter settlements 2. To provide basic services and amenities such as water supply, electricity and refuse disposal 3. To provide community and family development activities such as preschool education 4. To promote community participation in local activities 5. To focus the urban poor as the beneficiary group
Lahore Walled City Project	1. To improve basic living conditions in the Walled City 2. To conserve places of cultural and historical importance 3. To provide or improve services such as water supply, electricity, street lighting, sewage, solid waste disposal, schools, and loans for house construction
Integrated Social Services Project, Seoul	1. To provide basic services to meet the immediate needs of the poor in the area 2. To assist the urban poor in becoming self-reliant 3. To encourage community participation through grass-roots organizations
Lahore Katchi Abadis Project	1. To facilitate community participation in activities dealing with the improvement of environmental conditions 2. To provide infrastructural facilities such as roads, drainage system, community halls, and sewage system 3. To mobilize community resources for self-sustaining development 4. To provide social services such as health and education for children and illiterate women 5. To provide income generating opportunities
Environmental and Community Development Project, Colombo	1. To provide physical amenities wuch as water supply and sanitary toilets 2. To promote health education 3. To create a trained cadre of community workers, for example, Health Wardens 4. To establish community organizations in order to elicit popular participation in the project

Table 3.3 *continued*

Project	Stated Objectives
Dandora Community Development Project	1. Providing shelter through serviced sites 2. Providing community facilities such as public market and primary and nursery schools 3. Providing adult literacy, maternal health and child-care facilities 4. Promoting employment generating activities
Chaani Upgrading and Services Project	1. Providing basic infrastructure such as roads and water supply 2. Providing survey plots for house construction 3. Providing community services and facilities
Olaleye-Iponri Slum Upgrading Project	1. Providing basic urban services such as public water supply, community clinics and sanitary and sewage facilities 2. Encouraging community participation through women's associations and community development committees
Surabaya Block Grants Project	1. To make up for deficiencies in sectoral coverage of urban services 2. To facilitate community participation 3. To encourage local initiative to solve particular problems of an area 4. To strengthen local capacity for planning and management
Hyderabad Urban Community Development Project.	1. To promote self-help activities by creating a sense of participation among people 2. To provide basic physical amenities 3. To promote opportunities for income generation 4. To create an increased awareness among the people by promoting educational activities

care health clinics in selected squatter settlements. Because the squatters have higher priority to the provision of such basic amenities as piped water and electricity, the original recommendation was modified to include the provision of preschool education and income-generating activities. The project was named Sang Kancil (symbolically adopting a favorable image from Malay folklore) and was gradually extended to cover thirteen settlements. In 1979, the Sang Kancil Project was merged with the National Family

Planning Board's project that was aimed at combining parasite control for children with family planning. Thus, the Nadi (pulse) project came into existence. In addition to the first two components, other services needed by the poor urban communities were added to the new project; these include: multiagency delivery of urban services; community-based operation with an active participation of the community organization; and focus on the urban poor as the beneficiary group. Three types of services are provided through this project: comprehensive health services, such as mother and child health; services and basic amenities, such as water supply and electricity; and community and family development activities, such as preschool education and income-generating opportunities.[36]

Lahore Walled City Project

The Lahore Walled City is extremely overpopulated with about 285,000 people in an area of 3.09 square kilometers. Three or four decades before, all income groups had been represented in the population of this area. Gradually, however, more affluent families have moved to suburbs, and at present most of the residents are small traders, craftsmen, or low-paid workers. The average monthly income of the households is close to the country's absolute poverty line. The area has multistoried houses built on small plots and connected by narrow winding lanes. More than 17 percent of the houses are classified as "dilapidated premises." The drainage system in the area is also used for sewerage and there is an increasing discharge of solid waste into open drains. The water pipes are continously leaking and subject to contamination. There are very few spaces or community centers in the area.

In 1980, the Lahore Development Authority undertook "Urban Development and Traffic Study" in collaboration with the World Bank. Based on the study, the Lahore Urban Development Programme was initiated. The Walled City Upgrading Project is one of its main components. The main objectives of the upgrading project were to improve basic living conditions in the Walled City and to conserve places of cultural and historical inportance. The project is focused on the improvement of water supply, electricity, and street lighting; the provision of sewerage, community centers, and solid waste disposal; upgrading of schools; and the provision of loans for house construction.[37]

Integrated Social Services Project, Seoul

The Integrated Social Services Project in Bongchun-dong, Seoul, Korea was initiated in 1975. Bongchun-dong is a typical urban squatter area with a population of about 125,000 persons, most of whom are poor. There are ten field-administration units. Designated as a resettlement site for the victims of 1965 floods, Bongchun-dong had become one of the largest slum and squatter areas in Seoul. Most housing units were illegal and temporary, and therefore the government agencies tended to be reluctant to provide infrastructure facilities for the area. The identification and formulation of this project resulted from several consultations between concerned ministries and organizations such as the Economic Planning Board, the Ministry of Science and Technology, the Seoul City Government, research institutions, and UNICEF. The main objectives of the project were to (1) provide basic services to meet immediate needs of the poor in the area; (2) assist the urban poor in becoming self-reliant; and (3) encourage community participation through grass-roots organizations. The services provided through the project included government donations of food grains and cash grants to the poorest families, government employment service on a daily basis, income-generating activities and vocational training, child nutrition improvement, primary health care, and preschool education.[38]

Lahore Katchi Abadis Project

Most of the Katchi Abadis (slums) in Lahore resulted from a large-scale influx of refugees from India at the time of independence in 1947 and rapid rural-urban migration over the past three decades. In most cases, residents of these settlements did not have legal occupancy of land and were below the average household income in the country. Most of the inhabitants were illiterate. Some of these settlements were subject to frequent flooding and were badly damaged during the rainy season. The quality of the dwelling units was poor, and most residents did not have an access to basic urban services.

The Lahore Katchi Abadis Project began in 1981. Responsibility for implementing the project was entrusted to Lahore Development Authority (LDA) and government departments such as social welfare, health, and education. UNICEF provided assistance for the project, the strategic objectives of which were to facilitate community participation in various activities dealing with the improvement of environmental conditions and income generation; increase educational opportunities for children and illiterate women; and reduce infant mortality. Four components of the project were to provide infrastructural facilities such as roads, drainage systems, street lights, community halls, and sewage systems; to encourage self-sustaining development; to provide social services such as health and education; and to provide income-generating activities.[39]

Environmental Health and Community Development Project

It had been estimated that in Colombo about half of the city's total population lived in slums and shanties. In most of these settlements there was a relatively high incidence of infant and child mortality, prevalent water-related diseases, poor sanitation, lack of environmental hygiene, and inadequate basic urban services. It was within this context that the UNICEF-assisted Environmental Health and Community Development Project began in 1979. Four main objectives of the project were to provide physical amenities such as water supply, sanitary toilets, and bath facilities; raise the health standards through mass media health education programs, immunization campaigns, promotion of family planning, and increased awareness of personal hygiene; create a cadre of community workers, that is, health wardens who were to serve as a link between the communities and project authorities; and establish community organizations in order to elicit participation of the people in the project.[40]

Dandora Community Development Project

As in other developing countries, in Kenya there has been a massive rural to urban migration that has put additional strain on available urban services and housing facilities. By the late 1970s, one-third of Nairobi's population was estimated to be living in squatter settlements that lacked basic standards of shelter and sanitation. Thus, the Nairobi City Council felt the need to formulate a housing program to meet the needs of the city's population, to improve existing squatter settlements, to provide sites with basic services, and to encourage aided self-help housing.

The Dandora Community Development Project was launched in 1975, with the World Bank providing 55 percent of the funding. Dandora, formerly a private farm, was acquired by the government to provide land for the people to construct their houses on. The project was aimed at providing shelter, community facilities, and income-generation opportunities intended to benefit low-income urban dwellers. The community facilities to be provided included public markets, primary and nursery schools, and public open spaces. The project also provided for adult literacy and maternal health and child-care activities. Over 16,000 people applied for the 6,000 plots made available under the project. Home construction was the responsibility of the allotee.[41]

Chaani Upgrading and Services Project

In 1976, the government of Kenya and the municipality of Mombasa decided to upgrade the Chaani settlement with the assistance of the World Bank. The Chaani Upgrading and Services Project was to cover 941 existing structures and 544 plots for sites and services. Objectives of the project were to provide basic infrastructure such as paved roads, water, and a sewage system; prepare plots for house construction; and provide community facilities such as primary schools, community centers, garbage disposal, and electricity.[42]

Olaleye-Iponri Slum Upgrading Project

The Olaleye-Iponri slum in Lagos was characterized by overcrowded shanties built close together without adequate space for vehicular movement and without proper drainage, water, or electricity. The system for garbage disposal was a hazard to public health; the average household income was below the national poverty line; and most of the residents were illiterates or primary school dropouts. The occupants did not have security of land tenure.

The main objective of the Olaleye-Iponri Slum Upgrading Project was to improve the residents' quality of life. More specifically, the project aimed at providing basic urban services to meet the immediate needs of the residents and encouraging community participation through existing neighborhood groups (such as women's associations and community development committees). The services to be provided through the project included improved roads, community clinics, public water supply, and sanitary and sewerage facilities.[43]

Surabaya Block Grants Project

In Surabaya, Indonesia's second-largest city, there were serious deficiencies in basic urban services. Access to piped water was limited to 17 percent of the households, and immunization was available to only 40 percent. About 70 percent of the solid waste went into ditches, canals, or rivers. The infant mortality rate was high, particularly for Kampung (village) areas in the city. In 1979, the government launched the Block Grants Project with the assistance of UNICEF. The main objectives of the project were to make up for deficiencies in sectoral coverage of basic urban services; enhance community participation in the delivery of services; encourage local initiative in solving particular area problems; and strengthen local capacity for planning and management of development projects and activities.[44]

Hyderabad Urban Community Development Project

In Hyderabad, the slum population was estimated to be about 50 percent of the city's total population. There were two types of slums in the city: old housing areas that were in dilapidated condition and the squatter settlements or shanty towns that have developed more recently. The pilot project in Hyderabad to upgrade the slum area began in December 1967.

In the 1960s, the government of India established the Rural-Urban Committee, which suggested encouraging people to exercise their own initiative in planning and implementing development projects and providing more government resources to meet the felt needs of the people. Based on the committee's recommendations, experimental projects were initiated in

Delhi, Ahmadabad, Baroda, and Calcutta and were extended to Hyderabad in 1967. After three years, the project was transferred from the central to the state government and thus began to function as a part of the Municipal Corporation. The main objectives of the project were to promote self-help activities by creating a sense of participation among the people; provide basic physical amenities; promote opportunities for income generation; and create an increased awareness among the people by promoting educational activities.[45]

The evolution and rationale of these projects can be better understood within the context of peculiar social, economic, and political conditions in the respective countries. Yet, there are several similarities relating to the evolution of the projects that could be summarized as follows

1. The selected projects reflect the governments' responses to the failure of conventional approaches to providing shelter and basic urban services to low-income groups.

2. In most cases, political expediency necessitated the recognition of squatter settlements and initiation of improvement strategies.

3. Active community participation was considered a prerequisite for the success of the selected projects. Therefore, one of the main objectives of most projects is to promote active participation of the people in identifying local needs, mobilizing community resources, and implementing development activities.

4. The projects are based on the assumption that security of tenure and physical upgrading would encourage residents to improve their houses on a self-help basis.

5. Each of the projects emphasizes the provision of basic urban services such as potable water, garbage disposal, drainage, and community centers.

6. International agencies (in particular the World Bank and UNICEF) have played an important advocacy role in government's recognition of the need for formulating poverty-oriented urban projects and have provided financial and technical support to implement most of the selected projects.

7. Most of the projects were experimental in nature and were designed to be replicatated in order to reach the largest number of urban poor.

NOTES

1. Charles Abrams, *Housing in the Modern World: Man's Struggle for Shelter in an Urbanizing World* (London: Faber & Faber, 1964); and John F. C. Turner, *Housing by People: Towards Autonomy in Building Environments* (London: Marion Boyars, 1976).

2. Turner, *Housing by People*, p. 124.

3. Rod Burgess, "Petty Commodity or Dweller Control? A Critique of John Turner's Views on Housing Policy," *World Development* 6:9–10 (1978), 1105–33.

4. Ibid., p. 1126.

5. Ibid., p. 1130.

6. Ibid.

7. Janice E. Perlman, "Strategies for Squatter Settlements: The State of Art of 1977," in United Nations Centre for Human Settlements (HABITAT), *The Residential Circumstances of the Urban Poor in Developing Countries* (New York: Praeger, 1981), pp. 170–71.

8. Aprodicio A. Laquian, *Basic Housing: Policies for Urban Sites, Services and Shelter in Developing Countries* (Ottawa: International Development Research Centre, 1983), pp. 17–18.

9. Shlomo Angel and Stan Benjamin, "Seventeen Reasons Why the Squatter Problem Can't be Solved," *Ekistics* 242 (January 1976).

10. Ibid.

11. United Nations, *Report of Habitat United Nations Conference on Human Settlements* (New York: United Nations, 1976).

12. Ibid.

13. David G. Williams, "The Role of International Agencies: The World Bank," in Geoffrey K. Payne, ed., *Low Income Housing in the Developing World: The Role of Sites and Services and Settlement Upgrading* (Chichester, England: John Wiley, 1984), pp. 173–86.

14. Douglas H. Keare and Scott Parris, "Evolution of Shelter Programmes for the Urban Poor: Principal Findings," Washington, D.C.: The World Bank, Staff Working Paper no. 547 (1983).

15. Michael A.Cohen, "The Challenge of Replicability: Towards a New Paradigm for Urban Shelter in Developing Countries," *Regional Development Dialogue* 4:1 (Spring 1983).

16. Ibid.

17. UNICEF, *Reaching Children and Women of the Urban Poor* (New York: UNICEF, 1984), p. 15.

18. Ibid.

19. United Nations Centre for Human Settlements (HABITAT), *Survey of Slum and Squatter Settlements* (Dublin: Tycooly International, 1982).

20. Madhu Sarin, *Slum and Squatter Settlements in the ESCAP Region* (Bangkok: Economic and Social Commission for Asia and the Pacific, 1980), pp. 9–10.

21. In-Joung Whang, "Managing Public Services for the Urban Poor in Korea" (Nagoya: UNCRD, 1984, mimeo), p. 6

22. J. O. Kayila, "Managing Urban Development: Kenya's Experience" (Nagoya: UNCRD, 1984, mimeo), p. 18.

23. Viqar Ahmed, "Managing Urban Development: Focus on Services for the Poor" (Nagoya: UNCRD, 1984, mimeo), pp. 17–18.

24. Hong Hai Lim, "Country Review for Malaysia" (Nagoya: UNCRD, 1984, mimeo), pp. 5–6.

25. H. R. Goel, "Indian Experience in Managing Services for the Urban Poor" (Paper presented to the International Seminar on Managing Urban Development, Seoul, 20–23 November 1984).

26. For an overview of these approaches and strategies, see, among others, UNICEF, *Social Planning with the Urban Poor: New Government Strategies* (Geneva: UNICEF, 1982): and Sarin, *Slum and Squatter Settlements.*

27. Arturo D. Aportadera, "Bagong Lipunan Sites and Services Program: The Philippine Experience in Rural Housing and Development," in Y. M. Yeung, ed., *A Place to Live.*

28. For an analysis of patterns of policy, see John D. Montgomery, Harold D. Lasswell, and Joel S. Migdal, *Patterns of Policy* (New Brunswick, N.J.: Transaction Books, 1979).

29. Yeung, *A Place to Live*, pp. 12–17.

30. Ibid., p. 12.

31. Alan Gilbert and Peter Ward, "Community Action by the Urban Poor: Democratic Involvement, Community Self-Help or a Means of Social Control," *World Development* 12:8 (August 1984).

32. World Bank, *Learning by Doing: World Bank Lending for Urban Development, 1972–82* (Washington, D.C.: World Bank, 1983).

33. Keare and Parris, "Evolution of Shelter Programmes."

34. On the reasons for the change of attitudes on the part of the governments, see, among others, Allan Gilbert and Josef Gugler, *Cities, Poverty and Development* (Oxford: Oxford University Press, 1982); Shlomo Angel et al., eds., *Land for Housing the Poor* (Singapore: Select Books, 1983).

35. Gilbert and Gugler, *Cities, Poverty and Development*, p. 113.

36. Hong Hai Lim, "Nadi Integrated Social Services Programme, Kuala Lumpur" (Nagoya: UNCRD, 1984, mimeo).

37. Viqar Ahmed, "Lahore Walled City Upgrading Project" (Nagoya: UNCRD, 1984, mimeo).

38. In-Joung Whang, "Management of Integrated Social Services for the Urban Poor: The Case of Bongchun-Dong, Seoul" (Nagoya: UNCRD, 1984, mimeo).

39. Feroza Ahsan, "Provision of Services to the Urban Poor: A Case Study of Lahore Katchi Abadis" (Nagoya: UNCRD, 1984, mimeo).

40. S. Tilakaratna, S. Hettige, and Wilfred Karunaratna, "Environmental Health and Community Development Project" (Nagoya: UNCRD, 1985, mimeo).

41. James O. Kayila, "Improving Urban Settlements for the Poor: Case Studies of Dandora and Chaani Projects in Kenya," (Nagoya: UNCRD, 1984, mimeo).

42. Ibid.

43. Paulina Makinwa-Adebusoye, "Upgrading Olaleye-Iponri Slum in Lagos Metropolitan Area" (Nagoya: UNCRD, 1984, mimeo).

44. T. Tarigan, Soedarjo and Saukat Sacheh, "Block Grants Project in Surabaya" (Nagoya: UNCRD, 1984, mimeo).

45. William J. Cousins and Catherine Goyder, *Changing Slum Communities* (New Delhi: Manohar, 1979).

4

CAPABILITIES OF
IMPLEMENTING AGENCIES

The success of government policies that deal with urban shelter and basic services for the poor depends, to a considerable extent, upon the degree to which agencies and concerned actors at the national, regional, and local levels have developed the capacities to effectively perform the planning, decision-making, and management functions given to them. To be effective these agencies should have a clear understanding of their roles and responsibilities; the technical and managerial skills necessary to perform their assigned tasks; adequate budgetary allocations and timely availability of funds; political support for the policies and programs at all levels of government; viable linkages with poor urban communities and project beneficiaries; and the capacity to coordinate and integrate their actions.

The planning and management of upgrading and sites-and-services projects require different types of structures and procedures from those needed for conventional public sector housing. These structures and procedures should facilitate increased participation by the residents in the design and construction of dwelling units, the modification and reduction of the construction standards, and the mobilization of community resources.

This chapter discusses lead agencies and multilevel responsibilities for implementing selected projects, technical and managerial skills of implementing agencies, their linkages with beneficiaries, and the degree of political support for the projects. It also examines the types of administrative responses and public management styles and an optimal distribution of responsibilities for urban services to the poor.

LEAD AGENCIES AND MULTILEVEL RESPONSIBILITIES

The case studies of selected urban projects aimed at providing shelter and basic urban services show that in most cases the lead agency at the national level is the ministry concerned with urban development. In some cases, training and research institutions also play an important role. At the regional level, usually the municipal government and semiautonomous urban development authorities are the lead agencies. At the local level, implementing agencies are local community organizations, local offices of municipalities and state governments and nongovernmental voluntary organizations. It is evident that one of the main features of these projects is that unlike most government-initiated development programs, at the community level people's organizations are relatively more actively involved in the process of project implementation (see Table 4.1).

Table 4.2 presents multilevel responsibilities for implementing the selected projects. In most cases, project identification and formulation have been undertaken by the concerned central ministry or the municipality in collaboration with UNICEF or the World Bank. In the case of Lahore Walled City Project, however, these tasks were performed by a semiautonomous development authority in collaboration with the World Bank and the Planning and Development Department. Research institutions played an important role in formulating the Integrated Social Services Project in Seoul. In federal systems such as India, Pakistan, and Nigeria, state governments have actively participated in the process of project identification and formulation. The allocation of funds has in most cases been the responsibility of the ministry or department of finance and the concerned municipality.

Project activities have usually been carried out by the municipality with the active participation of community organizations. Nadi Project, however, was based on a multiagency approach to project implementation that involved about twenty sectoral agencies. Implementation of the Lahore Walled City and Katchi Abadis projects involved semiautonomous urban development authorities. With the exception of Lahore Walled City Project, each project provides for active participation of community organizations.

Monitoring and evaluation tasks are performed by the municipality and/or the concerned ministry and department. International organizations such as UNICEF and the World Bank have undertaken ongoing and impact evaluations. In the case of Integrated Social Service Project in Seoul, research institutions have been actively involved in monitoring and evaluating development activities.

There are advantages to having a special authority to provide basic housing and services—it might facilitate coordination, attract dynamic and innovative personnel, succeed in mobilizing more funds from the central and regional governments, and be able to elicit political support from national leaders. The weaknesses of the special authority are that it might lead to

Table 4.1
Lead Agencies for Implementing Selected Projects

Projects	National Level	Regional Level	Local/Community Level
Nadi Project, Kuala Lumpur	Social Development Division, Ministry of Federal Territory Consultative Committee		Nadi Divisional Offices Local/Community Action committees
Lahore Walled City Project	Ministry of Housing and Urban Development as the national agency for coordination	Lahore Development Authority Water and Sanitation Agency Lahore Municipal Corporation Provincial Housing and Physical Planning Department	Local councillors
Integrated Social Services Project, Seoul	Economic Planning Board Chung-Ang University Social Welfare Centre Korea Institute for Research in Behavioral Sciences Korea Institute of Population and Health	Bureau of Health and Social Affairs, Seoul City Government	District Social Welfare Division Dong Office
Lahore Katchi Abadis Project	Ministry of Housing and Urban Development	Planning and Development Department Lahore Development Authority Social Welfare Directorate Lahore Municipal Corporation	Community Development councils

Table 4.1 *continued*

Projects	National Level	Regional Level	Local/Community Level
Environmental Health and Community Development Project, Colombo	Common Amenities Board Urban Development Authority Ministry of Finance Ministry of Local Government Housing and Construction	Municipal Government	Community Development Councils
Dandora Community Development Project	Ministry of Works, Housing and Physical Planning Ministry of Lands Ministry of Local Government	Housing Development of Nairobi City Council	Dandora Community Development Council
Chaani Upgrading and Services Project	Ministry of Works, Housing and Physical Planning Ministry of Local Government Ministry of Lands	Housing Development Department of Mombasa Municipal Council	Chaani Village Committee
Surabaya Blocks Grants Project	Directorate of Urban Development	Surabaya Municipal Council	Community organizations
Olaleye-Iponri Slum Upgrading Project	Federal Ministry of Works	Division of Urban and Regtional Planning Lagos State Government departments	Community Development Association
Hyderabad Urban Community Development Project	Ministry of Health, Family Planning and Urban Development	Municipal Corporation	Basti Welfare Committees Mahila Mandals (neighborhood organizations)

Table 4.2
Multilevel Responsibilities for Implementing Selected Urban Projects

Project	Identification Formulation	Allocation of Funds	Carrying Out Project Activities	Monitoring and Evaluation
Nadi Project, Kuala Lumpur	Ministry of Federal Territory UNICEF	Treasury Economic Planning Unit Ministry of Federal Territory	Social Development Division of Ministry of Federal Territory Concerned sectoral agencies and departments	Ministry of Federal Territory
Lahore Walled City Project	Lahore Development Authority Planning and Development Department World Bank	Planning and Development Department Finance Department Lahore Development Authority	Lahore Development Authority Lahore Municipal Corporation Water and Sanitation Agency Other relevant sectoral agencies	Planning and Development Department Provincial Department of Housing and Physical Planning
Integrated Social Services Project, Seoul	Economic Planning Board Seoul City Government University Social Welfare Centre UNICEF Korea Institute of Population and Health	Economic Planning Board Seoul City Government	Bureau of Health and Social Services of Seoul City Government through its branch offices and NGOs	Seoul City Government
Lahore Katchi Abadis Project	Planning and Development Department of Provincial Government UNICEF	Provincial Finance Department Planning and Development Department	Katchi Abadis all of Planning and Development Department Lahore Development Authority Lahore Municipal Corporation Social Welfare Directorate Community Development Councils	Planning and Development Department UNICEF

Table 4.2 *continued*

Environmental Health and Community Development Project, Colombo	Municipal Government Ministry of Local Government, Housing and Construction	Municipal Government Ministry of Finance	Relevant departments of municipal government Urban Development Authority Other supporting agencies	Ministry of Local Government, Housing and Construction
Dandora Community Development Project	Nairobi City Council World Bank	Ministry of Finance Nairobi City Council	Housing Development Department of Nairobi City Council Concerned government departments	Nairobi City Council Ministry of Local Government
Chaani Upgrading and Services Project	Mombasa Municipal Council World Bank	Ministry of Finance Mombasa Municipal Council	Housing Development Department of Mombasa Municipal Council Concerned government departments	Mombasa Municipal Council Ministry of Local Government
Surabaya Block Grants Project	Directorate of Urban Development UNICEF	Ministry of Finance Directorate of Urban Development	Community with the technical assistance of Surabaya Municipality	Surabaya Municipality Directorate of Urban Development
Olaleye-Iponri Slum Upgrading Project	Lagos State Government UNICEF	Lagos State Government	Division of Urban and Regional Planning Community	Lagos State Government
Hyderabad Urban Community Development Project	Municipality State Government UNICEF	State Government Municipality	Community Development Department of Municipality Basti Welfare Committee Neighborhood committees	State Government Municipality UNICEF

functional and geographical fragmentation of government functions, increase administrative costs of government programs, and antagonize line agencies. Because the provision of shelter and services requires contributions from many agencies and different levels of government, in some countries shelter programs have been placed under the central government ministries (such as finance, local government, or housing), which facilitates the mobilization of political support for such programs.

TECHNICAL AND MANAGERIAL SKILLS

The experience of developing countries shows that while in most cases agencies responsible for implementing shelter projects have adequate technical skills, their ability to work effectively with poor communities is extremely limited. Formal advanced education and managerial skills do not necessarily prepare the project personnel for organizing poor communities, working with local leaders, or eliciting the community's support for government programs. In his case study of the Nadi project, Lim summed up the weaknesses of the concerned project personnel in their attempts to work with poor communities:

The majority of officials lack the appropriate training, the sense of professionalism, and the strong commitment for the complex and demanding task of working for and with the people. . . . Many kinds of undesirable behaviour observed in the programme are, at least in part, manifestations of this lack of professionalism and commitment, including the sense of status superiority and the inability and reluctance to interact with the poor on an equal basis, the refusal to work outside office hours, and the unwillingness to work or to spend time in the villages.[1]

In the case of the Hyderabad Community Development Project, close teamwork developed among the project personnel over the eight years that they worked together. All the staff members had university degrees and had previous experience with the Rural Community Development Programme. Furthermore, eight volunteer social workers were recruited and given adequate training. The community organizers and the project personnel worked in close cooperation with Basti (settlement) welfare development committees to promote self-help activities to meet the felt needs of the people. Thus, the background, training, and teamwork of the project personnel enabled them to work effectively with the people.[2]

The agencies responsible for implementing the Integrated Social Services Project in Seoul had adequate technical and managerial skills. The Social Affairs Division of the city government had eighteen officials; there were twenty-two working in the Dong office, three of whom were college graduates. The Korea Institute for Research in Behavioral Sciences, the Social Welfare Centre, and the Korea Institute for Population and Health were

actively involved in the project. Each of these research institutions had a
highly competent staff. Community development committees were established to facilitate communication between implementing agencies and the
people.[3]

The Katchi Abadis Project in Lahore has intensive administrative input.
The lead government agency, that is, the Lahore Development Authority,
is a semiautonomous organization that has a relatively more competent staff
and the flexibility required to design and implement development activities
for the urban poor. UNICEF has provided necessary training particularly
related to community participation in social services and income-generating
activities.[4]

The design of the Environmental Health and Community Development
Project in Colombo provided for health wardens to work in co-operation
with the people.[5] The implementing agencies have the technical skills to
carry out development activities, but their relations with the local communities have not been very smooth. During the early years of the project,
several implementing agencies (the Urban Development Authority, for example) carried out their activities without taking the priorities of the communities into consideration. In some cases these agencies provided services
and facilities to areas in which community development committees had
not yet been established. Furthermore, initially these agencies failed to appreciate the significance of the community work undertaken by the health
warden and the community development committees.

The case studies show that in most cases implementing agencies had
adequate technical skills required to carry out development activities. Where
the concerned staff utilized human skills to elicit the community's response
to government initiative and where there was relatively more flexibility in
the administrative structures and procedures, the project staffs were more
successful in improving the access of the poor to urban services.

Because the tasks involved in planning and managing shelter projects are
multidisciplinary in nature, the conventional dominant roles of architects
and engineers ought to be modified or attenuated in relative power to allow
for greater participation by professionals from other disciplines, such as
economics, public administration, or sociology. This should enhance the
abilities of the implementing agencies to organize poor urban communities,
mobilize community resources, and elicit the necessary support of the target
communities in the government-initiated programs.

INTERAGENCY COORDINATION

Ineffectiveness of interagency coordination is one of the most critical
weaknesses of urban shelter and basic services projects in low-income settlements. The most common tendency of the project personnel is to over-
emphasize their own agency's approach and requirements and to be

reluctant to appreciate the needs and difficulties of other agencies. The result is a fragmentation of governmental activities and an inability of implementing agencies to respond effectively to the felt needs of the poor communities.

In the case of Katchi Abadis Project, the Lahore Development Authority (LDA) was responsible for the main physical infrastructure upgrading; the Water and Sanitation Authority for sewerage, drainage, and water supply; the Water and Power Development Authority for electricity; and the Lahore Municipal Corporation for solid waste collection. The project design provided for establishing an interagency coordinating committee as well as various working groups to resolve operational problems. In actual practice, however, the LDA retained for itself the role of general coordinator, and a single-dominant-agency type of management has emerged. Other agencies are called upon to provide specific services. The Interagency Coordination Committee and the working groups do not exist.[6]

In the case of Nadi Project, the Consultative Committee in the Ministry of Federal Territory was created to plan and coordinate development activities. The committee, however, has remained inactive. The career prospects of government functionaries are dependent upon agency-specific performance and they are, thus, usually not anxious to share or coordinate their activities with those of other agencies. As Khairuddin Yusof has pointed out, "Kuala Lumpur's experience has indicated that a multiagency approach, where twenty agencies are called to a meeting and have tasks allocated to them, tends to be counterproductive."[7] An organizational responsibility chart was suggested as a way of making agency commitments more concrete. However, the chart was not actually used by the ministry. One of the problems was that several key personnel from the Consultative Committee were transferred and their replacements did not adequately understand and appreciate the rationale and the strategy of Nadi Project. The Ministry of Federal Territory lacked formal authority to issue directives to other agencies concerning the extent of their contributions to the project. The participation of these other agencies in the program was on a voluntary basis. The transfer in 1982 of the secretary general of the ministry, who had been keenly interested in the project, might also have negatively affected the interest of the ministry in the project. His successor, who was also the mayor, "was by all accounts fully occupied by his mayoral duties to have much time and inclination left for playing an active leadership role in the Nadi Programme."[8] The inability of the Consultative Committee to effectively perform its coordination role partly led to the failure of the divisional action committees and the local action committees to coordinate related activities at their respective levels.

Because the Nadi Project was not designed to be implemented by a single agency, budgetary requests for carrying out the project activities were included in the respective agencies' budgets. Though an attempt was made to make joint budgetary requests for the project activities, it did not succeed, and the agencies continued to make their own budgetary requests. An equally important factor impeding the process of coordination was that the interest and support of key actors in project implementation declined.

In the case of the Integrated Social Project in Seoul, government activities related to the project were coordinated by the Kwanak District Office and the Bongchun-Dong office. However, there were no formal arrangements for coordinating the activities of nongovernmental organizations. One of the important channels for ensuring interagency coordination was a series of workshops and review meetings organized by UNICEF. Representatives of concerned government and nongovernmental agencies participated in these meetings and discussed their work performance. It should be pointed out, however, that this arrangement was ad hoc, and the concerned government agencies and NGOs lack adequate authority and motivation to play the coordinating role.[9]

The coordination of activities in the Olaleye-Iponri Slum Project is achieved through the meetings of the Urban Development Committee, which are attended by senior officials of the concerned government agencies and nongovernmental organizations. Since the Urban Renewal Committee is located in the governor's office, it is in a position to exercise formal and informal authority in seeking the cooperation of the concened agencies. The committee is perceived to be the lead agency for coordinating slum upgrading projects in the metropolitan area.[10]

The Environmental Health and Community Development Project in Colombo was implemented through the existing administrative machinery. This arrangement led to minimal overhead cost and strengthened implementation capacities of the municipality and concerned government agencies. However, the existing structure was not conducive to interagency coordination. The project design stipulated the appointment of a coordinator in Urban Development Authority (UDA) from the Slum Upgrading Project. However the appointment was not made nor were all the required services delivered by the concerned agencies in the project areas. For example, the Common Amenities Board (CAB) failed to upgrade physical amenities in some areas where the community development committees (CDCs) had been established, while providing physical amenities in those areas without CDCs. As Tilakaratna and his associates pointed out:

This situation not only created a credibility gap between the project personnel and the potential beneficiaries, but it also violated a basic principle, namely, that a measure of social preparedness on the part of the communities is a prerequisite to the delivery of services. The CAB appeared to have considered the selection of sites for upgrading of amenities as its prerogative which would not be compromised with requests emanating from the CDCs.[11]

The lack of coordination between UDA and CAB is indicated by the cases of demolition by UDA of the new amenities constructed by CAB. UDA's argument was that demolition was needed for urban redevelopment programs. Another example was the lack of recognition within the administrative system of the special nature of tasks performed by health wardens (HWs) who had to undertake most of their activities in the evenings when the residents could be found at home in their shanties. In 1981, however, the situation improved. A special-projects unit was established to implement UNICEF-assisted activities. In the process of providing facilities, preference was given to those communities in which CDCs had been established, and the choices of location were made after consultation with UDA. A coordinating committee under the chairmanship of the mayor of the municipality was established to review the progress of the project at regular intervals.

The experience in developing countries indicates that the need for interagency coordination is recognized, and institutional arrangements are often made for this purpose. Yet, the sectoral orientation of agencies impedes effective coordination. In some cases, the coordinating agencies do not have adequate authority, while in other cases, the key actors responsible for coordination do not give sufficient time and the attention necessary for this purpose. The studies show that adequate authority is necessary but usually not sufficient for coordinating policies, programs, and projects for the poor. Equally important are the interest and support of senior officials. In some cases, informal channels for coordination prove to be more effective than formal ones.

LINKAGES WITH BENEFICIARIES

Effective management of poverty-oriented urban policies and programs necessitates viable linkages between government agencies and program beneficiaries in order to identify local needs and priorities, mobilize local resources, and elicit active involvement of the people in the process of implementation. This is particularly true for those projects that are aimed at providing basic services such as water, public health, sanitation, community halls, drainage, or sewerage. Lack of rapport between implementing agencies and the people leads to passive responses on the part of the people, and, in some situations they even resist the government initiative. Conversely, where viable linkages exist, there appears to be a greater probability that people will identify with the project, organize themselves to undertake collective actions, and contribute funds and labor to achieve project objectives. In the case of urban shelter and basic housing projects, for example, viable linkages would facilitate the recovery of user charges and the cost of infrastructural improvements, the investment of residents' savings to upgrade their housing units, and integration of social and physical improvements in low-income urban settlements.

The experience of developing countries reflects a variety of approaches that have been utilized, with varying degrees of success, to create better rapport between implementing agencies and the residents of the concerned low-income settlements. In most of the selected projects, specific provisions have been made to create channels for continuous communication between the implementing agencies and the beneficiaries. In practice, however, the effectiveness of those channels shows differences.

As mentioned above, the design of the Environmental Health and Community Development Project in Colombo stipulated the establishment of CDCs through which basic services were to be delivered to the slums and shanties in the project area.[12] In addition, health wardens were to be appointed to work in close cooperation with the communities in order to safeguard public health. Initially, the concerned government agencies failed to coordinate with program beneficiaries. With improved coordination, however, these agencies were able to work more effectively with the program beneficiaries. One hundred and twenty-three health wardens were recruited and trained. They served as the most important channel of communication between the communities and the concerned government agencies. With the assistance of local communities, the health wardens organized voluntary campaigns for cleaning up the environment. The City Development Council, consisting of concerned project officials and representatives of CDCs, was established to review project activities. This provided another channel for communication between officials and representatives of program beneficiaries.

The two projects in Kenya show significant variation in the effectiveness of linkages between implementing agencies and program beneficiaries.[13] In the case of the Dandora Project, the Community Development Division of the Housing Development Department was responsible for publicizing the project, undertaking public relations tasks, providing training to the allottees prior to the occupation of plots, and encouraging residents to organize themselves for development of their communities. The allottees worked in close cooperation with the Community Development Division and formed building groups that facilitated community interaction and cooperation for construction of dwelling units and maintenance of common facilities. In the case of the Chaani Project, the Village Development Committee was not formed during the planning stage, nor were the beneficiaries asked to contribute labor, money, or land. Most of the work was undertaken through contractors. Thus, the linkages between the implementing agencies and program beneficiaries remained weak. The Chaani Project was a replication of the Dandora Project, yet in actual practice, the linkages between implementing agencies and program beneficiaries were much more viable in Dandora than in Chaani, leading to the former's relatively greater success.[14]

In the case of Lahore Walled City Project, there were hardly any formal linkages between implementing agencies and beneficiaries.[15] The nongovernmental organizations within the area did not serve as a communication channel between the residents and the concerned agencies. However, the beneficiaries were able to communicate their suggestions and complaints through some of the informal channels. They could approach the local councillor for the Lahore Municipal Corporation (which is represented in the managing body of Lahore Development Authority) and file complaints through branch offices of the Water and Power Development Authority (WAPDA). In practice, one finds that linkages between beneficiaries and implementing agencies were not effective.

The agencies involved in programming and implementing the Block Grants Project in Surabaya were either official or quasi-official, but both had formal and informal linkages with the community leaders. For example, project locations and beneficaries were invariably chosen by the community in consultation with the project coordinator. Since the Block Grants Project was designed to initiate and promote small-scale development activities directly affecting the community, the implementing agencies have found viable linkages with community leaders a prerequisite to achieving the project objectives.

The design of Nadi project in Kuala Lumpur provided for neighborhood development offices and local action committees as formal linkages between the implementing agencies and the community. However, these committees have not been actually established. Implementing agencies have not been active in communicating needs of the communities to the concerned government agencies. The most important communication channels between the local community and the concerned government agencies are the branches of political parties that are organized along ethnic lines. In Malaysia's plural society, local demands and aspirations are communicated through the United Malay National Organization (UMNO), the Malaysian Chinese Association (MCA), and the Malaysian Indian Congress (MIC), which are the main partners in the national coalition government, that is, Barisan National.[16] The heads of local branches of these parties are the most influential among the local leaders. They use their formal and informal links with government officials and politicians to get the community demands accepted.

A flexible approach and a recognition of the need to work in close cooperation with the community were two of the main features of the Hyderabad Urban Community Development Project.[17] The concerned government agencies and the community organizers worked alongside the Settlement Welfare Department Committees and voluntary groups within the community. This enabled the project personnel to utilize resources from the lower middle class and the urban poor to undertake developmental activities. The implementing agencies also attempted to discover and channel resources from municipal and government departments and nongovernmental agencies to the selected settlements. This further improved the rapport between the project personnel and local residents. In addition, the project staff initiated a number of development activities that were specifically requested by the community. Cousins and Goyder have summed up the need for a flexible approach:

The necessity of forward planning for programmes and budgets, and the need for indices for monitoring and evaluation, too often lead to the establishment of fixed targets. And these bring in their train an increased rigidity. Thus, the needs of the people tend to become subordinated to the bureaucratic needs of the project which originally set out to help them. The success of the Hyderabad Project in maintaining a high degree of flexibility is a rare accomplishment and one of the sources of its strength.[18]

POLITICAL SUPPORT

The formulation of urban policies and projects aimed at improving low-income settlements is a result of pressures and demands by the residents and, consequently, the recognition by policymakers, planners, and administrators of the need to take concrete actions. The implementation of these policies, programs, and projects, however, requires continued political support at the national, regional, and local levels. There are competing demands on the allocation of scarce resources for national development. Within the urban sector, residents of high- and middle-income settlements are more likely to be able to exert greater pressure to divert a major portion of funds to provide urban services and improve infrastructure in their own areas. Therefore, continued support for urban shelter projects for low-income groups at the highest levels as well as pressure from the residents are necessary conditions for the successful implementation of these projects. Political support for a policy or project should be reflected in the allocation of funds and the provision of adequate administrative resources to carry out the activities in close cooperation with the communities.

The experience of developing countries indicates that one of the most difficult tasks in implementing programs for the urban poor is ensuring continuity of support. The tendency of most governments is to respond to the pressures from the urban poor in an ad hoc manner and there are usually very few explicitly stated policies being pursued over a longer period of time. Thus, successful experiments cannot be replicated. As compared to the 1950s and 1960s, however, there is a clear shift in the degree of political and administrative support for poverty-oriented urban projects.

To an extent, the political support for Katchi Abadis in Pakistan has existed since the 1970s. Political parties and potential candidates in national and provincial elections had to pay attention to the situation in these settlements. Ahsan has pointed out that the improvement of Katchi Abadis "predominantly figured in election manifestoes of main political parties in

1970 and 1977 and also in many speeches and declarations by national political leaders."[19] The residents of these settlements are organized in local associations and welfare societies, frequently issue statements in the press, and meet concerned high-level government officials and policymakers to draw their attention to the situation in their localities. In the absence of representative institutions in the late 1970s and early 1980s, however, the extent of their influence on the allocation of funds depended upon their informal linkages with the policymakers and the councillors of Lahore Municipal Corporation.

The Hyderabad Urban Community Development Project could not have succeeded without the political support of the central, state, and municipal governments. While the flexible approach of the project and the motivation and commitment of the project personnel led to the enthusiastic response of the communities, the governments at the central, regional, and municipal levels, respectively, provided the necessary resources and administrative support for the project. Hyderabad was one of the twenty cities that were chosen by the central government to implement its Urban Community Development Project in 1967. Eight community organizers headed by a project officer and eight volunteer social workers were appointed. After the initial success of the project, the state government and the Municipal Corporation provided facilities and resources to extend the activities under the project. One of the additional responsibilities was the construction of 13,000 houses for slum dwellers who had been given legal ownership of the land they were occupying; eight commercial banks with eighty-six branches agreed to lend up to Rs.4,000 to each family for house construction.[20]

When the Nadi project in Kuala Lumpur was initiated, it had support at the highest levels. The administrative head of the Ministry of Federal Territory showed keen interest in the project and spent time mobilizing necessary support from the concerned government agencies for the project. At the community level, the support for the project was elicited through local branches of the three political parties—UMNO, MIC, and MCA—and the local action committees. After a few years, however, the support for the project declined. As mentioned earlier, the administrative head of the ministry was transferred and his replacement did not (due to his additional responsibilities) spend the time and energy needed to coordinate the activities of various agencies, leading to the decline in enthusiasm of officials at the lower levels. In the meantime, the country was passing through a tight economic situation. Though local residents have continued to put pressure from below and communicate their demands to the policymakers, the actual support for the project has declined from M $10 million to M $5 million and there seems to be no guarantee of continued government support. In order to compensate for declining government support, a nongovernmental organization called Sang Kancil Organization for Social Services has been formed to raise funds.

As the case of Nadi project shows, the problem of the urban poor cannot be resolved unless there is a clear national policy and a financial commitment of the government on a continuing basis. The magnitude of the problem is such that existing programs need to be significantly expanded. In most cases, however, such a commitment has still not been made.

The Olaleye-Iponri project has strong political support at the local level.[21] Community development associations were formed in most of the neighborhoods to mobilize support at the grass roots. The Lagos State Government provided a significant percentage of funds, and its role in improving slums and squatter settlements is likely to increase in the future due to its recent policy of gradually eliminating subsidized conventional housing schemes.

TYPES OF ADMINISTRATIVE RESPONSES

The case studies indicate differenty types of administrative responses for implementing urban shelter and servics projects (Table 4.3). Lahore Walled City, Katchi Abadis, Dandora, and Chaani projects were implemented by a single, dominant type of agency while other projects were carried out through multiagency type of structures. In most cases project formulation, allocation of funds, and monitoring and evaluation were undertaken in a highly centralized manner, primarily through government agencies or their field offices. The Lahore Katchi Abadis, Environmental Health and Community Development, Block Grants, and Hyderabad projects had relatively more flexibility in their respective approaches.

The selected projects are equally divided between those in which coordination took place through a single agency and those in which a multiagency coordination committee was established for this purpose. The implementing agencies in the Nadi, Lahore Walled City, Integrated Social Services, Dandora, Chaani, and Olaleye-Iponri projects had top-down types of linkages with the beneficiaries, while the other projects were characterized by a bottom-up, participatory approach. Most projects had significant political support, though in some cases, this could not be sustained.

PUBLIC MANAGEMENT STYLES FOR URBAN SERVICES

One of the critical issues in the provision of urban shelter and services is the role of the state in the performance of such functions as needs assessment, determination of standards, financing, planning, implementation, cost reduction, and financing and quality control. It would seem that, given the magnitude of the problem, the role of the government should change from that of being the primary service provider to that of being one of many service providers. But the government must still retain a leading role in facilitating any self-help activities. As a facilitator of self-help, the functions

Table 4.3
Types of Administrative Responses for Implementing Urban Shelter and Services Projects for the Poor

Types of Administrative Response	Nadi	Lahore Walled City	Integrated Social Services	Lahore Katchi Abadis	Environmental Health & Community Development	Dandora	Chaani	Block Grants	Olaleye-Iponri	Hyderabad
Implementing Agencies:										
Single Agency Dominant		X		X		X	X			
Multiagency	X		X		X			X	X	X
Multilevel Responsibilities:										
Standard	X	X	X			X	X		X	
Flexible bottom-up				X	X			X		X
Interagency Coordination:										
Single Agency Coordination		X		X		X	X		X	
Multiagency Coordination Committee	X		X		X			X		X
Linkages with Beneficiaries:										
Top-down approach	X	X	X			X	X		X	
Bottom-up participatory approach				X	X			X		X
Degree of Political Support:										
High	X			X	X	X			X	X
Low		X	X				X	X		

of the state would include dispersal of information, upgrading standards incrementally, and assisting communities and local governments in the process of planning and implementation.

Other functions of the state as facilitator would be to encourage local governments and communities to generate their own revenue, allow communities and local governments to undertake planning with the guidance of professionals and to control local development activities, and encourage community self-help. The differences in roles and management styles are described in Table 4.4.

OPTIMAL DISTRIBUTION OF RESPONSIBILITIES FOR URBAN SERVICES TO THE POOR

Urban basic services for the poor can be provided by the central government, regional governments, municipalities, or the informal service sector (ISS)—either individually or, as is most common, collectively.[22] Each of these levels has advantages for providing some of the services.

The services in which the ISS can play an important role are those that have a relatively higher "potential incentive" for community participation. For example, housing can (and usually is) provided more effectively through an active involvement of individuals and small groups. The need for sanitation services also motivates communities to be actively involved. Montgomery has identified "three conditions under which the informal sector may serve better than public action: services in which individual needs differ significantly from person to person, those that have to be provided frequently but not routinely, and those that require the individuals to be served to change their behaviour significantly in order to gain the desired benefits."[23]

Municipal governments can facilitate the provision of services to the urban poor in several ways. Among those are building infrastructure for sanitation, public safety, health, and transportation: providing security of land tenure to squatters and slum dwellers; providing standards and training for informal sector activities; and reviewing locational decisions. Municipal governments can also establish employment centers in poor settlements; train concerned government officials in the organization and supervision of voluntary activities; and serve as a link between national planning groups and local communities.

The central government's functions should be those that cannot be performed more effectively by ISS or municipal governments. The main advantages of the central governments, however, are that they can plan and deliver services over larger geographical areas; and that they have more resources in capital and personnel.[24]

In practice, the responsibilities for providing shelter and services are carried out at each level. The optimal distribution of responsibility for services to the urban poor would differ from one place to another depending upon

Table 4.4
Public Management Styles for Urban Services

| Function | Management Styles | |
	State as Provider	State as Facilitator
Needs assessment	Surveys, census, field visits and statistical analysis, centralization of information	Communities' self survey direct consultation, dispersal of information
Determination of standards for services	Professionally established standards; uniform and high level technical performance	Incrementally upgradable standards based on adaptation of existing situation and technologies
Financing	Greater dependence on national government grants and international loans	Local governments and communities generate revenue
Planning	Professionals in government and parastatal agencies	Communities and local governments with guidance of professionals
Implementation	Centrally controlled and managed by authorities, directorates, and public corporations	Controlled and managed by communities with local government support
Financial and quality control	monitoring and evaluation by central authorities through reports, auditing, and strict adherence to numerous and uniform rules, regulations, procedures, standards, and designs	Service providers accountable to community residents and local officials and judged on final effectiveness of service rather than adherence to procedures, etc.
Service personnel	Few professionals assisted by large support staff	Community volunteers and paraprofessionals supported by small group of professionals
Cost reduction	"Efficient" management, competitive bidding, and "economies of scale"	Community self-help, adapting standard to local situation and affordability; elimination of "overhead" costs
Relationship of service providers	Separated and often opposed to communities' demands; government controls	Merging of providers and users; communities control government supports

Note: Most successful experiences of urban services involve elements of two management styles. We are thankful to Clarence Shubert for preparing the first draft of this table.

Table 4.5
Toward an Optimal Distribution of Responsibility for Services to the Urban Poor

	ISS	Municipality	Region or Nation
Housing	Building, leasing	Inspection and technical aid; subsidies	Housing development if needed
Transportation	Bicycles, rick-shahs, jitneys, roadways or alleys	Licensing and supervision; construction and maintenance	Road networks
Sanitation	Water carrying, sewage carrying, water sales	Standpipes, residential service; open and closed sewers	Metropolitan systems, reservoirs; pollution standard
Public safety	Preventive patrols; bonfire control	Supervision and police and fire departments	Networks; national police
Social services	Literacy, traditional health, supervised recreation	Schools, teachers, clinics, staff; parks, staff	Accreditation, higher education, high technology, career development, referral networks, national parks

Source: John D. Montgomery, The Informal Service Sector as an Administrative Resource (Nagoya: UNCRD, 1985), Table 4.

management capacities at each of the three levels. Yet, one could partly redesign the distribution of responsibilities according to the advantages that each of the three levels has in providing a specific service. Table 4.5 shows a prototype of functions in each of the sectors or services to be carried out by the ISS, the municipality, or the central or regional governments.

Montgomery has suggested three steps for the optimal distribution of responsibility. First, an inventory of the current practice, based on a fact-finding survey, must be taken. Second, the analysts could review various combinations of responsibilities to examine the degree to which "restructuring would strengthen the sectors that are least effectively administered."[25] The third step would be to delineate possible problems of coordination among various types of actors and to agree on structures and procedures for interagency coordination in the provision of services.

NOTES

1. Hong Hai Lim, "Nadi Integrated Social Services Programme, J. Kuala Lumpur" (Nagoya: UNCRD, 1984, mimeo), p. 15.

2. William J. Cousins and Catherine Goyder, "Hyderabad Urban Community Development Project" (Nagoya: UNCRD, 1985, mimeo), p. 15.

3. In-Joung Whang, "Management of Integrated Social Services for the Poor: The Case of Bongchun-Dong, Seoul" (Nagoya: UNCRD, 1984, mimeo), pp. 6–9.

4. Feroza Ahsan, "Provision of Services to the Urban Poor: A Case Study of Lahore Katchi Abadis" (Nagoya: UNCRD, 1984, mimeo), pp. 8–9.

5. S. Tilakaratna et al., "Environmental Health and Community Development Project: A Case Study in the Slums and Shanties of Colombo" (Nagoya: UNCRD, 1985, mimeo), pp. 5–7.

6. Viqar Ahmed, "Lahore Walled City Upgrading Project" (Nagoya: UNCRD, 1984, mimeo), pp. 8–9.

7. Khairruddin Yusof, "Urban Slums and Squatter Settlements: Variations in Needs and Strategies" (Paper presented to WHO Workshop on Child Abuse and Urban Slum Environment, Montreal, September 1981, p. 11.

8. Hong Hai Lim, "Nadi Integrated Social Services Programme," p. 6.

9. In-Joung Whang, "Management of Integrated Social Services."

10. Paulina Makinwa-Adebusoye, "Upgrading Olaleye-Iponri Slum in Lagos Metropolitan Area" (Nagoya: UNCRD, 1984, mimeo), pp. 15–17.

11. Tilakaratna et al., "Environmental Health and Community Development Project," p. 6.

12. Ibid.

13. James O. Kayila, "Improving Urban Settlements for the Poor: Case Studies of Dandora and Chaani Projects in Kenya" (Nagoya: UNCRD, 1984, mimeo), pp. 22–24.

14. Ibid., pp. 22–24.

15. Ahmed, "Lahore Walled City Upgrading Project."

16. G. Shabbir Cheema, "Malaysia's Development Strategy: The Dilemma of Redistribution with Growth," *Studies in Comparative International Development* 13 (Summer 1978), 40–55.

17. Cousins and Goyder, "Hyderabad Urban Community Development Project," p. 18.

18. Ibid., p. 10.

19. Ahsan, op. cit., p. 7.

20. Cousins and Goyder, "Hyderabad Urban Community Development Project," pp. 21–22.

21. Makinwa-Adebusoye, "Upgrading Olaleye-Iponri," p. 18.

22. Montgomery has used the informal service sector (ISS) as a concept "to identify hidden service functions, communal, semi-commercial, familiar, or voluntary, that substitute for, or enlarge the reach of, government agencies in dealing with the needs of the urban poor." John D. Montgomery, "The Informal Service Sector as an Administrative Resource" (UNCRD, 1985, mimeo), p. 2.

23. Ibid., p. 8.

24. Ibid., pp. 17–18.

25. Ibid., p. 24.

5

COMMUNITY PARTICIPATION

Many of the basic premises of development theory have come into question during the last two decades, and the direction and priorities of development policy have shifted dramatically. The very concept of development was stretched beyond the previously cherished goal of maximizing gains in gross national product and, indeed, beyond the concept of economic growth as the primary objective. Planners and policymakers began to recognize that truly effective development requires the creation of appropriate structures through which the poor are able to participate in decisions affecting their own welfare and that more attention needs to be given to providing for the basic needs of the poor to enable them to become more productive participants in the progressive development of society. Thus, governments in Asia, Africa, and Latin America have launched equity-oriented programs and projects aimed at, among other things, improving the living environment in slums and squatter settlements by eliciting the active participation of the residents of these communities.

This chapter examines the theory and practice of community participation in urban shelter and services. In the next section, the concept of participation is discussed. This is followed by an examination of the role, modes, and forms of community participation; a review of relevant community participation experiences; an identification of critical factors facilitating community participation; and a discussion of implications for action.

THE CONCEPT OF PARTICIPATION

It is widely recognized that participation is essential for any realignment of political influence more favorable to disadvantaged groups and for more meaningful social and economic development. It is a channel through which the people ensure their effective influence on the decision-making process at all levels of social activity.[1]

According to one view, participation could be defined as "the organized effort to increase control over resources and regulative institutions in a given social situation on the part of groups and movements of those hitherto excluded from such control."[2] Yet, meaningful participation goes beyond the control over resources and institutions exercised through periodic elections, since such control may only be nominal. Mere adult franchise and going to the polls may not mean much unless there are self-protecting and self-realization avenues for the dispossessed. The whole system could be operated in such a way that it becomes apparent that a majority of the people have no real stake in it, and in frustration then may opt to not actively participate.[3] Broadly speaking, participation means a share in decision making by all those who are influenced or affected by the decision. This requires appropriate distribution of decision-making powers among individuals and groups at the national, regional, local, and community levels.

In relation to development, a United Nations study has defined popular participation "as active and meaningful involvement of the masses of people at different levels (a) in decision making process for the determination of societal goals and the allocation of resources to achieve them and (b) in the voluntary execution for resulting programmes and projects."[4] According to this definition, the decision-making process refers to a broader set of behavioral activities. The term *masses* implies most of the residents of the community. The *active* involvement of the people on the basis of their free will is differentiated from *passive* involvement through pressure. An underlying assumption in this definition is that when people are actively involved in decision making, they can contribute more fully to the intended development.

Another study has identified four types of participation: (1) participation in decision making, (2) participation in implementation, (3) participation in benefits, and (4) participation in evaluation.[5] Participation in decision making involves making choices among various options and formulating plans to put selected options into effect. The decisions in this regard could be "initial," "ongoing," or "operational." Popular participation in implementation could involve resource contributions, administration and coordination, or program enlistment activities. Resource contribution on the part of the people could take the form of labor, cash, information, and so on. Their participation could also be in the form of either locally hired employees or members of advisory and decision-making boards or as members of voluntary organizations. Program enlistment implies responding to facilities provided by the government. The third dimension of participation implies three types of possible benefits: material, social, or personal. Finally, participation in evaluation includes involvement in the ongoing process of influencing public opinion and critically examining whether intended objectives are being met.

Four levels of popular participation should be differentiated: national, regional, local, and community. The nature of popular participation is different at each of these levels. Obviously, only a few can directly participate at the national level where the main policy decisions are made. The scope of active participation is relatively greater at the regional level but again probably through representative advocates. However, it is at local and community levels that most of the direct involvement of the people in the process of development takes place. There are several reasons for this. First, more interaction takes place over a longer period of time among individuals and groups at the local and community levels. Second, local issues and problems affect individuals and groups more directly than national issues. Third, the feeling of belonging to a community provides an impetus to the people to involve themselves in development activities. Fourth, even the national-level development projects consist of subprojects that are implemented at the local level, thereby necessitating grass-roots support for the success of national programs.

Community participation has been defined "as the involvement of the local population actively in the decision making concerning development projects or in their implementation."[6] This definition is not concerned directly with broader goals of democracy or income distribution. If defined broadly, community participation could be equated with "political democracy."

For the purposes of this study, community participation is defined as the residents' active involvement in collective activities aimed at improving their living environment, including physical structures of the community. Such activities may include establishing community-development committees, making demands on behalf of the community through various channels, identifying and implementing local development projects, mobilizing community resources, and disseminating information concerning improved hygiene and nutrition practices.

OPPORTUNITIES AND CONSTRAINTS

Three main viewpoints have been presented in the literature on the nature and possible role of community participation in the provision of shelter and basic urban services. According to the first view, deficiencies in shelter and basic urban services and, subsequently, the need for community participation and local action are the symptoms of internal and external "dependencies" and the exploitation of the poor by the rich.[7] The second view is that the importance of community participation in determining service provision "is shaped more by governmental constraints and needs than by local or settlement conditions."[8] The third view is that active participation of communities in collective actions has tremendous potential for providing shelter and basic urban services and should, thus, be promoted and strengthened.[9]

Several reasons could be advanced in favor of participatory methods of providing shelter and basic urban services. Some of these are summarized below.[10]

Reduction of Cost

Participatory approaches to shelter and basic urban services for the poor may lead to cost savings. The government's financial and human resources contributions can be reduced if the community undertakes some of the tasks otherwise performed by government agents. The communities are often more willing to provide labor, materials, or financial contributions if they are actively involved in the identification of local needs and the planning and management of local development projects or activities. Furthermore, the organizational or technical solutions adopted by local participants to meet urban shelter and services deficiencies are usually both cheaper and more appropriate than those that might be imposed from above by the government. This is substantiated by experiences of developing countries. As discussed in Chapter 8, sites-and-services schemes and squatter settlements upgrading projects planned and implemented with active community participation have reduced the cost of services and improved the access of the urban poor to these services.

Extensions of Services to All Communities

Community participation facilitates the dissemination of needed services to more recipients, often faster than is possible through conventional government services agencies. Administrative costs associated with the delivery of services through government agencies are usually very high, and this is one of the reasons why the urban poor cannot afford government-initiated low-income housing schemes. The reduction of costs through participatory approaches would enable the government to extend services to more low-income urban settlements, provided the funds thus saved are not diverted to the government's urban development programs and projects in middle- and higher-income urban settlements.

Mobilization of Community Resources

Community participation is conducive to the mobilization of local resources for providing shelter and basic services. Communities are more likely to contribute funds, labor, or management in situations where the people are actively involved in decisions concerning project location, the choice of implementing agencies and individuals, the choice of community leaders for the project, the selection of beneficiaries, and the allocation of project resources within the community. In the case of Vila El Salvador in Lima, for example, the community organization elected by the residents was actively involved in mobilizing internal funds for community projects through a self-managed community bank that contributed significantly to the success of the project.

People's Identification with the Project

Community participation in the provision of shelter and basic services increases the people's identification with and commitment to the project. Where they have been actively involved in the development activities, they tend to look at the results of these as their own creations, and they are more inclined to maintain and preserve the community services and facilities. It has been argued, however, that special provisions should be made in project documents to sustain the interest of the community in the project and, hence, in its maintenance. The sense of community responsibility is a necessary but not sufficient condition to sustain its interest.

Identification of Felt Needs

Active community involvement is the most effective way of identifying felt needs of the people. Where the people have actively participated in identifying their needs and aspirations and are willing to contribute funds and resources to carry out the activities to meet such needs, there is no doubt about the relevance of these activities to the community. Conversely, the identification of local needs through government functionaries without adequate involvement of the people does not ensure that real community needs are reflected in government programs and projects for upgrading low-income urban settlements. In such situations, the response of the people to the government initiative usually tends to be that of passive recipient.

Use of Indigenous Knowledge and Expertise

Community participation in shelter and basic urban services leads to an increase in indigenous knowledge and expertise and, to varying degrees, reduces the dependence of poor communities on professionals. The indigenous techniques are usually appropriate and well adapted to the existing situation. They utilize local labor and raw materials, are easier to maintain and repair, and are less dependent on skilled manpower. There are, however, limits to the use of indigenous knowledge and expertise. Several activities concerning design, planning, or management might still have to be undertaken by professionals.

Accumulation of Local Experiences

Active community participation in poverty-oriented urban projects leads to the accumulation of local experiences that would facilitate future community-development efforts. While there is no guarantee that community-development committees established for a particular project would be utilized in implementing other projects, past experience in making collective decisions improves the capacity of the community to identify local priorities, mobilize local resources, and plan and implement development activities. With the accumulation of local experiences, community leaders have more confidence with which they can negotiate with government officials and elicit the response of the people to community-development activities.

Increasing Awareness of the People

Community participation increases the people's socio-political awareness. The community involvement in activities affecting urban services makes the people aware of the ways through which their community problems could be resolved. Community organizations established to plan and implement local services and facilities provide a mechanism through which the people can put pressure from below to get their demands accepted and to ensure the responsiveness of government officials to community needs and aspirations.

Accumulation of Information about Socioeconomic Characteristics of Communities

People-based programs and projects for upgrading low-income urban settlements can provide the government with a great deal of information concerning socioeconomic characteristics of residents without installing costly data-collection systems. This information can be used to formulate and implement future development activities by concerned government agencies.

Ideally, community participation in shelter and basic urban services could result in each of the aforementioned benefits. In real-world situations, however, there are several constraints that impede effective community participation. These could be summarized as follows:

1. internal sociopolitical hierarchies, such as class, sex, age group, religion, or political affiliations, that lead to community factionalism and different economic interests;
2. the inability of the urban poor to participate in community activities dealing with shelter and basic services due to limitations in time and technical knowledge;

3. weak community organizations that result in lack of collective actions and inability of the community to exert pressure from below for increased allocation of funds;

4. government fears about the community participation being vulnerable to popular movements;

5. difficulties involved in coordinating the community's own activities with those of local governments;

6. the paternalistic attitude of government bureaucracy, partly due to which the urban poor in slums or squatter settlements become passive recipients of government services rather than active participants in mobilizing the community's own resources and implementing development activities;

7. the lack of adequate experience by government officials and professionals in working in close cooperation with communities in upgrading low-income settlements, largely because of their training in conventional housing techniques and methods;

8. the highly centralized mode of decision making within the administrative system, which results in the determination of basic program design and budgets for personnel and equipment at the national or regional levels;

9. evaluation systems that are focused on completion of tasks and targets by government officials and not on strengthening the community's capacity to participate in local issues;

10. the lack of an appropriate community organization through which collective community action could be undertaken; and

11. the rigidity of bureaucratic structures and procedures, which impedes flexibility of approaches needed to seek community participation.

MODES AND FORMS OF COMMUNITY PARTICIPATION

In the literature, several modes and forms of community participation in planning and management of shelter and basic urban services have been identified. These delineate the extent and style of people's involvement in decisions concerning their communities.

Hollnsteiner has identified six modes in planning and management of human settlements: Unofficial representation by a "solid citizien" group that endorses outside planned programs; appointment of local leaders to positions in government bureaucracy; community's choice on a final plan from among predetermined options; ongoing consultation starting with plan formulation; people's representation on decision-making boards; and community control over expenditure of funds. These modes are differentiated based on the "identity of participants," "locus of power," and "functions."[12]

Nawawi has identified four modes of participation. "Individual participation" implies activities such as voting, campaigning, or contacting government officials. "Communal participation" refers to common interests, and it emphasizes "mutuality and interaction." "Relational participation" refers to forms such as patron-client relationships, relations between the headman and members of his community or that between the headman and government officials. "Organizational participation" means that participants are members of the same group and that the extent of a member's participation depends mostly upon his or her position in the organization.[13]

UNICEF has proposed a checklist for use in identifying participatory components of projects that covers the extent of community involvement in project-planning processes, the identification of needs, the resource mobilization for the project, the identification of project workers, the development of social and/or technical skills, the project implementation, and the periodic monitoring and evaluation of the project.[14]

Gilbert and Ward have identified three basic mechanisms employed by Latin American governments to enlist the support of neighborhood associations in planning and management of human settlements. These are (1) "cooptation of leaders," meaning a situation in which a group led by its leader is affiliated with a supralocal institution; (2) institutionalization of "channels of political mobilization, social control, and neighbourhood improvement" through the government or a political party; and (3) patron-client relationships.[15]

At the program and project levels, community participation in upgrading irregular urban settlements takes place through (1) attendance at community meetings; (2) involvement in delivering petitions; (3) participation in public rallies; (4) lobbying of government officials; and (5) involvement in community work.[16]

Turner has delineated four alternative forms of citizen participation in housing activities.[17] The first form is one in which "sponsors decide and users provide." The sponsor "selects the site, plans the dwelling, and arranges the financing and administrative procedures before selecting the participants."[18] The second form is one in which "users decide and users provide." Owner-occupiers in older urban neighborhoods earmarked for redevelopment could be convinced about the feasibility of their houses being rehabilitated at much lower cost and could then take steps to improve their living environment. In the third form, "users decide and sponsors provide"; this is the form that could involve private developers. The fourth form is that of "central planning and local control" where two types of controls could be identified: (1) in one, what needs to be done and procedural lines to be followed are specified, and (2) in the other, a limit to what may be done is established and actors have flexibility within those limits.[19]

In the research design for the UNCRD-sponsored case studies of slums and squatter settlement upgrading projects, six modes of community participation were identified:

1. community involvement in the location of project activities;
2. the choice by the community of implementing agencies and individuals;

3. the selection of the community leaders to plan and manage a project by the residents of a settlement;

4. the selection by the community of the beneficiaries and clients of the project;

5. the involvement of the community in the allocation of project resources within the community; and

6. the contribution by the community of money, labor, time, and ideas for planning and managing community projects.

URBAN COMMUNITY PARTICIPATION EXPERIENCES

The case studies commissioned by UNCRD on the selected slums and squatter settlement upgrading projects indicate a variety of modes of participation under different socioeconomic and political situations. Yet, several similarities can be discerned related to community participation in project location, the selection of local leaders and beneficiaries, and the mobilization and allocation of local resources. In this section, urban community participation experiences in Asia, Africa, and Latin America are discussed and similarities among the selected cases are identified.

Examples from Asia

The Hyderabad Urban Community Project in India emphasized the active involvement of the community in project activities. Its aim was to create in problematic urban areas stronger communities with their own leaders who could plan and implement self-help projects. The first site selected was a predominantly Muslim neighborhood with numerous mosques and religious organizations. The work within these communities was carried out by community organizers (COs). In order to understand and resolve local conflicts, the COs brought different groups together. They spent most of their time in the field and some of them established small offices where they could discuss local problems for a few hours a week. Several new community organizations, including the Bustee welfare development committees, were established because most existing organizations did not include all segments of their local community. The new organization helped to diversify community leadership and bring together the various factions and ethnic groups. The result was that the project led to a significant improvement in the living environment in slums and squatter settlements. As Cousins and Goyder reported, the project "shows that despite the central problem of poverty, there are enormous potential economic resources in most slum communities which can be actualized with the help of sensitive community workers."[20]

The squatters in the Nadi project areas in Kuala Lumpur are well organized because of their insecurity of land tenure. Most squatter settlements are predominantly mono-ethnic, and this has "encouraged a vertical and ethnically structured political mobilization of the squatters by the major

mono-ethnic political parties operating at the national level."[21] The headman of the squatter settlement is also usually the chairman of the local
political party branch. The squatters expect their leaders in the settlement
to communicate their demands to higher levels of decision making, and
demands are usually made through political party channels. To obtain specific services, letters and petitions are sent to concerned government agencies.
Political pressure is then used to secure attention to these requests.

The designers of the Nadi project sought to provide three channels for
demand making by squatters: (1) the Local Action Committee, (2) the Divisional Action Committee, and (3) the Consultative Committee. The first
did not materialize, and the other two are not frequently used by squatters.
Some divisional officials do not regard frequent contacts with squatters as
desirable. They hold the view that squatters make too many demands, that
what they want is difficult to meet, and that they are already "spoiled" by
the government. Lim points out that "not surprisingly, the squatter leaders
on their part do not regard administrative channels as the most effective
method for getting what they want: only political pressure right from the
top can overcome bureaucratic inertia and reluctance."[22]

The analysis of the Nadi project suggests that informal mechanisms of
community participation can be as, if not more, important than formal
channels. If only formal channels are considered, it would seem that there
is only a minimal level of community participation in project implementation. In reality, squatters and their leaders exercise considerable influence
over the location of community services, the selection of project beneficiaries, and the mobilization and allocation of community resources. Officials
consider it desirable (and at times essential) to seek the support of leaders
of squatter settlements in the process of carrying out development activities.

The design of the Katchi Abadis project in Lahore emphasized active
community participation. Community development committees (CDCs)
were established. The members of CDCs were trained and, subsequently,
all project activities were carried out and coordinated through CDCs. In a
survey of CDC members and Sectoral Committee members, it was found
that about 98 percent had taken an active part at the planning stage, 56
percent in the selection of project locations, and 56 percent in decision
making concerning allocation of funds and duties.[23]

Unlike Katchi Abadis, Lahore Walled City Project did not provide for a
formal structure of community participation. Of the respondents to a survey,
64 percent had come to know about the project only when work actually
started. Beneficiaries of the project have little formal linkage with implementing agencies. Informal channels of participation, however, exist, and
these, to varying degrees, are utilized by residents of the project area. In
case of problems related to the project, elected local councillors are contacted
because they are represented on the managing body of Lahore Development
Authority, which is the implementing agency for the project. Other channels

of participation are newly elected national and provincial assemblies and the mass media.

In his review of major slum and squatter settlement projects in Pakistan, Ahmed has identified the following mechanisms that are used more frequently in the country:[24]

1. representation on town committees in small cities, municipal committees in medium-size cities, and metropolitan corporations in big cities;

2. indirect representation in governing bodies of urban development authorities;

3. establishment of community development councils;

4. participation through slum dwellers' associations that have their own federation at the city level; and

5. informal channels, such as local influential persons, family and caste affiliations, and mass media.

Three types of community organizations existed in the Integrated Social Services Project area in Seoul. The first group consisted of organizations established by the government that had been in operation within the framework of Saemaul Undong (Community Movement). The second, the Community Development Committee (CDC) was set up by the Social Welfare Centre in collaboration UNICEF to identify local needs and interests. The CDC consists of twenty-nine Saemaul leaders, thirty-three Tong chiefs, and thirty-three mothers' clubs. Its chairman is elected for a two-year term by the committee members. The third type, consisting of several organizations including the House-maid Self-help Club, and the Dong Housing Renewal Club were established to undertake specific tasks. Whang notes that residents in the area have a heterogeneous background, and they perceive their stay in the area to be temporary. Therefore, the residents are usually reluctant to identify themselves as members of the community and the CDC members find it difficult to mobilize the residents for collective tasks. Though the CDC and specific-purpose organizations such as the House-maids' Club have successfully carried out several projects, "both the lack of leadership commitment to community development and the high mobility of residents in this squatter area seem to be dysfunctional to community participation."[25]

In the case of the Sungnam New Town Development program, the Seoul city government adopted a top-down and centralized approach to project planning and implementation. Program enforcement was carried out through police action because the city government was reluctant to involve the beneficiary groups due to sensitivity of the issues involved. As a result, the migrants to the new town expressed their grievances through a series of demonstrations.

In the case of Environmental Health and Community Development Project in Colombo, the community development councils (CDCs) were established to be the principal instrument for achieving community participation in project implementation. More specifically, the CDCs were to be involved in the maintenance of common physical amenities, health care, environmental hygiene, and other social and economic activities for improving the quality of community life. In a random sample field survey of the communities, it was noted that the communities with active CDCs were smaller, homogeneous, and had a tradition of working together. Leadership in inactive CDCs often represented only one group in the community. There was a significant relationship between active community participation and health and environmental conditions.[26]

All the organizations involved in planning and managing the Block Grants Project in Surabaya, Indonesia, were official or quasi-official. Yet, the participation of formal and informal community leaders was high. Project locations where chosen by the community in meetings attended by the project coordinator. The community provided the list of candidates for training, using existing community leaders for the project. Decisions about the identification of beneficiaries was made at the same time that the project type and location were decided

Table 5.1 shows the extent and modes of community participation in planning and management of selected upgrading projects in Asia. The table and the preceding discussion indicate the following:

1. The community participation in selected projects is greater in choice of locations, beneficiaries, or community leaders and minimal, if existing at all, in control over the allocation of project resources, the mobilization of community resources, and the choice of implementing agencies/individuals.
2. The extent of community participation is the highest in the Hyderabad project and Katchi Abadis project and the lowest in the Lahore Walled City Project.
3. Most projects are relatively new and participatory management in these is not institutionalized.
4. In most cases, both formal and informal channels for communicating with senior officials and politicians are utilized.
5. UNICEF has played an important role in the advocacy of participatory approaches to planning and management of squatter settlement upgrading projects in the region.
6. Where an appropriate structure was provided and the projects dealt with activities directly affecting the people, the community participation has been forthcoming. The examples show that poor urban committees are willing to actively participate in improving their living environment under appropriate circumstances.

Examples from Africa

Two prominent community organizations existed in Olaleye in Lagos before the upgrading project was initiated, the Council of Elders and the

Table 5.1
Modes of Community Participation in Selected Projects

Project	Choice of Location	Choice of Beneficiaries	Choice of Community Leaders	Control of Allocation of Project Resources	Mobilization Community of Resources	Choice of Implementing Agencies/Individuals
Nadi	X	X	X	O	O	
Lahore Walled City			O			
Integrated Social Services	X	X	X		O	
Lahore Katchi Abadis	X	X	X	O	X	O
Environmental Health and Community Development	X	X	X	O	O	
Block Grants	X	O	O		O	
Hyderabad Urban Community Development	X	X	X	O	X	O

Key: X = active involvement
O = partial involvement

Community Development Committee (CDC). The council consisted of representative elders from all areas, who occasionally met to discuss social, political, and economic aspects of the community. The CDC consisted of people chosen from different districts, and it served as a communication channel between state government and the people. On the recommendation of the Division of Urban and Regional Planning, it was enlarged to include representatives of the Council of Elders, market groups, women's associations, and youth and religious organizations. The enlarged CDC was involved in all stages of the upgrading project. Due to the community's active involvement in the project, acquisition of land for public buildings (such as clinics and market stalls) has been easy, and the previous owners have been allocated new, comparable sites in the area. In cases where no adequate alternative sites were available, owners have accepted land allocations within the Lagos Metropolitan Area, actions indicative of a positive attitude toward the project. In order to motivate the residents to participate in the project activities, special lectures, film shows, and consultative meetings were organized for members of the CDC, the Council of Elders, and concerned NGOs. The visible impact of some of the ongoing activities has also been a motivating factor.

The design of the Lusaka Squatter Upgrading and Sites and Services Project in Zambia provided for a mechanism to establish a two-way relationship between the project staff and the community. The structures through which community participation has been encouraged consist of cadres of community development and construction adviser staff, working together in the field team under the field team leader, the party organization, and the Ward Development Committee. Several techniques and procedures have been employed to make these structures into an "innovative package." "These include the briefing system, the road walks, the seminar for leadership, and the various communications techniques."[27] Furthermore, Zambia has a long tradition of mutual help. "This tradition survives undiminished throughout the country's squatter settlements."[28]

In the case of the Dandora project in Kenya, community organizations were established to elicit people's participation. The project beneficiaries were expected to participate in the construction of their own houses. However, project planning and the construction of the infrastructure and services was done by the relevant agencies and the contractors prior to the establishment of community organizations. Neighborhood committees under area chiefs were used to maintain security in the area. The committees helped resolve minor disputes among residents, thereby facilitating collective community actions. After taking possessions of their plots, the beneficiaries of the Dandora project organized themselves into building groups to pool financial resources and labor for construction work. They were given technical assistance by the community development staff of the project.

Examples from Latin America

In the case of Bogota, Colombia, community action programs and projects have been promoted. Gilbert and Ward reported that at the community level, "juntas" can be established by as few as fifteen neighbors. Since 1969, the members of the junta have been elected democratically by the affiliated members of the community. Initially the juntas functioned as effective channels of local participation in development projects. Later, however, attempts were made to strengthen central government control over them. A competitive users' organization was created and the federation of juntas was replaced. Despite these constraints, the Department of Community Action "has been successful in stimulating community self-help around projects such as schools and community halls, encouraging communities to form juntas, chanelling requests for help to the servicing agencies, and in mobilizing limited funds to help with community services."[29]

In Mexico City, patron-client relationships have been the main form of linkage between high-level government officials and the urban poor. The benefit to the clients is that they have access to influential persons who might intervene on their behalf to have their demands accepted. Around election time, political parties are also active in low-income urban settlements. After the election, however, their interest in these settlements declines.

The relationship patterns between low-income urban communities and the government in Mexico could be divided into three periods. Before 1970, little attention was given to the creation of an appropriate structure to elicit community participation in local-level development. Between 1979 and 1976, the government interest in low-income housing and land issues increased. The new Federal District Constitution provided for the election of block representatives and a community "Junta" that were to report on urban service deficiencies and to make suggestions for their improvement. Since 1977, local mayors have been given the responsibility for the provision of street paving, street lighting, water, and drainage. The community organizations are asked to petition their local mayors to get their demands accepted.

In Venezuela, an emergency plan was initiated in 1958 that provided for improvements in housing, education, sanitation, and paving. Improvement committees were established in each barrio, and community initiative and participation were encouraged. With the change of government in 1969, two new agencies, the Secretariat of Popular Promotion, and the Department of Barrio Urbanization and Servicing, were created to improve the situation in low-income urban settlements. The first agency was aimed at increasing the level of community participation, while the second sought to increase banks' interest in physical improvements in barrios. In 1974, a new strategy for barrio development that focused on physical improvements in low-income settlements was initiated by the administration of Carlos Andres Perez. A survey of all low-income urban communities was to be undertaken and the provision of services was to be coordinated. The new strategy deemphasized community participation.

The new administration of Herrera-Campins again shifted the focus to active participation of communities in upgrading low-income urban settlements. The establishment of neighborhood associations was encouraged. In summing up the experiences of community participation and action in Venezuela, Gilbert and Ward commented that:

a long series of efforts to encourage community participation has failed to establish a reliable and trusted procedure by which barrio inhabitants can address the government. There are two major explanations for this. One is that the community action had generally been encouraged only so far as it has been in the interest of national and local governments to do so.... Second, government support for community participation, like most other areas of public activities in Venezuela, is part and parcel of the process of party political competition.[30]

In Peru, the project for the young towns of the Cono Sur of metropolitan Lima was launched in 1978 with the assistance of UNICEF. The project design provided for the establishment of 100 operational centers, the development of the community's specific skills and abilities, and the active involvement of the people in all activities. The leaders in the selected settlements are highly politicized and have trade-union experience in companies and factories. The project agencies have worked with the existing community organizations to implement the project. Neighborhood associations have been strengthened, and "greater grassroots involvement has been generated in dealing with concrete problems of direct concern to the population."[31] Project locations are chosen with the participation of "young towns" and "follow a selection process based on predetermined criteria."[32] The community participation in implementing projects, however, has been confined to specific or ad hoc activities and the relationship between the community and local governments in implementing the project has been minimal.[33]

In 1971 about nine thousand squatter families in Lima were relocated to the outskirts of the city. The new area, named Vila El Salvador, was provided with only such minimal services as unsurfaced roads and street lighting at the entrance. R. J. Skinner noted that after five years of its existence, the community organizations were actively involved in several activities, which included: "the identification of land speculation by plot occupants; securing internal financing for collective projects through a self-managed community bank...; disseminating information on improved hygiene and nutrition practices through a community health centre; running a small bus service; selling key building materials at controlled prices; funding a construction company...; [and] creating employment by establishing a clothing workshop."[34]

Several conclusions emerge from the Latin American experience in promoting community participation in low-income urban settlements:

1. Many organizations established to elicit community participation for barrio upgrading have existed since the late 1950s.
2. The extent of the commitment by governments to community participation has varied from one country to another and within the same country from one administration to another.
3. Mechanisms that governments have used to "deflect" opposition in poor urban settlements include provision of services, co-optation of leaders, making incremental concessions to meet residents' demands, and coercion.
4. The need for responding to community demands is widely recognized.
5. The residents of squatter settlements have little control over allocation of resources to improve the quality of life.

FACTORS CONDUCIVE TO COMMUNITY PARTICIPATION

There is an increasing recognition by planners and policymakers in developing countries of the need to actively involve communities in upgrading slums and squatter settlements. As discussed in the previous section, several poverty-oriented urban programs have been initiated to mobilize local resources and provide more opportunities to the urban poor to participate in improving their living environment. In order for communities to participate effectively in decision making concerning the provision of shelter and services, however, conditions in cities and communities must support the involvement of the poor. While the significance of some of the factors conducive to community participation might vary from one country to another, several common themes that recur in the case studies seem to emerge. A number of conditions that seem to contribute to effective community participation are briefly described in this section.

Smallness of Unit

Where the geographic and demographic unit for the delivery of basic urban services is small, effective community participation in local decision making is more likely to take place. In the case of the Environmental Health and Community Development Project, community development committees elected by the people were more effective in those communities that were relatively smaller in size. In his comparative study of "people-based mechanisms," Yeung reported that "kelurahan" and "barangay" (in Indonesia and the Philippines, respectively) "are convenient building blocks for urban services to be extended in urban areas" because of the small size of these units.[35] In Korea, however, the "Dong" level, in which participatory urban services are organized, was considered "too large a functional unit to be really effective."[36] Small size of the unit increases the residents' interest in community activities, enhances the resident's trust in community leaders, and facilitates communication between government officials and the community.

Strong Leadership

The communities that have strong leadership are more likely to be actively involved in decisions concerning the choice of project locations, the mobilization of community resources, the allocation of project resources, and the choice of beneficiaries. Community leaders serve as the most effective channel between residents and concerned government agencies. Their capacity to mobilize local people to put pressure from below and to negotiate with government officials partly determines government decisions to provide services and facilities in their communities.

As the Nadi project in Malaysia illustrates, community leaders in squatter settlements should not only have good rapport among themselves, they also need adequate linkages with politicians and administrators at higher levels in order to effectively communicate the people's needs and aspirations. In addition, they must have human skills to mobilize the community and to convince administrators and politicians at the state and national level about the necessity of providing basic services.

Leadership may be formal or informal. In some situations, there may be one strong leader for the community, while in others an extensive network of leadership might exist, each leader representing different formal and informal organizations. Different leadership styles can be effective in different situations. In small communities, the first style might work adequately. In heterogeneous communities, however, the second style of leadership is more conducive to community participation.

The relationship between participatory urban services and strong leadership is summed up by Yeung:

The important finding to emerge from all country studies is that leadership is perhaps the most critical factor in the success of any participatory urban service. Many studies identified weaknesses in present training, and poor communication skills. Almost every case study pointed to the need of, and ample room for, improvement of leadership qualities if participatory urban services were to further improve.[37]

When a heterogeneous community does not have leaders representing the interests of its diverse segments, there is a danger of minority opinion becoming the basis of government programs. As Minerbi has noted, in such situations "the autonomy of leaders, their lack of accountability and their self-serving demands can create problems."[38]

In his study on Lima, Dietz found that the role of leadership at the community level was indispensable:

The emergence of effective leadership is a crucial final success factor. Leadership exerts an influence in a variety of ways: these include the formation and maintenance of (by the perception of the majority of the pobladores) a strong, effective community organization, the exclusion or suppression of intra-community conflict, and the capacity to resolve perceived problems. . . . [39]

Threat to the Survival of the Settlement

Where there is a real or perceived threat to the survival of a squatter settlement, the community tends to participate more actively in the articulation of the need to legitimize the occupation of land, mobilization of community resources for upgrading the settlement, or implementation of development activities. This is substantiated by the case of Katchi Abadis in Lahore. The squatters have their own associations, which are quite vocal, and frequently attract the attention of policymakers and planners at the national and regional levels through the mass media and through their contacts with concerned government officials. When the planning and development department initiated a settlement upgrading project in cooperation with UNICEF, the community responded favorably. Community development committees were elected by the people who, despite their heterogeneity, worked collectively to improve their living environment.

Solidarity in squatter settlements, when forged by external threats, could override even those cleavages that are based on ethnicity, geographical place of origin, income level, or occupation. This is also illustrated by the case of the Tondo squatter area in Manila. Though each of the barrios in the settlement had numerous associations, until 1963 these had been strictly of a specific-purpose type. It was only "when a serious threat to eviction from the city government loomed over most residents in 1963, [that] these groups realigned and united to protect themselves from the hostile outside world of law-enforcement agencies," resulting in a high level of community participation.[40]

In their survey on community participation in Bogota, Gilbert and Ward found that the level of community participation was high in only one of the five settlements studied, that is, in Juan Pablo I. The fact that this settlement was "faced by recurrent threats from the police" was the main factor leading to active involvement of the community.[41]

Provision of Framework by the Government for Community Participation

The extent and modes of community participation are affected by the government's attitude toward organizations of the people at the grass roots. Where the national government is afraid of community organizations changing to mass movements to restructure society, participation of residents in low-income settlements has to take place within official guidelines. Conversely, where central and regional governments are more tolerant of inevitable conflict emerging from community organization, there are more opportunities for residents to express their views about issues affecting them directly or indirectly. Community participation in the Hyderabad Urban Community Development Project and the Block Grants Project was affected partly by policy framework for participation in Indian and Indonesia, respectively. In the case of Indonesia, Tarigan and his associates reported that there was a "strong reluctance, for political and other reasons, to single out a group of people as poor. As a result Kampung residents are very unlikely to point out a neighbour as being part of a target group."[42] The government policy framework in Hyderabad was conducive to urban community participation. Elected councils at the municipal and local area levels provided an institutional framework for communicating the needs of the urban communities to the decision-making structures at higher levels. The central and provincial government encouraged the organization of the urban poor for self-reliant development.

In Vila El Salvador in Lima, the high level of community participation has been attributed, along with other factors, to the fact that "in 1971 Peru as a whole was passing through a period of social and political change under a government which propounded an ideology of participation and mobilization in all popular sectors [industry, agriculture etc]."[43]

Flexibility of Approach

Rigid administrative structures and procedures are not conducive to effective planning and management of slums and squatter settlement upgrading projects. To an extent, each community is different than the other. Flexibility of approach and methods is, therefore, a prerequisite in eliciting the community's positive response to upgrading projects. The Lahore Walled City Project and the Hyderabad Urban Community Development Project provide two contrasting examples. The Walled City project was planned by the concerned government agency in collaboration with the World Bank without the involvement of the residents. The provision of infrastrucutre improvement and community services such as sewerage and drainage are being carried out by government officials from the concerned agencies. There is minimal involvement of residents in implementation of these activities.

In the Hyderabad Urban Community Development Project, however, a flexible approach was adopted. Several of the activities were started at the request of the residents. Resources from lower-middle-class areas were utilized to carry out upgrading activities in poor localities. Attempts were made to discover and channel resources to improve the living environment in slums. Voluntary organizations within the communities were established to encourage self-reliance. Initially the project emphasized social welfare activities, but in response to the felt needs of the people, activities of direct economic benefits were emphasized at a later stage. Cousins and Goyder summed up the need for a flexible approach in upgrading low-income urban settlements:

The necessity of forward planning for programmes and for budgets and the need for indices for monitoring and evaluating, too often lead to the establishment of fixed targets. Thus, the needs of the people tend to become subordinated to the bureaucratic needs of the project which originally set out to help them. The success of the Hyderabad project in maintaining a high degree of flexibility is a rare accomplishment and one of the sources of its strength.[44]

Homogeneity of the Community

Where the residents in a low-income settlement are more homogeneous, they are more likely to participate in the community activities. Heterogeneity within the community usually leads to factionalism and lack of adequate interest in the community's affairs. In the case of the Integrated Social Services Project in Seoul, for example, Whang pointed out that due to their heterogeneous geographical backgrounds, residents tend to be reluctant to identify themselves as members of the community and that the members of the Community Development Committee find it difficult to put pressure on residents to consider collective rather than factional interests. Heterogeneity of residents is more pronounced in slums and squatter settlements of Karachi where differences in language, ethnicity, and place of origin frequently lead to factionalism within the community, impeding efforts of community workers and change agents to promote collective actions.

In addition to cleavages based on ethnicity and regional identity, the urban poor might be rigidly specialized by occupations "which are quite specified in technical or education requirements."[45] The urban poor could also be seriously divided in terms of income level. About the impact of these cleavages, Nawawi has written that "the existence of these cleavages prevents the development of broad horizontal solidarity and organizations which are necessary for the nourishment of wide-ranging political interest and concerns."[46]

Positive Experience with Past Collective Actions

Views of residents about the usefulness of community participation are partly shaped by their past experiences. Where in the past a community has been able to safeguard common interests through collective action, residents tend to be more willing to devote their time and energy to promote community activities. The success of residents of Vila El Salvador in Lima in initiating several collective activities soon after their relocation to the area led to mutual trust and solidarity even though in most cases their places of origin were different. In the case of the Hyderabad project, the original project objectives were modified in response to the felt needs of the communities selected during early phases of the project. Once successful in undertaking collective actions, residents were willing to cooperate with each other despite linguistic, ethnic, and religious differences.

Similarities in Perception of Needs

Where services providers and residents have similar perceptions of needs, a strong basis for active community participation exists. Residents invariably and for obvious reasons prefer to be involved in those community activities that affect them more directly and immediately. If the perception of those needs by government functionaries is similar, a viable partnership between concerned government agencies and the community would emerge. One of the reasons for the continued participation of communities in the Hyderabad Urban Community Development Project was that in response to the felt needs of the people, project implementers shifted their emphasis from social welfare to income-generating activities. On the basis of case studies of participatory services, Yeung concluded that "different perception of the needs of an urban community by the residents as opposed to the delivery organizations bedevil many of the well-intentioned efforts and result in low rates of participation and success."[47]

Diversified and Integrated Nature of Project Activities

Where project activities are more diversified and well integrated, various segments of the community are more likely to participate in their planning and implementation. Though single-purpose projects are easier to plan and manage, these might not respond to the needs of some of the groups who would, obviously, not be involved. A diversified and integrated package of basic services provides opportunities to more groups to benefit from project activities and, thus, gives more legitimacy to the project within the community. In a case study of participatory services in the Republic of Korea, it was found that the activities pursued in these selected urban communities were not wide enough in scope "to cater to a broad spectrum of needs."[48]

This affected the extent and effectiveness of community participation. The main reason for a holistic view of urban services is that beneficiaries have interrelated needs for services, and if these needs are adequately met, beneficiaries tend to be more willing to identify with the provider and the project.

Information Flows and Training

A community's involvement in settlement-upgrading projects is also affected by the frequency, relevance, and adequacy of information available to each individual and household, as well as by the training of community leaders to use the information to meet their respective communities' socioeconomic needs. The case studies of selected shelter and basic urban services projects show that different mechanisms have been developed to improve information flow in either direction and to provide training.

In the case of the Environmental Health and Community Development Project in Colombo, for example, health wardens were appointed to perform these tasks, and thus enhanced community participation. In Lahore Katchi Abadis Project, members of the community development committees were trained to plan and manage local activities, and women were trained to participate effectively in income-generation activities.

The Hyderabad Urban Community Development Project emphasized the training of community organizers and, through them, the urban poor. Free flow of information was encouraged to identify opportunities for improving the living environment of the communities.

The Squatter Upgrading Project in Lusaka, Zambia, employed several procedures and mechanisms to promote two-way communication. These have included the briefing system, the "road walk," and seminars for leadership. In the case of the Olaleye project in Lagos, adequate information was provided to the Council of Elders and the Community Development Committee through seminars, field visits by officials, or informal dialogue sessions to make them aware of the need for the project. In most Latin American cities, structures were created to facilitate communication between policymakers and planners at the national levels and residents of squatter settlements.

Visible Gains from Services Provided

Past experiences of communities with regard to implementation of government projects for upgrading low-income settlements influence their motivation to participate in existing community-level development activities. As examined in Chapter 2, many social, political, administrative, and economic constraints impede the access of the urban poor to shelter and basic services provided through government-initiated programs and projects. The urban poor, therefore, become passive in their attitude. In the case of slums and squatter areas in Metro Manila, for example, Einsiedel and Molina reported that "many years of neglect and unfulfilled commitments of government" made residents of these settlements "indifferent and suspicious of any proposal to develop or upgrade their areas."[49] Therefore, the "people-centered approach" to upgrading low-income areas was evolved and intensive community relations and information campaigns to elicit community support and participation were initiated.

The Extent of Service Deficiencies

Where urban service deficiencies are the greatest, the communities tend to be more willing to participate in demand making, mobilizing local resources, and implementing development projects. Because servicing and regularization problems affect such communities more seriously, they are likely to cooperate to achieve their common goals. One of the reasons for different levels of community participation in the Katchi Abadis project and the Lahore Walled City Project is that the former have minimal basic services while in the latter, several of these services and facilities, such as electricity and water, are available to at least a segment of the community.

Project Type

The degree of community participation is also affected by the type of urban project. In squatter settlements, residents have developed their own internal system of interaction over a period of time. They might have their own organizations for undertaking collective community actions. The security of land occupation is invariably their main problem. Because of these and other factors, squatter upgrading projects are more conducive to community participation. In the case of sites-and-services projects, the residents might not have known each other before. They have legal occupation of land. Physical services are frequently provided by the government agencies before they move to the site. Therefore, the areas of their cooperation are somewhat reduced. The inner-city slums usually have well-established organizations and, in some cases, deep-rooted factionalism. The residents of such settlements are more willing to participate in upgrading projects if they are owner-occupants. When the majority of the residents are tenants, they might not be enthusiastic about the upgrading project because of their fear that rents in the area might go up.

It should be pointed out, however, that project type is only one of several factors affecting community participation. For example, where other conditions are favorable, active community participation might take place even in sites-and-services projects. On the other hand, a heterogeneous squatter settlement might not be conducive to collective actions by the community.

IMPLICATIONS FOR ACTION

The nature, scope, and determinants of community participation in upgrading slums and squatter settlements vary, as shown in this chapter, among countries and, indeed, among projects within the same country. Experiences of developing countries during the past three decades indicate the significance of several actions that are required for successfully implementing participatory upgrading projects. Table 5.2 presents some of these actions.

The responsibility, authority, and resources for the provision of urban basic services needs to be decentralized and delegated to local governments and community organizations. After adequate decentralization, the government should encourage the formation of organizations among urban communities through support of community organizers, training of residents and leaders, and utilization of existing social networks. Service provision should be integrated at the community level.

In order to identify community needs, regular dialogues between government functionaries and communities should be held and existing formal as well as informal organizations should be used. To ensure active community participation in the process of project planning, existing planning procedures need to be modified to facilitate bottom-up planning. Furthermore, the project staff should work with more than one group so that all segments of the community are enthusiastic about the project and participate in collective actions.

Continuous efforts should be made to encourage consensus within the community concerning the location of services and the choice of beneficiaries and community leaders. Where consensus is not feasible, working with more than one group yields better results in terms of community participation.

In order to effectively choose project beneficiaries, actions needed are the delineation of criteria by the community, increasing the role of the community development committees, and higher level of consultation with the community.

Mobilization of community resources is important for the provision of participatory services. The actions needed to mobilize financial and human resources of the community are: the involvement of both formal and informal leaders; providing more information to communities before asking them to contribute; seeking community contributions initially about those activities that affect them directly and immediately; and encouraging consensus in the community before launching the drive to mobilize community funds.

Project activities should be carried out under the control and supervision of the community. Furthermore, the community development committee should be empowered to undertake periodic monitoring and evaluation of community development projects. To enable the community to implement projects and monitor activities, however, adequate training needs to be

Table 5.2
Actions Required for Implementing Participatory Approaches

Modes of Participation	Most Common Existing Patterns	Actions Required
Identification of community needs	Local needs identified by government agencies and reactions of communities to these is sought	Regular dialogue between government functionaries and communities before community needs are identified
	Some highly participatory projects but these are mostly experimental in nature	Using existing formal and informal organizations to identify community needs
	Demand for services is communicated to government officials through opinion leaders	Training concerned government officials in communication skills and participatory approaches
Participation in project planning process	Project planning is mostly considered to be a technical task to be undertaken by professionals and technocrats	Training for community leaders to plan community projects
	Top-down project planning process linked with centrally sponsored schemes	Changes in procedures to ensure bottom-up planning process
	Government sponsored organizations are occasionally involved	Working with more than one group and organization during the planning process
Choice of location of services	Usually communities consulted in decisions concerning location of services	Involvement of community in choice of locations to be sought during planning phase
	Services in sites and services schemes located without community participation	Working with more than one community
	Community's cooperation needed for acquisition of land in slums and squatter settlements to locate community services	Seeking community's consensus through community workers
Choice of beneficiaries	Community leaders consulted in choosing beneficiaries	Delineation of criteria by the community for choosing beneficiaries
	Strong linkages between traditional community leaders and concerned government officials	Increased role of community development committee needed
	Choice of beneficiaries mostly	Higher level of community

Table 5.2 *continued*

Modes of Participation	Most Common Existing Patterns	Actions Required
	based on patron-client relationships	consultation needed to ensure that benefits are not pocketed by a few
Choice of community leaders	Community Development committees elected by the community or nominated by project staff are created	Training of community leaders in planning, organization, management, and monitoring skills
	Each community has, in addition, traditional leaders	Regular dialogue between community leaders and project staff
	There exist leaders of indigenous organizations and groups in the community	Eliciting support of informal leaders for implementing community projects
Control over allocation of project resources	Control over allocation of project resources exercised by government officials and/or project staff	Decentralization of financial and administrative authority
	High level of financial centralization in the country	Increased role of Community Development Committee in allocation of project resources
	Low capacity at community level in financial management	Training of community leaders in financial procedures and management
Mobilization of community resources	Communities contribute for activities affecting them directly	Involvement of both formal leaders in mobilizing community resources
	Labor main form of community contribution	Providing more information to communities before asking them to contribute
	Percentage of community contribution to overall project cost is small	Seeking community contributions only about those activities affecting communities directly and immediately
		Encouraging concensus in the community before the drive to mobilize community funds
Choice of implementing agencies/workers	Implementing agencies/workers chosen through project staff	Increasing the role of CDC in choosing project workers
	CDC involvement in choosing unskilled workers	Upgrading skills of community by choosing workers from the community

Table 5.2 *continued*

Implementing project activities	Projects implemented with some community involvement Work usually carried out under the control and supervision of concerned government agencies	Standardization of procedures for project implemen ation under community control and supervision Provision of adequate training to community leaders and works concerning implementation of project activities
Periodic monitoring and evaluation of the project	Monitoring and evaluation responsibility of government agencies Community leaders convey their views about the effect of ongoing activities to higher level officials	Giving the responsibility for project monitoring and evaluation to Community Development Committee Training community leaders in methods of monitoring and evaluation of project performance

provided to leaders and residents in methods of needs identification, financial management, communication, and project monitoring.

NOTES

1. Andrew Pearse and Matias Stiefel, *Debater's Comments on Inquiry in Participation: A Research Approach*, occasional paper (Geneva: United Nations Research Institute for Social Development, 1980), pp. 11–12.

2. Ibid., p. 25.

3. George Kent, "Community-Based Development Planning," *Third World Planning Review* 3:3 (August 1981), 313–26.

4. United Nations, *Popular Participation in Decision-Making for Development* (New York: United Nations, 1975), p. 4.

5. John M. Cohen and Norman T. Uphoff, "Participation's Place in Rural Development: Seeking Clarity through Specificity," *World Development* 8, 221–35.

6. Alastair T. White, "Why Community Participation: A Discussion of the Arguments," in *Assignment Children 59/60* (Geneva: UNICEF, 1982), pp. 18–19.

7. Burgess, "Petty Commodity or Dweller Control?," pp. 1105–33.

8. Alan Gilbert and Peter Ward, "Community Participation in Upgrading Irregular Settlements: The Community Response," *World Development* 12:9 (September 1984), p. 913.

9. Turner, *Housing by People.*

10. For a more detailed discussion of the significance of community participation, see, among others, White, "Why Community Participation"; Yue-man Yeung, "Provision of Basic Urban Services in Asia: The Role of People-Based Mechanisms" Paper presented to the Expert Group Meeting on Policy Issues in Urban Services for the Poor, Nagoya, Japan, 13–17 August 1985; Turner, *Housing by People*; and Gilbert and Ward, "Community Participation."

11. For discussion of constraints on community participation, see, among others, R. P. Misra and G. Shabbir Cheema, "Group Action and Popular Participation," in R. P. Misra, ed., *Local Level Planning and Development* (New Delhi: Sterling, 1985), pp. 231–339; and Frances F. Korten, Community Participation: A Management Perspective on Obstacles and Options," in David C. Korton and Filipe B. Alfonso, eds., *Bureaucracy and the Poor: Closing the Gap* (West Hartford, CT: Kumarion Press, 1983).

12. Hollnsteiner, "People Power," pp. 11–48.

13. Mohammad A. Nawawi, "Political Participation, Basic Services and the Urban Poor in Developing Countries," in G. Shabbir Cheema, ed., *Managing Development: Services for the Poor* (Nagoya: UNCRD, 1984), pp. 169–90.

14. UNICEF, *Report of the Community Participation Workshop* (New Delhi: UNICEF, 1981), pp. 13–16.

15. Gilbert and Ward, "Community Action."

16. Gilbert and Ward, "Community Participation," p. 913.

17. Turner, *Housing by People*, p. 139.

18. Ibid., p. 141.

19. Ibid.

20. William J. Cousins and Catherine Goyder, "Hyderabad Urban Community Development Project" (Nagoya: United Nations Centre for Regional Development, 1985, mimeo), p. 27.

21. Lim, "Nadi Integrated Social Services Programme," p. 24.

22. Ibid., p. 28.

23. Ahsan, "Provision of Services to the Urban Poor," p. 24.

24. Viqar Ahmed, "Policy Issues in Urban Services for the Poor: Country Paper on Pakistan" (Paper presented to the Expert Group Meeting on Policy Issues in Urban Services for the Poor, Nagoya, Japan, 13–17 August 1985).

25. Whang, "Management of Integrated Social Services for the Poor," p. 14.

26. Tilakaratna, Hettige, and Karumaratma, "Environmental Health and Community Development Project."

27. Pasteur, *Management of Squatter Upgrading*, p. 146.

28. Harrington Jere, "Lusaka: Local Participation in Planning and Decision-making," Payne, ed., *Low-Income Housing in the Developing World*, p. 61.

29. Gilbert and Ward, "Community Action," p. 175.

30. Ibid., p. 780.

31. Willy Bezold Salinas and Falvio Moreno Jimenez, "Integrated Basic Services for Lima's 'Young Towns,' " *Assignment Children 57/58* (Geneva: UNICEF, 1982), p. 132.

32. Ibid., p. 133.

33. Ibid.

34. Skinner and Rodell, *People, Poverty and Shelter*.

35. Yeung, "Provision of Basic Urban Services," p. 22.

36. Ibid.

37. Ibid., p. 23.

38. Lucinao Minerbi, "Beneficiary Organizations and Mobilization of Local Resources for the Delivery of Urban Services to the Poor" (Nagoya: UNCRD, 1985, mimeo).

39. Henry A. Dietz, *Poverty and Problem Solving Under Military Rule: The Urban Poor in Lima* (Austin: University of Texas Press, 1980), p. 84.

40. M. A. Sembrano et al., *Case Studies on Development of Slums, Squatter and Rural Settlements: The Philippines* (Quezon City: Ateneo de Manila University, Institute of Philippine Culture, 1977), p. 42.

41. Gilbert and Ward, "Community Participation," p. 917.

42. Tarigan, Soedarjo, and Sacheh, "Block Grants Project in Surabaya," p. 11.

43. Skinner and Rodell *People, Poverty and Shelter*, p. 133.

44. Cousins and Goyder, "Hyderabad Urban Community Development Project," p. 18.

45. Joan M. Nelson, *Access to Power*, p. 135.

46. Nawawi, "Political Participation," p. 176.

47. Yeung, "Provision of Basic Urban Services," p. 24.

48. Ibid., p. 25.

49. Nathaniel von Einsiedel and Michael L. Molina, "Policy Issues in Urban Services to the Poor: The Case of Metro Manila" (Nagoya: UNCRD, 1985, mimeo).

6

FINANCING, COST RECOVERY, AND AFFORDABILITY

Patterned in large part on Western developed country experiences, the application of conventional approaches to the provision of shelter and services for the urban poor in the Third World has not yielded meaningful results. The reasons for this, to a considerable extent, are economic. Costs of the acquisition of land, the construction of dwelling units, and the provision of infrastructural facilities are extremely high vis-à-vis the financial capacity of these governments. Furthermore, income levels and savings of the urban poor are low, hence they are not able to afford basic shelter and services at the prevailing market rates. Governments of the developing countries have attempted to partially subsidize the effort to meet the needs of the poor through public sector housing schemes from their limited resources. However, even with such subsidies, conventional public sector housing is usually still beyond the affordability levels of the urban poor. Thus, only a very small minority of the large targeted group have actually benefited from such schemes. It is, therefore, now widely recognized that much in the conventional models, approaches, or standards for public housing is not relevant to situations in slums and squatter settlements in densely populated cities of the Third World.

Financing, affordability, cost recovery, and replicability are interrelated and interdependent concepts. Affordability is key to cost recovery, and cost recovery is crucial for replicability. If the targeted groups are unable or unwilling to pay for their urban services and facilities, it would be "unlikely, if not impossible, to design appropriate cost recovery or resource mobilization measures without large scale subsidies."[1] Caught between the lack of funds for subsidies and the inability to recover the costs on such shelter projects as can be financed, replicability remains an elusive goal for these governments.[2]

The problems related to financing, particularly affordability and cost recovery, have become increasingly serious over recent decades and are now being widely discussed by governments in developing countries and international lending and aid agencies, especially the World Bank. In this chapter we will examine pertinent issues in the financing and affordability of shelter and services. The following sections discuss recent policies and programs to finance shelter projects, resource mobilization strategies, affordability and cost-recovery approaches, standards and codes, and mutual aid and self-help. Also discussed are actions needed to improve financing and affordability of shelter and services.

POLICY AND PROGRAM RESPONSES

Urbanization and urban development issues have, for the most part, received inadequate attention in the process of national planning. This is particularly the case with issues concerning financing of low-income urban settlements. National planning in developing countries is usually directed toward economic development planning with a sectoral orientation, while urban planning has conventionally emphasized physical/spatial development with an intersectoral, comprehensive focus. Economists at the national level and physical/town planners at the local level "shy away from policy and institutional analysis and have largely been divorced from decision-making and programmatic considerations."[3] Furthermore, government policies and programs lack adequate flexibility, and thus are unable to cope with the diversity among different urban areas and target groups.

In the past, policies and approaches were created rather pro forma and without adequate analysis or understanding of the peculiarities of the problems they sought to solve. Conventional housing policies "have generally been based on estimating normative requirements—current and future deficits in respect to housing needs."[4] In most cases the designated standards did not recognize or give due consideration to the availability of resources or the economic capabilities and willingness of the target group to pay. A recent World Bank report summarized the situation as follows:

Unfortunately the need for sound policy and appropriate investments was not fully appreciated in the 1960s in most countries. Governments frequently mounted expensive public housing schemes, extended water supply networks and built roads without considering how each project related to the others or anticipated needs. Policymakers and technicians often lacked adequate technical and financial solutions to the problems they anticipated. . . . By 1970, the urban dilemma appeared particularly difficult to resolve to development specialists, because their awareness of urban needs had developed at the same time as an international consensus was emerging that the rural sector should be the priority for assistance. . . . It was therefore essential that a new approach be found which acknowledged that the urban sector could and should pay for itself and which provided services the urban poor needed and could afford.[5]

Upgrading and Sites-and-Services Projects

As discussed in Chapter 3, several projects aimed at providing shelter and services in low-income urban settlements have been initiated during the past two decades. Through these projects, governments have attempted to mobilize community resources, provide credit for home construction, improve on-site infrastructure, and provide developed sites including basic services for house construction on a self-help basis. Most of the shelter projects have been implemented with the financial assistance of international lending agencies, such as the World Bank, which has played an important role in the recognition of the need to delineate a package of policies aimed at providing shelter and related basic services to the urban poor. While the seriousness of the urban situation has been recognized in the developing countries, Prakash noted, "the public policy, planning, programming, resource allocation, and financing aspects of housing and urban development have generally been unintegrated and disjointed."[6]

Sources of funding for shelter projects have varied among countries and, in some cases, among projects within the same country. In the case of the Hyderabad project in India, for example, initially about half of the project expenditure was met by the central government with the remaining 50 percent being shared between the state government and the municipality. After about three years, 50 percent was provided by the state government and the rest by the municipality. Two aspects of the project financing should be pointed out: First, development activites undertaken through the project were "people-intensive" with most of the budget being spent on staff. Second, due to the people's active participation, the total cost of the community development activities was relatively less than most government-initiated activities of a similar nature.[7]

The bulk of funding for the Nadi Programme in Malaysia was provided by the central government. Financing by UNICEF for one of its components (i.e., the Sang Kancil Project) formed only a small portion of the total expenditure of the Nadi Programme. In 1983, however, the funding was reduced from M $5 million (U. S. $1.00 = M $2.10). A nongovernmental organization, the Sang Kancil Organization for Social Services, was established to make up for the declining governmental budget. Whether the new organization will be able to raise sufficient private funds to offset the declining government support remains to be seen.

The Kampung Improvement Programme (KIP) has already been instituted in all the larger cities of Indonesia. In addition to government support, the World Bank and the Asian Development Bank have provided loans, and numerous other donors have provided grants. "The cost per capita for both the KIP physical improvements and social services are quite low (approximately $50 and $20, respectively) and, therefore, full coverage is affordable, both by the government and the communities concerned."[8]

The direct cost of the Environmental Health and Community Development Project in Colombo over a four-year period was about U.S. $1.3 million, that is, less than U.S. $20 per capita for the 70,000 people who benefited from it. UNICEF provided about two-thirds of the direct project funds. The overhead costs were covered in routine government budgets. Community participation in the project has been fully integrated into existing government operations. Because of its low cost, this type of slum and shanty improvement is being continued in Colombo and expanded to other cities in Sri Lanka.

Of the total cost of the Katchi Abadis Project in Lahore, 77 percent was financed by UNICEF, 13 percent by the government, 7 percent by nongovernmental organizations, and 3 percent by the community. In the case of the Lahore Walled City Project, the local and foreign components are Rs.45.35 million (U. S. $1.00 = Rs.15) and Rs.5.90 million, respectively. It is estimated that about 80 percent of the project cost would be recovered over a period of twenty years. The recoverable costs include those related to the water distribution network and sewer installation. These are to be recovered through connection fees and water and sewerage tariffs, respectively. The cost of improvement to footpaths, electricity supply, street lighting, and solid waste collection are to be recovered through an increase in property tax. No attempt will be made to recover the costs of other project components, such as the upgrading of schools and community facilities, community development, and conservation.

The Dandora and Chaani Sites-and-Services Projects in Kenya were funded by the government and the World Bank. In the case of the Dandora Project, each plot was to be provided with either the wet core (toilet, shower facilities, and a kitchen) or a wet core and a living room. The project participants were expected to develop their own plots based on the predesigned plan, although variations could be made with the prior approval of the concerned agencies. Each applicant was required to be the head of a household, to be within a monthly income range of Kshs 250 to Kshs 680, and to have been a resident of the city for a minimum of two years. Those who owned other plots in Nairobi were excluded. The project participants organized into building groups for the purpose of pooling their resources to construct their houses. They were allowed to rent out some of the rooms to supplement their income. In the case of Dandora Project, the planned monthly charges for two types of plots (A or B) ranged from Kshs 73 to Kshs 153. The option A and B plots accounted for 95 percent of the total plots in the project area. Based on the assumption that the project participants would spend 25 percent of monthly household income on shelter and services, it was estimated that "option A plots (65 percent of the total) would be affordable by households as low as the 20th percentile in the city's income distribution curve in 1975" and that option B plots (30 percent of the total) "would be affordable to households in the 30th and 40th percentile."[9]

The Arumbakkam Project in Madras, India, was funded by loans from the central government of India, direct fund allocations from the Tamil Nadu state government, and by a World Bank loan. The loan by the World Bank accounted for about 50 percent of the total project costs. The revenue from the sale of the plots is deposited in a revolving fund established by the Tamil Nadu Housing Board. The project aims at complete recovery of cost of land, land development, on-site infrastructure, and on-plot developments.

RESOURCE MOBILIZATION

Efforts to mobilize resources for providing shelter and services have been made at international, national, local, and community levels. At the international level, the World Bank has been very active in lending funds for sites-and-services schemes and other slum and squatter settlement upgrading projects. As discussed in Chapter 3, the World Bank's lending program for shelter projects was initiated to demonstrate (1) feasibility of low-cost technical solutions for shelter; (2) the possibility of providing services for most of the urban poor on a nonsubsidized basis; and (3) the replicability of such projects, that is, their ability to be self-financing and self-sustaining.[10] The projects assisted by the Bank were sites-and-services projects, as well as those aimed at upgrading existing settlements. Projects were funded in those countries that, among other things, were willing to reduce subsidies and improve pricing policies for land and housing.[11]

The United States Agency for International Development (USAID) has been supporting housing finance through its Housing Guaranty Program and through technical assistance. The main objectives of the USAID Housing Guaranty Program are to strengthen national housing finance institutions and develop national housing finance strategies in recipient countries. Major activities of the program are to borrow from the U.S. capital market under U.S. government guarantee, to finance infrastructure upgrading, and to provide mortgage credit through local financial institutions. In the case of Asian Development Bank (ADB), slum improvement and sites and services have usually been included as components of the ADB-supported integrated urban development projects. The ADB has also assisted in housing, regional development, and new town projects; extended credit to national development banks; and provided technical assistance dealing with shelter and urban development projects. The United Nations Centre for Human Settlements (UNCHS) has supported housing activities through technical assistance and through its support for establishing regional housing finance institutions.

Experience shows that two critical elements of a successful public sector shelter strategy are (1) strong emphasis on cost recovery and affordability; and (2) the initiation and development of programs that can be replicated on a large scale.[12] There are many ways through which cost effectiveness in shelter projects can be brought about. These include dissemination of standardized designs, standardization of building components, increased efficiency in production, improved delivery of services through adequate administrative and institutional coordination and the removal of inappropriate regulation.

Urban local governments need to play a substantial role in mobilizing local resources and financing for shelter and urban services in their respective areas. In practice, however, urban local governments in most financing countries are too weak to perform such a role. They are financially dependent upon state and central governments either because they are not authorized to levy sufficient taxes to fund their designated tasks, or because they are unable to collect the already authorized local taxes. In both cases, local governments end up as losers in the trend toward centralization of financial and administration decision making.

A major portion of low-income housing is financed, for lack of alternatives, through private domestic savings. These savings are usually mobilized through voluntary schemes that include demand and time deposits, contractual savings, and housing lotteries. Informal financing arrangements, therefore, play a significant role in mobilization of local resources for shelter and services. Examples of informal arrangements can be found within the individual family, in family contacts and neighborhood relationships, in informal rotating credit systems, or in savings clubs. Other examples of informal groups that may provide funding sources are nongovernmental organizations such as religious and charitable groups, labor unions, credit unions, and local social or political associations related to housing. While such informal arrangements have significantly contributed to the mobilization of resources for shelter, it is difficult to incorporate them into wider national programs.[13] An ADB report summed up the difficulties as incorporating these arrangements.

Formal financial institutions had not learned to accommodate the methods, the understanding of collateral, and collection techniques that operate successfully in the informal sector.... Banks were generally reluctant to extend services to lower-income families, based on a combination of perceived high risk, conservative management attitudes, and traditional practices.[14]

There are several steps that can be undertaken by public sector institutions to encourage private savings through informal channels. These are:

1. ensuring perceived security of tenure;

2. providing access to urban land at an affordable price;

3. adjusting regulatory controls to accommodate the conditions of poverty and the financial realities of low-income families; and

4. providing other incentive mechanisms such as building materials at a reduced price.[15]

The urban poor often have to resort to several methods to finance their housing. For example, a survey conducted in Karachi showed that the most common methods used by the slum dwellers were savings (55 percent), loans (48 percent), "bisi" (32 percent), the sale of property (19 percent), or some combination of any of these (thus resulting in an indicated total of more than 100 per cent). Conventional institutional credit is not readily available to these people because they typically occupy their land space illegally and do not have stable incomes. Therefore their borrowing sources are most commonly their relatives or friends (indicated in the survey at 70 percent), blockmakers or small contractors (20 percent), or some combination of these. The "bisi" method involves a neighborhood or common-interest organization. Each member contributes a specified amount monthly or periodically and is then eligible, in turn, to draw the combined total fund. For those selling property to finance their home investments, the properties sold included ornaments, land or other assets in rural areas, or part of their businesses.[16]

There are three main elements to be financed in shelter projects: land, on-site infrastructure, and off-site infrastructure. Probably in most of the cases, the land will be, at least incrementally, the most expensive of these elements. In already crowded urban areas, residential land is the scarcest and least replaceable of all the capital investments of shelter projects. However, where the intended residents/beneficiaries are already occupying the land illegally, it may be comparatively easy to vest them with legal ownership at little or no cost. Given the factors of low utility and neglect that give rise to opportunities for illegal occupancy in the first instance, the value of the land is arguably very low already. If it is government land, then its distribution is a noncash subsidy not requiring any revenue raising at all. If the land is privately owned, the true market value (based on its neglected state) can be further discounted by the amount of the expenses that the owner would probably incure in evicting multiple tenants and the additional costs that would be incurred in clearing and renovating the property to make it salable. The government, armed with its powers of eminent domain, could probably persuade the absentee landowner(s) to sell at lower than market rates, or an arrangement may be made for an exchange for government-owned land situated elsewhere that may have more utility to such owners (the latter again being a noncash transaction). Even the more recalcitrant landlords can be persuaded to settle on fairly favorable terms when faced with legal condemnation proceedings, and those that hold out to the bitter end usually have an empty victory at best given the usual lengthy and costly complex litigation and the tendency of awards to favor government. Mechanisms for making land available to the urban poor for shelter are analyzed in Chapter 7.

Concerning the other elements of off-site and on-site infrastructure, it may be that the financing burden of the urban poor can also be eased. Arguably, the shelter project tenants should not have to pay for the off-site infrastructure that would probably have to be built and maintained whether their project existed or not. At least these costs to the poor can be lessened through disproportionately higher charges to wealthier neighborhoods or other sectors that share the benefits of such off-site facilities. On-site infrastructure costs most conceivably have to be recovered from the occupants/users, but these costs can be lessened by means (such as community participation) discussed previously. Also much assistance can be given to the poor—especially as incentives to self-help—through the location of the projects near centers where employment opportunities exist.

The prerequisites of a successful financing strategy for each of the three elements are (1) government commitment and responsiveness to the housing and public service needs of the urban poor; (2) economically realistic standards of shelter for which the poor have the ability and willingness to pay; (3) minimization of subsidies, thereby reducing the financial burden on the public sector and increasing the chances of replicability; and (4) appropriate government intervention in the urban housing and land markets to promote and facilitate increased private investment.[17]

As regards long-term financing for residents, there are usually two main issues that need to be resolved. First, the issue of collateral or guarantees is important. The possibilities for long-term finance range from small loans secured on the borrower's character to government-guaranteed mortgage loans with land and structure as collateral. Second, the organizational issue has to be paid adequate attention in both upgrading and sites-and-services programs. Since loans given to residents are relatively small, overhead costs might be disproportionate. The urban poor are less likely to default as borrowers than middle- and high-income groups provided the expected payments are within their capacity, payment procedures are flexible enough to accommodate seasonal income fluctuations, and counseling systems are built into the lending programs.

In most developing countries a large number of agencies of all levels are involved in financing basic services to the urban poor. Two approaches are generally followed: (1) a "systematic approach" in which needs of the urban poor are not isolated from those of others, and (2) a "schematic approach" designed to provide shelter and specific services to the urban poor. The financing requirements under both approaches are usually met through revenue receipts or loan assistance. The centrally sponsored schemes have, in most cases, been based on loan assistance to subnational governments, which, in turn, give financial assistance to the implementing agencies as soft loans or grants.

The entities that participate in the financing of urban shelter include developers, owner-occupants, squatters, absentee landowners, national and subnational governments, and financial institutions. There are wide variations among developing countries concerning the roles of actors from public and private sectors.[18] In Singapore and Hong Kong, for example, public authorities play a leading role in the provision of housing and urban services for high-, middle-, and low-income households. In most other countries, however, public sector housing finance institutions tend to benefit mainly the middle-income groups. A World Bank report summed up the situation in developing countries:

In most countries little financing is available for low income housing. Some financing, usually heavily subsidized, is passed through public institutions, such as social security agencies, and is available only for housing in public developments. Little of this reaches the poor. There are very few institutions in the private sector that offer financing for housing in developing countries, and those that do offer it only for short terms and only to members of higher-income groups.[19]

AFFORDABILITY

Affordability implies the extent to which the purchase price and continued servicing charges are within the financial means of the intended beneficiaries. According to Keare and Parris, "a certain level of urban services is affordable to a low-income beneficiary household if the amount from monthly income that a household is willing and able to pay for shelter related expenditure is sufficient to cover the monthly costs of providing these services."[20] If a project is not affordable, it will not reach the target population without the use of subsidies, and given limited financial resources in developing countries, subsidies usually cannot be sustained. Affordability of shelter projects is important for two reasons. First, the policy should be replicable in the country with minimal or no subsidy. Second, these projects should be accessible to the urban poor who are the target group. There are several factors that may be used to gauge affordability: (1) household incomes; (2) the proportion of income the residents are able or willing to devote to housing; (3) the monthly cost for housing to the families; (4) the composition of the households; (5) the spending patterns of the households; and (6) the demand and supply of shelter in the area.

Estimating Income

While income is the most widely used criterion to determine the capacity of an individual to participate in a low-income housing scheme, it is also the most difficult to estimate. The difficulties involved in estimating a family's income are that it might be derived from many sources; it might not be regular; it might be increasing or declining; and it might be understated in income surveys to obtain lower payment rates. Sources of income in poor urban settlements include "money earned in exchange for labour, production for one's own consumption, the sale of items produced but not consumed, the increased value of assets owned, proceeds from the sale of assets, gifts from relatives and friends, or transfer payments from the government."[21] In order to determine affordability, a project designer might define income in terms of salary of the head of household, or add the income of the head of household and family members, or might consider all sources of income both regular and irregular. Each of these criteria would lead to different affordability levels. Obviously, the second and the third criterion would increase the accessibility of the project to low-income families.

Experience shows that in some situations, irregular sources might account for a significant portion of a family's income. A survey in El Salvador showed that one-third of the families surveyed received transfer income during the period studied and that gifts and transfer income accounted for more than 10 pecent of the recipient's household income.[22] A similar study in the Tondo area of Manila showed that "extra-regular sources" accounted for 10.7 percent of the monthly income of the households surveyed.[23] When the families are building new houses or improving the existing ones, income from cash gifts accounts for a greater percentage of the household income than would be the case in normal situations. Female-headed households receive more money through transfers than those headed by males. Similarly, households headed by unemployed workers receive more transfer payments than those headed by working members.

During the last decade, a large number of skilled, semiskilled, and unskilled workers from developing countries such as India, Pakistan, the Philippines, and Egypt, have found employment in the oil-rich Middle East countries. These expatriate workers not only support their immediate families but also their distant relatives. A significant portion of their remittances is invested in construction of new houses or improvment of existing dwelling units.

Lanquian summed up the complexity of income as a criterion for determining affordability level:[24]

The main dilemma for project designers, then, is where to set the cutoff for income to qualify for participants in basic housing projects. Setting too low an income requirement would run the risk of defaults, as well as force certain families to spend more for housing than they could really afford. ... Too high an income ceiling, on the other hand, would result in a "leakage" of project benefits to families who might be able to afford more economic housing elsewhere. ... Because of the inherent difficulties in estimating income, it is often better to be flexible when setting income requirements. Often, a range of incomes, proposedly weighted by family size and other considerations, seems to be the best approach.

Proportion of Income for Shelter

As regards the second criterion, the general rule of thumb is that the participants in shelter projects can be expected to allocate 20 to 25 percent of their monthly household income to housing. In actual practice, however, the range may be a much broader range of from 10 to 50 percent, since the proportion of income a family is willing to spend on housing depends upon many factors. Families purchasing ownership interests in a house are more willing to commit a higher percentage than those who are just renting. Large families might spend more because they need more space. Poor families have to "spend proportionately more for housing even though they need more money for food and other basic necessities."[25] During the construction phase, families participating in shelter projects spend not only their savings but also other resources such as transfer payments, gifts, or loans. The proportion of income that can be assumed to be spent for shelter is also partly influenced by climatic conditions, colder climates requiring heavier construction and heating requirements. Based on a review of some of the World Bank-assisted projects, Keare and Parris pointed out that willingness to pay for housing "varies with total family income, type of tenure (ownership vs. renting), the package of services being purchased, perceptions about the investment potential of the shelter (especially through subletting), and certain household characteristics."[26]

Cost of Shelter Package

The third criterion for determining affordability is the cost of the housing package. Monthly costs to a project participant usually consist of mortgage or loan repayments, service charges, cost of building materials, labor costs, and administrative and management costs. One of the most critical issues in shelter projects is how to reduce the allocated costs to the extent that basic per-unit housing charges are within the means of the low-income families. The project cost is influenced by many factors. The project participants may have to pay for the land and development costs. Standards set by zoning or building codes, such as plot requirements, might be too high, as was the case in the World Bank-assisted sites-and-services project in Zambia where these increased the overall cost. The prices for new construction materials also influence the cost. In some projects in India, participants could be provided only a serviced site, but they were allowed to bring used or old materials from their previous shanties to use for building on the new sites. In contrast, the Zambia project required permanent, modern-technology materials that increased the cost. In most countries, however, "project costs continue to be unrealistically high because of the insistence of participants for beautiful finished houses located in well regulated subdivisions that are nestled in landscaped surroundings."[27]

Composition of Household

Another difficulty in quantifying household income is that the concept of who constitutes the household is very fluid. In certain situations the household grouping that is applying for an allocation in a housing project may be quite different in composition from the household that actually occupies that allocation. Obviously, the applicant will be the most ideally qualified in the group and presented in the best possible light to increase the chances of success. The occupying group usually expands, and the income or existence cost bases also expand correspondingly.

Spending Patterns

Household life-styles and spending patterns are also important factors that should be considered in assessing affordability.[28] Household spending patterns are influenced by the occupation of the family members. White-collar workers tend to spend more on clothing, children's education, and transportation, for example, than blue-collar workers with similar levels of income.

Supply and Demand of Shelter

Affordability of low-income housing is closely linked with the supply and demand of housing in a city. The demand for shelter is influenced, among other things, by tenure, on-site services, and growth of urban areas. The supply of low-income housing depends largely on investment in the housing sector by public and private sector institutions. Where the supply of low-income housing does not keep pace with the demand, the prices are likely to further increase.

Steps in Assessing Affordability

Data on affordability of shelter and related urban services to intended beneficiaries could be derived from household-expenditure surveys. Average expenditures for housing and urban services by different income groups could be estimated. Davidson and Payne have identified seven steps in determining affordability:[29]

1. Determine the income distribution (in percentiles) of the target population;
2. determine the average net monthly household income for each percentile group;

3. determine the proportion of net monthly household income available for total expenditure housing;

4. determine the amount of income available monthly after deducting for property taxes and utility charges;

5. amortize monthly payments to calculate the investment potential of project beneficiaries;

6. calculate the "all-in" land and infrastructure costs per plot; and

7. determine the residual amount that can be afforded for initial superstructure development.

In practice, there seem to be few options other than for the project designers to adopt a more open, flexible, and "inquiring attitude" to the question of how the households look at their own problems of affordability. Lee has suggested that, "in many instances two complementary project changes would be beneficial: encouragement of potential beneficiaries themselves to determine what they can afford, basing the project design and principles of cost recovery on the outcome; and, simultaneously, taking a less dogmatic approach to income targetting."[30]

BUILDING CODES AND HOUSING STANDARDS

Building codes and standards are considered necessary by housing administrators for public safety and economy. In developing countries, however, many planners and practitioners question the usefulness of those existing building codes and standards that inhibit construction for the poor more than they serve the general welfare. It is argued that strict adherence to technical codes and standards will limit the number of dwelling units, that it would make home construction too expensive, and that it would constrain provision of even basic housing to the urban poor. One of the problems with the building codes and housing standards is that in many Third World countries, these are outdated vestiges of colonial administration or are patterned on conditions applicable only in more developed countries.

The Dandora Sites-and-Services Project provides an illustration of the significance of building by-laws and standards in shelter projects. During the project preparation stage, Grade II by-laws of the building code were adopted for the project area. The development control and law enforcement officers, however, would not approve the plans when implementation of phase I started—leading to a long controversy and subsequent delay over infrastructure design standards. This resulted in cost overrun because of both required changes in the designs and the increase of construction costs due to inflation and price escalation.[31]

In the process of planning and implementing shelter projects, a number of concerns regarding building codes and standards have to be taken into consideration. These concerns and issues have been resolved differently in different situations.

Plot Size

The size of plots is an important area of controversy. It is argued that small plots lead to too high densities and overcrowding. Yet, large-size plots increase the total cost of the shelter projects. Therefore, plot sizes need to be regulated in terms of the project capacities "to accommodate more people, more equitably allocate a scarce commodity such as land among project participants, prevent land speculation, and reduce project cost."[32]

Size and Design of Dwelling

The size and design of dwellings in a shelter project is primarily a saftey concern. If a house is too small, it would mean overcrowding, leading to sanitation problems and a rapid deterioration. Too big means essentially unaffordable. Most shelter projects provide a serviced site and a sanitary core or a sanitary core with one or two rooms. A look at the model houses built under most shelter projects demonstrates that housing authorities prefer relatively high standards in size, style, and building materials. Engineers and architects prefer durable, permanent dwellings. The main problem, of course, is that the poor cannot afford these houses. Some project designers have suggested that housing authorities should construct models of dwelling units "being progressively developed." One of the arguments against maximum housing standards is that it would further polarize social classes. It is difficult to tell the poor that they do not know how much they should spend on the house while no such restrictions are put on the rich.[33]

Building Materials

Safety is usually the main reason given for discouraging the use of materials such as grass, bamboo, or scrap wood in densely populated cities. Housing project designers strongly prefer permanent materials. The experiences in slum and squatter areas have shown, however, that cheaper, affordable building materials can be used in basic housing projects.

Sanitation Standards

In most shelter projects supported by the World Bank, sanitation services account for from 40–50 percent of total on-site infrastructure costs and water for about 20 percent. Most upgrading and sites-and-services projects provide waterborne sewerage systems, while from 30–50 percent of the houses usually do not have toilets. One of the reasons given in support of high-standard sanitation systems is that such projects do not exist in isolation from the city. The experience, however, shows that there are alternative sanitary systems that could be used to reduce costs. In the Mombasa project in Kenya, for example, pit latrines were accepted by project authorities as meeting minimum standards. In the case of Kampung Improvement Programme (KIP) in Indonesia, the sanitary model consists of communal toilet, artesian well, and a water storage system.

Density Standards

Density control is also usually justified for the sake of safety. Density standards may vary from one project to another. In the case of Dandora project in Nairobi, a minimum of two persons per room was accepted. In 1979, however, it was found that 95 percent of the households in Dandora exceeded that standard. About 50 percent of the plots surveyed were occupied by two or three families. High density in the Dandora project was attributed to two-thirds of the plot owners subletting at least one room at the time of the survey. Subletting was allowed by the housing authorities to enable families to increase their income. It was felt that subletting should be encouraged, because there was high demand for rental accommodations in the area, and because it would increase the chances of cost recovery.

While the significance of safety and health factors in basic housing is recognized, planners and practitioners also feel a strong need to accommodate as many people as possible and to increase the cost-effectiveness of the project. Furthermore, financial rewards for renting are so strong that as long as it increases the chances of recovery of costs, the project designers are likely to tolerate it.

Mixed Use of Land and Houses

Planners and professionals usually argue that allowing commerce or industry in residential areas would produce safety problems or lead to environmental degradation. The reality of the situation in low-income settlements, however, is that production, leisure, community affairs, and other activities often take place at the same time in the same area. Thus, there are wide gaps between "world views" of professional planners and the urban poor. The answer is not to eliminate standards but to identify more appropriate ones.

COST RECOVERY

As mentioned earier, cost recovery is essential for replicability and sustainability of shelter programs and projects. Cost can be recovered in three ways: by direct payment from residents; by a surcharge on utility connections and consumption fees for water, electricity, and sewage; and by general tax revenues such as increased collection of property tax from all urban residents.

The fiscal devices for cost recovery include land pricing/leasing policies, taxation of land and buildings, user or service charges for specific services, other tax or nontax revenues, and intergovernmental fiscal transfers. Cost recovery of services can take two basic forms. Under the "direct method," beneficiaries pay for services (water, refuse collection, etc.) and goods (house construction and maintenance materials) provided under the project through monthly house loan repayments, recurrent utility tariffs, and other user charges. "Indirect methods" include recovery through municipal and central government taxes.

Factors Determining Cost Recovery

There are five main factors that determine the extent of cost recovery from shelter projects. These are:

1. level of rates of repayment;
2. types of participants selected for the project;
3. measures and procedures for collection;
4. communities' role in the process of cost recovery; and
5. the extent of "political will" on the part of concerned agencies to recover cost.[34]

The determination of the extent of the project costs to be recovered was a crucial factor during the mid–1970s. Most World Bank loans for basic housing were given an interest rate of 7–8 percent per year for periods of twenty to twenty-five years. The housing agencies usually reloaned these funds at interest rates of 12 percent or more over fifteen to twenty years. One of the key project issues in shelter projects is whether there should be full recovery of project costs or whether a percentage of the costs should be subsidized. Those who favor subsidies argue that the urban poor have low wages and thus a low capacity to pay for shelter; that the credit institutions fail to adequately respond to the needs of the urban poor; that government spends huge amounts for infrastructre improvements in middle- and high-income settlements; and that better housing will improve the living environment of the urban poor.

The other arguments against full cost recovery are that it would push out the poorest households in the community; that the municipal services should be routinely provided as a part of local government responsibility without capital costs being charged to local residents; and that the squatters would be reluctant to pay for leasehold title to property and upgrading costs in situations where they already have a de facto security of tenure.

Table 6.1
The Total Investment Required in Order To Provide Each Household Living in
Poverty in the Year 2000 with a Basic Unit of Shelter
(billions of 1975 U.S. dollars)

Region	In Urban Areas	In Rural Areas	Total
Latin America and the Caribbean	62.0	7.0	69.0
Europe, the Middle East, and North America	11.0	3.0	14.0
Eastern Africa	6.0	5.5	11.5
Western Africa	4.0	2.0	6.0
South Asia	25.0	20.0	45.0
East Asia and the Pacific	8.0	8.0	16.0
Total	116.0	45.5	161.5

Source: World Bank, Shelter (Washington, D.C.: Poverty and Basic Needs
Series, 1980), Table 2.

Im most cities, local government decisions in the past have favored high-income groups and prestigious projects. Local governments developed and sustained infrastructure for the modern industrial sector, high-income residential areas, or commercial centers, and allocated a low percentage of the overall municipal budget to the provision of infrastructure in slums and squatter settlements. In view of the above, Baross argued that the strategy of direct cost recovery of government investments from residents of low-income settlements seems to be politically unfeasible.[35]

Those who favor full cost recovery argue that "subsidized programmes typically have severely limited supply capacities; and, in such situations where output is artificially restricted, higher income families have proven very adept in capturing the 'rationed' benefits."[36]

The main reason given in favor of cost recovery is that governments in the developing world do not have adequate resources to provide each household in poverty with shelter and services. The estimate of the total global investment needed to provide each such household with a basic unit of shelter by the year 2000 is about U.S. $161 billion (see Table 6.1). Prakash's studies of twenty-five Asian countries show that the total investment required to provide minimum urban services and facilities for new migrants to cities over the next twenty years could range from U.S. $147 to $210 billion. Even if these countries' total savings were mobilized to provide other services, they would fall short of the amount needed.[37]

The cost of a shelter project is significantly influenced by the government's policy decision whether to include or exclude the cost of land and infrastructure. In the World Bank-assisted project in Zambia, for example, cost of land was not included, while in the El Salvador project it was added to the project cost. In the Tondo project in the Philippines, project participants were asked to pay only a small percentage of the cost. As regards infrastructure costs of shelter projects, the policy of most governments is to include these in recoverable government expenses. Here again the issue is whether to include off-site infrastructre, such as roads to connect the area with the main networks, since these might be used by both the project participants and outsiders.

The second issue concerns the selection of participants. Usually the factors included in sites-and-services projects are household income, family status, residence in a project site or city, and good moral character. It would seem that the percentage of income a family is able and willing to spend on housing is the most critical factor in cost-recovery-type projects. Studies in Senegal, Zambia, Kenya, and Jamaica show that "single parent households tend to have more difficulty in meeting project payments than nuclear or extended families."[38]

The third issue concerns the collection machinery and procedures. Based on his evaluation of the World Bank-assisted shelter project, Laquian has identified six factors that determine the effectiveness of the collection machinery. These are: the provision of information to project participants; the development of those sanctions in cases of default that are fair, equitable, and have been adequately communicated to the participants; the incentives that the public authorities might establish to reward those people who pay regularly; appropriate collection procedures, such as the collection of payment through payroll deduction or authorization of community leaders to collect payment in neighborhoods; the identification of the level of satisfaction with the services provided; and the utilization of community pressure in ensuring cost recovery.[39]

The fourth factor is the extent of community participation in the process of project implementation. Active community participation in project implementation has a positive effect on achieving cost-recovery objectives efficiently. Therefore, the collection mechanism should be designed with community participation in mind.

Finally, "political will" to recover full or partial cost of the shelter project is a crucial factor. More often than not, community leaders and residents seek large-scale government subsidy and would delay payment even after the project with the government subsidy has been initiated. The tendency on their part is to seek the support of some of the national political leaders who are dependent on grass-roots support for reelection. Unless the government has adequate political will to enforce cost recovery, local administrators will not be able to accomplish project objectives

Selected Experiences

The performance of shelter projects in terms of cost recovery has been uneven. In the case of Lusaka program, for example, it was found that more than 50 percent of the families in some upgrading projects were in arrears and that some households had not made any payments. Evaluation studies showed that a more direct factor in the slow rate of collection appeared to be "weak political will on the part of the Zambian United National Independence Party to seek repayment."[40] Another hindering factor was "the absence of an efficient recordkeeping system to maintain up-to-date information on defaulters and amounts owed, as well as the lack of a flexible mechanism for collecting payments."[41]

The Kampung Improvement Programme (KIP) was initiated by the local government. However, its enlargement to cover the whole city and to extend it to other Indonesian cities required external assistance from the World Bank and other bilateral agencies. The World Bank has also supplemented the budget to upgrade programs in Bangkok and Manila.

Cost recovery in most shelter programs in India has not been effective. Even where a highly subsidized price or rent is within the affordability range of the urban poor, recovery has been dismal. In the case of resettlement schemes in Delhi, "it was found that when the 80 square yard developed plots with a latrine, a water tap, and plinth, on which a family could build a hut or house according to its needs, was given to allottees with an income of Rs.250 or less, on a 99 year lease on payment of a monthly instalment of Rs.12.75 for ten years, the bulk of the beneficiaries were unable to pay."[42]

One of the exceptions in India is the Arumbakkan Project in Madras, which aims at complete cost recovery through a number of strategies. Costs of land, land development, and on-site infrastructre are recovered through the sale of developed plots for residential, commercial, and industrial purposes.[43] Costs of on-plot developments are "fully charged to the respective categories of beneficiaries."[44] In case an allottee fails to make payments for more than two months, notice is served and action is taken to cancel the allotment and evict the allottee. In practice "bill collectors regularly warn allottees whose payments are in arrears before official notice is served."[45] As of 1981, an average repayment rate of 95 percent had been achieved. Nationalized banks provide loans for house construction and extension activities. The interest rate charged is 4.5 percent for scheduled castes and tribes and 12.9 percent for other categories.

Allottees' active participation in the construction of their houses was encouraged in the case of the Dandora project in Kenya. The predominant methods of house construction were (1) self-help building by allottees; (2) self-help building using subcontracted labor; and (3) self-help building by building groups. The second method was the most popular. The Community Development Division and Technical Division of HDD assisted the allottees in forming building groups. By the end of 1978, these groups had completed about 194 rooms for their members.

A World Bank report pointed out that one of the difficulties in implementing some of the shelter projects has been cost recovery. Initially the payment by beneficiaries was reasonably good. "Problems developed, however, after the start-up period, as the necessary follow-up services, such as maintenance and social services, were not provided as promised."[46] Therefore households became increasingly reluctant to pay. This situation was exacerbated by inadequate collection methods, the lack of sanctions for nonpayment, and the absence of political will to enforce collections."[47] Thus while the capacity to pay existed, lack of willingness to pay and the ineffective collection system led to declining performance.

Enforcement of cost recovery has, in some cases, been impeded by political bankers who like the rates to be reduced in order to gain political support among squatters and slum dwellers. Problems can begin even before the project is formally launched. In the case of the Lyari Slum Improvement Project in Karachi, Pakistan, the International Development Association (IDA) had declared its willingness to lend U. S. $40 million provided the Karachi Municipal Corporation (KMC) used this amount as seed capital for a revolving improvement fund. In 1976, the provincial government proposed the promulgation of legislation to establish the Slum Improvement Revolving Fund, which was to use the amount collected for land lease and improvement charges in the area, with similar projects in other slums of Karachi. In February 1977, however, during an election campaign, the chief minister of Sind Province declared in a public meeting in Karachi that the government had decided to immediately regularize the plots of residents of Karachi and that rates were to be fixed at Rs.4 for residential and Rs.6 for commercial plots. The rates that had been proposed by KMC to make the project self-financing ranged from Rs.5 per square meter for the first 100 square meters to Rs.105 for every square meter exceeding 400 square meters. For commercial plots the proposed rates were even higher. Thus the announcement by the chief minister "undermined the self-financing character of Lyari Improvement Project. With these rates, lease proceeds from Lyari would cover only a fraction of the actual cost of the scheme."[48] The loss of the self-financing character of the project led partly to the decision of IDA not to extend the loan, thereby ending the project.

MUTUAL AID AND SELF-HELP

"Mutual aid" describes the cooperation of families participating in sites-and-services and community upgrading programs in constructing basic parts or project infrastructures as a team. "Self-help" implies using a family's skills, labor, and other talents in the process of constructing and improving its own house. One of the commonly expressed views is that a dwelling unit designed by an architect; constructed by carpenters, masons, and electricians; and managed by a professional manager would cost more than that same unit built by friends and with technicians or professionals hired only to carry out such technical tasks as installation of plumbing and electricity. One of the assumptions in self-help approaches is that there is surplus labor in low-income settlements and that the low-income people have the basic skills to build a house. The World Bank experiences, however, indicate that self-help might not have as significant a role in shelter projects as was originally perceived because the amount of surplus labor within the household appears to be limited.

One of the views expressed about slum dwellers and squatters is that because most of them are migrants from rural areas, they carry with them the traditions of mutual self-help such as *gotong royong* in Indonesia and *panchayat raj* in India. In the Tondo project in the Philippines the residents organized themselves into informal *bayanihan* groups to move houses. However, it was found that such groups were not effective in the work, which required a continuous effort.[49]

In a sites-and-services scheme, three construction choices of allottees could be identified: individual self-help, mutual self-help, and employing a contractor. These have different implications concerning the time necessary to complete a house, its cost, skills required, and control over the construction process.[50] For example, the cost of construction through self-help would be lower and the allottee would be in full control of the construction process within the project limits. However, it would take him a longer time to complete the house and, furthermore, he might not have the skills to construct the housing according to the required standards.

The advantages of construction through mutual self-help are that its cost is lower than the other two choices and it enables the group to control the construction process. Yet, it might take a long time to construct houses for all members of the group, who might require intensive training to be able to construct according to the specified standards.

Construction through the contractor is faster, partly because he is able to provide skilled labor. However, the contractor-built houses are more expensive and provide less opportunities to the allottee to control the construction process.

The degree to which self-help is used in shelter projects varies from one country to another. In the World Bank-funded projects in the Philippines and El Salvador, for example, the role of self-help was significant in housing construction and improvement. In the case of Zambia project, however, about 90 percent of the households in a sites-and-services project used hired labor to improve their houses.

There are many factors that limit the use of self-help in basic shelter projects. These include lack of time for self-help housing; types of building materials commonly used; the higher status given to professional construction; difficulties with the material and loans; and problems with techno-logical assistance.[51]

REPLICABILITY

The main objective of shelter policies in developing countries should be the replicability of innovative approaches and strategies to meet the demand of the growing number of the urban poor. Attempts should be made "to create a framework that allows government to expand the housing supply system and to assist in mobilizing resources for housing provision without it dominating and controlling the process, since centralization of this sector is likely to inhibit innovation and progress."[52]

Replicability of projects requires more than merely repeating what has already been done. It requires the identifying of alternative ways of resolving problems of institutional capacity, public sector finance and trained man-power as well as facing "policy questions concerning the most appropriate division of labour between the public and private sectors in housing insti-tutional finance and urban management."[53]

The role of the public sector should be restricted to the provision of organization, finance, technology, materials, and information. Governments could encourage private participation by removing "overly restrictive" building codes and regulations. Furthermore, the government should en-courage new experiments and approaches to provide shelter. As Cohen has pointed out, "it can only be through the multiplication of new efforts—and not through replication of demonstration projects alone—that the growing demand for housing among low-income urban families can realistically be met."[54]

In order to ensure replicability, financial support has to be mobilized from many sources: agencies such as the World Bank, national government agen-cies, local governments, nongovernmental organizations, and the poor urban communities themselves. The availability of financial support, however, is a necessary, but not sufficient, condition for replicability, which, in addition, requires new policy orientation, resolution of legal issues, and identification of appropriate administrative arrangements. As discussed in Chapter 3, international agencies such as the World Bank and UNICEF have played an important role in the advocacy of upgrading and other self-help ap-proaches. Whether it will result in overcoming organizational deficiencies, vested interests, and related problems remains to be seen.

NOTES

1. Ved Prakash, "Affordability and Cost Recovery: Selected Urban Services for the Poor" (Nagoya: UNCRD, 1985, mimeo).
2. Ibid.

3. Ibid., p. 14.

4. Ibid., p. 17.

5. World Bank, *Learning by Doing*, p. 3.

6. Prakash, "Affordability and Cost Recovery," p. 3.

7. William J. Cousins and Catherine Goyder, "Hyderabad Urban Community Development Project" (Nagoya: United Nations Centre for Regional Development, 1985, mimeo).

8. Clarence Shubert, "Providing Urban Basic Services: A Comparative Analysis" (Nagoya: United Nations Centre for Regional Development, 1984, mimeo), p. 35.

9. T. S. Chana, "Nairobi: Dandora and Other Projects," in Payne, ed., *Low-Income Housing in the Developing World*, p. 22.

10. Cohen, "The Challenge of Replicability," pp. 88–99.

11. Ibid.

12. Asian Development Bank, *Financing of Low Income Housing* (Manila: Asian Development Bank, 1983), pp. 11–17.

13. Ibid., pp. 18–19.

14. Ibid., p. 22.

15. Ibid. pp. 18–19.

16. J. Van der Harst, "Financing Housing in Slums of Karachi," in J. W. Shoorl, J. J. Van der Linden, and K. S. Yap, eds., *Between Busti Dwellers and Bureaucrats: Lessons in Squatter Upgrading in Karachi* (Oxford: Pergamon, 1983), pp. 61–68.

17. Prakash, "Affordability and Cost Recovery," p. 28.

18. Ibid., p. 23.

19. World Bank, *Shelter: Poverty and Basic Needs Series*, p. 7.

20. Keare and Parris, *Evaluation of Shelter Programmes for the Urban Poor*, p. 46.

21. Laquian, *Basic Housing*, p. 28.

22. Ibid.

23. Ibid.

24. Ibid., p. 30.

25. Ibid., p. 31.

26. Keare and Parris, *Evaluation of Shelter Programmes*, pp. 49–50.

27. Ibid., p. 33.

28. Roger H. Tym, "Finance and Affordability," in Payne, *Low-Income Housing in the Developing World*, p. 211.

29. Forbes Davidson and Geoff Payne, eds., *Urban Projects Manual: A Guide to Preparing Upgrading and New Development Projects Accessible to Low Income Groups* (Liverpool: Liverpool University Press, 1983), p. 66.

30. Michael Lee, "Myth of Affordability," *Third World Planning Review* 7:2 (May 1985), 140.

31. Chana, "Nairobi: Dandora and Other Projects," p. 32.

32. Laquian, *Basic Housing*, p. 75.

33. Ibid.

34. Ibid., p. 104.

35. P. Baross, "Four Experiences with Settlement Improvement Policies in Asia," in Skinner and Rodell, *People, Poverty and Shelter*, p. 165.

36. Keare and Parris, *Evaluation of Shelter Programmes*, p. 85.

37. Ved Prakash, "Financing Urban Development in Developing Countries" (Nagoya, Japan: UNCRD Working Papers No. 82–86, 1982).

38. Laquian, *Basic Housing*, p. 109.

39. Ibid., p. 110.

40. Keare and Parris, *Evaluation of Shelter Programmes*, p. 86.

41. Ibid.

42. D. D. Malhotra, *Managing Urban Development: Policy Issues in Urban Services for the Poor* (New Delhi: The Indian Institute of Public Administration, 1985), p. 1983.

43. Peter Swan et al., *Management of Sites and Services Housing Schemes: The Asian Experience* (Chichester, England: John Wiley, 1983), p. 113

44. Ibid.

45. Ibid., p. 114.

46. World Bank, *Learning by Doing*, p. 26.

47. Ibid.

48. Yap Kioe-Sheng, *Leases, Land and Local Leaders: An Analysis of a Squatter Settlement Upgrading Programme in Karachi* (Amsterdam: Institute for Geographical Studies, Free University, 1982), p. 40.

49. Laquian, *Basic Housing*, p. 43.

50. HABITAT, *Community Participation in the Execution of Low-Income Housing Projects* (Nairobi: HABITAT, 1983), pp. 27.–29.

51. Laquian, *Basic Housing*, p. 39.

52. Michael A. Cohen, "Replicating Urban Shelter Programs: Problems and Challenges," in Dennis A. Rondinelli and G. Shabbir Cheema, eds., *Urban Services in Developing Countries: Public and Private Roles in Urban Development* (London: Macmillan, forthcoming), p. 152.

53. Ibid., p. 153.

54. Ibid.

7

LAND FOR THE URBAN POOR

Land is a crucial issue in the planning and management of human settlements. As was noted in the preamble to the Habitat Conference in Vancouver, "Land, because of its unique nature and the crucial role it plays in human settlements, cannot be treated as an ordinary asset, controlled by individuals and subject to the pressures and inefficiences of the market." Because the number of the urban poor illegally occupying public and private land has significantly increased during the last two decades, governments in developing countries have recognized the need to intervene in the land market to ensure adequate access to land for the urban poor and to control land use. One of the most complex problems in this regard has been how to grant security of tenure to infrastructures of these illegal settlements, particularly where land is privately owned.

There are several reasons for advocating security of tenure for squatters and slum dwellers.[1] The pride of ownership and the chance to create a family estate encourages residents to invest more capital and self-help in the improvement of their dwellings; stable and permanent infrastructures provide governments the opportunity to regulate and control irregular and haphazard growth of low-income infrastructures; and the sense of community is solidified, which greatly facilitates and economizes on the provision of settlement and basic urban services through community participation. With such benefits in mind, planners and practitioners in developing countries are experimenting more with innovative approaches and with appropriate mechanisms to provide the infrastructures of slums and squatter settlements with legal, permanent occupation of the land on which their homes are established.

In this chapter, we will look at the existing land arrangements in low-income settlements, describe interventions used by government to increase the availability of land for shelter and services, and identify appropriate mechanisms to make land accessible to the urban poor. The following sections discuss land shortages, processes of land supply, patterns of land occupation and tenure, and land use patterns. This is followed by an analysis of government interventions, that is, land use controls, landownership limits, security of land tenure, land transfer and taxation, and land acquisition and banking. Also discussed are alternative mechanisms to make land more accessible to the urban poor.

LAND SHORTAGE

The supply of serviced urban land, particularly for low-income groups, has not kept pace with the rapidly increasing demand. Furthermore, the supply has been lower through public agencies than through private agencies, which predominantly cater to the needs of middle- and high-income groups—a smaller segment of the urban population in most developing countries. The even more unfortunate reality seems to be that the scarcest land is that located near centers of employment, the kind that the urban poor need the most.

The shortage of land for the urban poor can be attributed to several factors. First, urban populations are generally increasing rapidly, expanding into the nearest available space and engulfing any land that will support habitation. Second, the rich acquire and hold land as a mechanism of storing wealth and as a hedge against inflation. They buy land not necessarily for their own use but as an investment; this not only deprives others of its use, but tends to bid up the price of the scarce asset.[2] In some cases large amounts of "black money" that needs to be "laundered" is channeled into land, further increasing land prices as a result of market pressures. Finally, as will be examined later, in most cases government controls and regulations have not been adequately enforced, a situation particularly convenient to speculators, who are then able to create artificial shortages to maximize their profits.

In the 1970s, in most of the major urban areas of developing countries studied by Hardoy and Satterthwaite, it was found that there was an inadequate supply of land for shelter; that the price of serviced plots was beyond the affordable range of the majority of households; that the private market did not respond to the need of the urban poor; and that squatting was the only option available to the vast majority of the urban poor.[3]

The failure of market mechanisms to ensure the poor adequate access to land necessitates intervention by public authorities to see that that function is served. Therefore, public authorities in most developing countries have attempted to increase their control over the urban land market. In the case of metropolitan Delhi, for example, a major portion of the land is owned and directly controlled by the public authority; this has enabled the city to respond to the demand for serviced land for the urban poor more effectively than other cities in the country where land ownership and control is weak.

As regards the intervention of public authorities in the land market, Hardoy and Satterthwaite reported that "many governments have been rather slow in recognizing that legalizing land tenure for squatters is more effective than destroying the settlements and that, with the exception of a few serviced site-and-squatter legalization programmes, public authorities have been reluctant to enter into urban land market on a large scale to reduce land speculation."[4] Tanzania and Singapore are the exceptions here. In Tanzania almost all land is publicly owned. In Singapore a major portion of the land is owned by public authorities that have efficient expropriation procedures and exercise revenue power through property taxes and development charges.

Processes of Land Supply

The practices of developing countries show different processes through which the urban poor get access to land for housing, or what Baross has referred to as the "articulation of land supply."

In identifying three forms of this articulation,[5] Baross used the term "noncommercial articulation" for situations in which those who build on land "either do not pay for its ownership or use right or, if they do, payment is a 'voluntary gift,' according to social customs."[6] There are four manifestations of the noncommercialized articulation of land supply. First, the use of customary land may be retained by tribes and ethnic communities and allocated in accordance with social customs. Muslim communal land holdings and temple land would also be in this category. With the increasing pressure on land in urban areas, customary land becomes an important potential source of land for the urban poor, particularly those migrating from rural areas. An example of this manifestation is the customary land in Port Moresby. Second, the colonial rulers alienated native land that after independence was passed on to the new government. This type of land reserves also became an important source for irregular settlements. The examples of such land being used for popular settlement are found in Lima, Istanbul, Karachi, and Ankara. Third, "abandoned properties" are another source of noncommercialized articulation of land for popular settlements. Properties might be abandoned because of wars, religious upheavals, or political factors. Squatting in Tondo in Manila after the Second World War and in some areas in Lusaka after independence are examples. Fourth, "marginal land" such as riverbanks, marshland, and slopes is another source of land supply for the poor. Squatter settlements on marginal lands can be found in Manila, Sao Paulo, and Bogota.

"Commercialized articulation" of land supply may take the form of "miniplots," "land rental," and "substandard subdivisions."[7] Those selling parts of their land might do it for such reasons as debt payment or home improvement. Those who buy probably are doing it largely for the security of tenure. The land rental system "offers the possibility of illicit property development for large landowners who anticipate that their land holdings can ultimately be sold for urban uses yielding higher returns than popular housing."[8] Subdivision of land into unserviced plots, usually carried out by property developers and entrepreneurs, has significantly increased in cities of developing countries.

"Administrative articulation" is manifested through government-initiated projects for owner-built housing development and various rules and regulations that are aimed at intevening in the urban land market, such as the land ceiling acts in India and Sri Lanka

PATTERNS OF LAND OCCUPATION AND TENURE

By definition a squatter is a person who occupies a piece of land without right or title. Land occupation patterns in squatter settlements, however, are complex. Some inhabitants in squatter areas might either own or have land use title. This is the case in many squatter settlements in Asia and Latin America where land occupation by some residents is legal while that of the others is not. In Manila, for example, about 75 percent of squatter families living in Tondo Foreshore occupied public land without paying rent. Before initiation of the improvement programs, 13 percent of the households had title to the land they occupied.

Another complexity emerges in situations where the modern concept of ownership is superimposed on the predominantly traditional or communal patterns of landownership. In Sub-Saharan Africa, for example, traditional landholding patterns "permit the possession of land to satisfy individual needs in respect of farming, trading, or housing but do not give absolute rights of ownership in the Western legal sense."[9] Thus, communal land laws and new concepts of landownership exist side by side, though there are frequent conflicts between these.

Mechanisms for Access to Land

In Malaysia, as in other developing countries, land occupation by squatters is considered illegal, however temporary occupation licenses (TDL) are given in some cases upon request to the District Land Office. If the land is needed for public use, these licenses can be revoked. In several squatter settlements in the capital city, Kuala Lumpur, residents have been occupying land for more than two decades. Large-scale removal of the residents does not seem to be politically feasible and concerned government agencies have recognized this fact.

Three main types of land occupation in squatter settlements in the Third World could be identified: legal, traditional, and illegal.[10] The dwelling units constructed on the occupied land may be owner-occupied, rented to others, or given to relatives and friends to use free of charge. Table 7.1 shows the proportionate use of these types of tenures in selected slum and squatter settlements. It will be noted that the majority of the buildings in selected settlements were rented out or had mixed tenure and that owner-occupied dwellings were predominant in the selected Asian and Latin American settlements.

In Indonesia, house ownership statistics usually refer to building tenure (rather than land) since construction of houses on rented, leased, or government-controlled land is a common phenomenon. In Surabaya, only 23 percent of the owner-occupied houses had the right of ownership to the underlying land. A major proportion of land in urban kampungs (villages) is under the control of the government. A common practice in the past has been to allow squatters to continue using land provided it is not contradictory to the city's land use plan. Long-term leases are being granted under the Kampung Improvement Programme in Surabaya and other selected cities in the country.

In Calcutta, there are eight types of slums and squatter settlements.[11] In the "conventional bustis," feudal lords lease out their land to middlemen (thika tenants) who construct huts and rent these to migrants. Legislation passed over the years protects the rights of the middlemen and bustis. In the "legal refugee colonies," refugees squat on vacant land and titles are given to the occupants; these are not considered legal by the government. The fourth type, "squatter settlements," grew slowly through squatting that was "organized illegally through the caretakers of the absentee landlords, through local agencies, or through relatives and friends of those who have already squatted.[12]

The other types of settlements in Calcutta are: "jute lines," which include official and unofficial dwellings provided by the jute mill owners to migrants from other regions; "private self-help housing"—temporary and semipermanent structures on unserviced plots in fringe areas that are purchased by occupants; "old rented walk-ups," which are old and permanent structures with community-type water supply and sanitation facilities and which have become slums because landowners have lost interest in maintaining the property; and "government tenements for low-income people" constructed by government and leased to the urban poor."[13]

In a survey of selected slums in Bangkok, it was found that 49 percent of the respondents were living on government-owned land, 46 percent on privately owned land, and 3 percent owned their own land. The rest did

Table 7.1

Types of Building Occupancy in Selected Slum and Squatter Settlements

City	Settlement	Owner occupied	Mixed Tenure[a]	Rented	Rent-free Occupancy	Total structures
Colombo	Punchi Harak Watte	11	--	88	1	100
Dacca	Suritola	10	60	30	--	100
Hong Kong	Yau Ma Tei	--	20	80	--	100
Lahore	Walled City	64		26	7	97[b]
Ahmadabad	Sabarmati Riverbank	95-100	--	-5	--	100
Delhi	Rouse Avenue	100	--	--	--	100
Istanbul	Rumelihisarustu	88	10	2	--	100
Kuala Lumpur	Kampong Pandan	86	--	14	--	100
	Kampong Maxwell	84	2	14	--	100
Manila	Tondo Foreshore	62	4	24	10	100
Alexandria	Kom-el-Decka	5	28	67	--	100
Kumasi	Ayigya Village	--	31	29	40	100
Lusaka	George Compound	81	5	14	--	100
Nairobi	Kawangware	22	59	19	--	100
Port Sudan	Deim Omna	80	12	8	--	100
Bogota	Las Colinas	90	6	4	--	100
Kingston	Drewsland	84	--	16	--	100
Lima	Villa El Salvador	95	5	0	--	100
San Salvador	El Manguito	96	--	4	--	100
Santiago de Chile	Manuel Rodriguez	100	--	--	--	100

[a] Partly rented out.

[b] Three percent of the structures in the Walled City are listed as having "another" type of tenure, which is not specified.

Source: United Nations Centre for Human Settlements, Survey of Slums and Squatter Settlements (Dublin: Tycooly International, 1982), p. 56.

not know to whom the land belonged.[14] Unlike in other capital cities in Asia, private landowners in Bangkok have verbal agreements or written land rental contracts of from one to three years with slum dwellers who are considered temporary occupants. The survey showed that 44.3 percent of the respondents had written contracts ranging from one to five years; 3.1 percent had verbal contracts; 25.8 percent had the landowner's permission to stay; and 22.5 percent had neither an agreement nor the permission to stay.[15]

The perceived security of tenure by squatters and slum dwellers is only partly dependent on the status of their legal tenure. The above survey in Bangkok showed that about 25 percent of the respondents perceived their chance of staying in the area over the next five years to be less than 40 percent; 30 percent perceived a 75 percent chance; and 18 percent felt certain about their stay.[16] The factors considered critical in determining the perceived security of tenure were the status of legal tenure, the attitude of landowners, any alternative plans for the use of the land, and rumors of eviction.[17]

During the past four decades, the access of the urban poor to land to housing has largely been through a number of informal arrangements that might vary from one country to another. In the case of Mexico City, for example, there are three mechanisms through which land alienation for irregular settlements takes place: subdivisions of marginal land for the sale of unserviced plots; land invasion by a group of the urban poor; and land cession to low-income residents.[18] The illegal alienation of land in the city "is a complex business, and each case is likely to be the outcome of a carefully orchestrated attempt to further the interests of the agents involved, be they realtors, vote catchers, radicals, do-gooders, ministers, unions, etc."[19]

In Fiji, the land issue is both complex and highly sensitive. Some of the land previously held under customary ownership has been converted to freehold title or leased out for agricultural, residential, or other uses. A major portion of the undeveloped land is still under customary ownership by native Fijians who depend on this land as the main source of their living. Three forms of land tenure can be identified in the country. "Freehold land," which constitutes about 10 percent of the total land area, was acquired by European settlers through negotiations with Fijian chiefs. "Native land" is owned communally by native Fijians and constitutes about 83 percent of land in Fiji. The third type is "crown land," which was purchased or transferred from native land for government purposes. The Fiji Housing Development Authority was established in 1957 to provide housing for workers. In 1971, the authority started producing more single-unit houses or housing sites and basic urban services as well as financing for self-building. In addition, the provision of services sites became its main approach to providing shelter and basic urban services to the poor. Squatting on the crown land has been common and the authorities have shown unwillingness to take strong measures to discourage the practice.[20] On native land, squatting has taken place with the permission of landowners. Some native landowners have allowed the migrants to urban areas to build houses on their land with payment in cash or kind, though such agreements are only verbal. Speculation on native or crown land is not possible because the sale or transfer of a lease is strictly controlled by Lands Department and Native Land Trust Board.[21]

Security of Tenure and Housing Improvement

It is widely accepted that where the people are assured in the security of their tenure, they improve their dwelling units to the fullest extent possible. The earliest observations on the relationship between the security of tenure and housing improvements were made by Turner based on his work in Peru. Studies in Karachi have also shown that there is a positive relationship between security of tenure and housing improvement.[22] Most of the land in Karachi is owned by the government, which has occasionally given ninety-nine-year leases. Households with higher perceived security of tenure have invested more for housing improvements.

Tenure security is a necessary but not a sufficient condition for increased investment in housing by the people. In Colombo, the Ceiling on Housing Property Law was introduced in 1973. It was hoped that tenants would then have more opportunity to purchase their own homes and that there would be increased improvement of housing. In 1977, however, it was found that there was no significant investment in housing improvements in tenement gardens due largely to the low income levels of residents.[23] Similarly, the economic status of households was found to be significantly related to people's investments in housing in Mexico City.[24]

Housing improvements could also be influenced by sociocultural considerations. People might have the potential to invest but do not do so for social and cultural considerations. In Port Moresby, for example, a migrant settlement program was initiated, but many people left their house unfinished. The tribal customs required the house owners to accommodate and feed members of their tribe or clan: therefore some clans put most of their energies into organizing periodic festivals and other communal activities.

Thus, while granting of security of tenure is a prerequisite for home improvements, it needs to be followed up with other measures, such as institutional financing, in an integrated program. There are also several other factors that influence slum dwellers to improve their houses. These include income level, age of dwelling unit, access to formal and informal housing finance, and household composition. A survey in Bangkok showed that most of those who improved their houses did it from their own savings or by pooling resources; that most residents were willing to improve their housing if formal housing finance was available; that those with a low level of perceived security are less likely to make improvements than those with a high level of perceived security; and that those with written land rental contracts with landowners improved their houses more often than those with verbal contracts.[25] It was also found that household income was positively related to house improvement; the average value of improvements increased both with the perceived degree of security and the income level. The period of stay in the dwelling and the age of the settlement did not seem to have any significant influence on the propensity to improve the house.[26]

There are many options that have been used to ensure the security of tenure. These include outright sales, long-term leases, and leasing with purchasing option. There are, of course, other factors that determine housing consolidation, and these might not be a direct result of the security of tenure. Such factors include initial condition of a dwelling, family income, the types of building materials used, and the value of existing houses.[27]

LAND USE PATTERNS

The pattern of land use in a squatter area develops along with the growth of the settlement and is determined mostly by the needs of the residents. One of the problems, though, is that the percentage of land utilized for residential purposes is very high and that dedicated to common area or communal needs is usually inadequate. Furthermore, "in most cases, plots of various shapes and sizes are packed together with little provision for a circulation network and even less provision for public open space. "[28]

A survey of slum and squatter settlements in developing countries showed several land use patterns.[29] In Latin America individual plots are used for residential purposes as well as for such commercial purposes as shops and service activities. In Africa, residential densities are lower, thereby providing more space for commercial activities and larger areas for community facilities. In Asia, individual plots are usually found to be relatively small in size, and are almost fully occupied by dwelling units. Several inferior plots do not have adequate access or roadways to walkways.

LAND USE CONTROLS

Land use controls are usually advocated for "(a) public safety and health; (b) order and efficiency in public services; (c) a desirable pattern of development; (d) the way land use affects land values and the distribution of wealth and (e) the impact of land use in aesthetics and urban forms."[30] Therefore various forms of land use controls have been introduced in developing countries. In Indonesia, for example, the Town Planning Ordinance was promulgated in 1948. The need for new legislation in view of the changing human settlement situation has been widely felt in the country, though no new draft law concerning city development has been adopted. In 1980, however, the directorate of Town Planning in the Ministry of Home Affairs issued a ministerial instruction for city planning based on which master plans are being prepared for all cities in the country.

In India effective use of zoning as a tool for planned development has been limited to a few large cities such as Delhi, Bombay, or Madras. The planning framework in most states is provided through the conventional master plan approach. More than five hundred master plans have been prepared, though very few of these have been implemented. As a report by ESCAP points out "the master plans' inherent rigidity in the face of rapid urban growth, and preoccupation with physical as against social and economic factors and their ambitious development proposals in disregard of financial and administrative realities have made their relevance very doubtful."[31]

Planning is one of the main mechanisms utilized to limit the use of land. Though the urban master plans are widely believed to be essential to the success of any urban land policy, "the basic problems with land use controls in Third World cities are that they are over-ambitious and that in their specific detail and philosophy they follow too closely systems of control in Western Europe and North America."[32] In India's Tamil Nadu State, for example, the Town and Country Planning Act of 1971 requires that development controls be based on plans. The Master Plan of Madras, the state capital, consists of the Land Use Plan and the Development Control Rules. Land in the Madras Metropolitan Area is divided into ten different use categories. The city of Madras is divided into sixteen planning divisions that are subdivided into ninety-nine planning units. The Development Control Rules are aimed at categorizing land in accordance with the "intensity of its development and its characteristics" and at controling subdivisions, parking requirements, and so on. There are wide gaps, however, between the statutory provisions and their actual practice. Since housing provided through the public agencies has not kept pace with the rapid increase in urban population, the number of squatters is increasing. There is a shortage of qualified staff to administer development controls, and concerned agencies have not been able to effectively coordinate their activities. Thus, the "system fails in practice because it is over-ambitious, given the capabilities of the administrative system."[33]

In most of the settlements in the developing countries, rapid population increases have been accompanied by unplanned and haphazard urban growth. Many countries have therefore attempted to improve the public control of changes in land use.[34] In the Philippines, for example, about 600 square kilometers were declared an urban land reform zone in 1979. No land could be sold or building constructed in that zone without the permission of the Regulatory Commission of the Human Settlements Ministry.

In Tunisia also, regulatory powers of municipal master plans have been strengthened.

During the period of Nigeria's 1970–74 plan, acquisition of land for public projects was found to be difficult. Among the factors impeding such land acquisition was the excessive compensation demanded by private land-owners. In 1978, therefore, the Land Use Decree was promulgated. According to this decree, all land is to be held in trust and administered for the common benefit of all under the supervision of the state governors. In Mexico the legal basis for effective land use control was provided by the General Law on Human Settlements. The law strengthened land use powers at the central, state, and municipal levels, respectively, and allowed for setting up research areas for future growth in urban development plans. In Tunisia two concerned public agencies have wide-ranging power to expro-priate land for housing. In Singapore clear expropriation procedures have been established and the extent of compensation to be paid has been defined.

The main reason that governments in developing countries have been unable to effectively enforce land use controls is that there are significant conflicts among various city groups that attempt to seek access to urban land. The main conflict is usually found between public authorities respon-sible for controlling and guiding settlement development and those who operate contrary to government regulation, such as squatters; those who illegally subdivide land; and those who establish commercial operations.

Bringing customary land into urban use is an important issue in providing land for housing to the urban poor. In the case of Port Moresby in Papua, New Guinea, several irregular settlements of rural migrants have emerged on customary land. The government has not been able to upgrade these settlement due to the unwillingness of traditional landowners to cooperate. Past efforts to create joint ventures or long-term leasing arrangements be-tween customary landowners and the migrants have not yielded positive results.[35]

Hardoy and Satterthwaite reported that among the seventeen countries studied in Asia, Africa, and Latin America, governments sought to increase public control over land use and, in some cases, attempted to limit private ownership rights.[36] Most of these actions by the governments were initiated in the 1970s. However, the scope of the government control over land-ownership and the effectiveness of this control have varied from one country to another. Though considerable progress was made during the 1970s in establishing the principle of public or community rights, "the legislation and the political will to follow this up have not been so forthcoming."[37] Public authorities in each of the selected countries were found to have the right to expropriate land in the public interest, and, in several countries, such government actions were limited in scope. In Indonesia, for example, the public authorities faced difficulties in acquiring land. In Singapore, Tun-isia, Sudan, and Tanzania, however, substantial progress has been made in carrying out land use regulations. In Tanzania almost all land is publicly owned, hence concerned public authorities are able to guarantee public rights in land tenure. Hardoy and Satterthwaite summed up the situation in the developing countries as follows:

There have been few successful attempts among the seventeen nations to improve land use control through negative controls—the enforcement of zoning, subdivision and building regulations, or master plans containing a combination of these. The rapid and unplanned physical expansion of urban areas which characterize Third World cities in the 1950s and 1960s is even more generally true today. The picture is one of municipal governments lacking the political power, the legislation, financial base, and the trained personnel needed to guide and control the growth and development of the area in their jurisdiction.[38]

LANDOWNERSHIP LIMITS

Some countries have attempted to regulate ownership of urban land by law. In India, for example, the Urban Land Ceiling and Regulation Act, enacted in 1976, imposed a ceiling on vacant holdings and limited the size of dwelling units to be constructed. The implementation of this regulation. Several exemptions have been granted to encourage low-income housing and housing cooperatives. Furthermore, the act reduced the supply of land in the urban market "by imposing a ban on transactions in land exceeding the specified limit and by putting a restriction on transactions of land below that limit."[39]

In Sri Lanka the Ceiling on Housing Property Law of 1973 regulates ownership, size, and cost of construction. The law was aimed at redistributing ownership of private rental housing. Surplus units were appropriated by the government and were either redistributed among the occupants or were used for redevelopment programs. Most of the surplus houses were found to be slum tenements. In 1978, the Slum and Shanty Improvement Programme in the city of Colombo was initiated. About 65 percent of the shanties under the project are located on government land. Since the implementation of the new law, however, serious procedural delays have been caused by new land tenure conditions.

In many Third World countries, central and local governments are increasingly using public ownership as an important instrument of urban land policies. In Tanzania and Sudan, public ownership of urban land has increased the supply of urban land for shelter and basic urban services. Hardoy and Satterthwaite noted that "the scale of both nations' housing plot schemes would not have been possible without public land ownership." Singapore too has made effective use of public land reserves. Without the public ownership, public authorities in Singapore could not have succeeded in their housing programs.[40] In the case of Bolivia the Law on the Reform of Ownership of Urban Land was passed in 1954. In the Philippines, in accordance with the urban land reform zone within Metro Manila, large landowners were asked to sell land to those squatters who had been oc- cupying land for more than ten years, and U. S. $20 million was allocated for land expropriation.

SECURITY OF LAND TENURE

Land tenure has many direct and indirect implications. It influences dens- ities and affects accessibility of land for shelter and basic urban services. More specifically, it affects land use, land acquisition and disposal, the development potential of land, land taxes, and credit supply. The experience in Asia shows that procedures to achieve security of tenure to the benefi- ciaries of squatter settlement upgrading schemes and sites-and-services proj- ects are "cumbersome." The granting of security of tenure has been extremely slow even though in some cases such as in Karachi, Pakistan, political support for such projects existed at the highest level.

Colonialism has had a lasting impact on land tenure patterns in developing countries. Two main forms of urban land tenure owe their origin in most cases to the colonial rule[42] One system, spread through the colonial empires of the Netherlands, France, and Spain granted outright ownership or rights in the land. The second, which is based on the English "common law" "gives more restricted ownership and rights to the land."[43] The latter system of land law makes it relatively easier to control land transfer, because the common law is utilized to limit absolute landownership in the "leasehold system," which gives the leaseholder the use of the leased land only for a specified period.

Doebele has identified seven major groups that are usually involved in or affected by actions concerning urban land. These are agrarian elites, urban elites, commercial and industrial elites, the middle class, low-income but well-established households, low-income renters, and low-income migrants with no previous claim on land.[44] Because of competing interests, opera- tional policies of relevant institutions are determined by the relative power of these groups within the political system.

Experience in developing countries shows that the security of land tenure for the urban poor is primarily a political issue, and it often necessitates government intervention in the land market. The process of granting security in land tenure involves several actors whose interests are usually not iden- tical. Landlords prefer market mechanisms that enable them to gain max- imum benefits from the land they own. Middlemen and land speculators seek maximum gain from their investment in real estate. Private land de- velopers are almost exclusively interested in middle- and high-income hous- ing. Bureaucracy tends to maintain the status quo. Some politicians might use the land security issue to mobilize the squatters' and slum dwellers' support against the government in power. The politicians who are in power attempt to utilize the land issue to legitimize their rule, on the one hand, and safeguard the interests of landlords and developers, on the other.

Government intervention to ensure land security for the urban poor emanates from two sources.[45] First, well-organized squatters and slum dwellers might be able to put pressure from below to get their demands accepted. Second, military governments might attempt to legitimize their rule through granting land security to the urban poor and implementing their decisions under strict military regulations. The cases of Manila and Karachi, respectively, are the examples of two types of political action.

In the Tondo Foreshore area in Manila, there was a large concentration of squatters. In 1970, various neighborhood associations formed the Zone One Tondo Organization (ZOTO) to pressure the government to grant them landownership rights. The unifying cause for the neighborhood associations was their common objective of securing tenure. The residents even defied martial law, and their persistent struggle resulted in a presidential decree establishing a land tenure system in the area in 1975. The decree provided, among other things, for rearranging houses and offering lots to residents on a lease basis.

In Karachi, the prime minister and other national political leaders publicly supported security of tenure in Katchi Abadis in 1973. But no concrete actions were taken. After the military government came into power, it conferred proprietary rights to the inhabitants of Katchi Abadis as of January 1978 and issued enabling legislation. The military regime had more power to press local authorities, semiautonomous organizations, and other concerned agencies and actors to implement the legislation. Most of the land occupied by the squatters belonged to the government, and this facilitated the implementation of the government legislation. Those squatting on private land have had to negotiate with their landlords, and progress in implementation of the law in such cases has been slow.

The provincial government also passed legislation for a change of land security in the slums of Karachi. Furthermore, the Karachi Municipal Corporation (KMC) established a directorate for slum improvement. Two upgrading strategies were followed: provision of security of tenure through legislation of occupancy; and upgrading settlements through the provision of infrastructure.[46] A revolving fund that included grant contributions from the government was established. The practice followed was to give each participant squatter land leases for a period of ninety-nine years, and a one-time charge was levied against the plot holder for the lease. Leaseholders were also to pay nominal annual rents. In the Baldia township, a pilot project was initiated in which residents were asked to obtain leasehold rights at nominal rates. The project designers hoped that increased security of land occupation and physical improvements in the area would encourage residents to pay for the nominal charges and obtain their legal leases. In reality, however, very few residents have come forward and paid their dues. It seems that government announcements giving them de facto security of tenure before the project was initiated eliminated the incentive they needed to make payment. They prefer to continue living on rent-free land as long as they have de facto security of tenure.[47]

In addition to political commitment, administrative support is a precondition to effective implementation of legislation for change in land tenure. More often than not, the bureaucracy tends to protect the interests of the more established landlords, real estate speculators, and middlemen. Even without such vested interests, land tenure systems might face several obstacles, particularly where they may lead to multiple ownership claims. A large number of actors might be needed in the transfer of all the rights in private lands. Negotiations between landowners and government to transfer privately owned land to slum dwellers often take long periods of time.[48]

While the security of tenure is a prerequisite for slum and squatter settlement improvement, there might be several adverse consequences of tenure change. Angel has identified three such consequences. First, once squatters gain informal and collective security of tenure, they are usually less willing to pay for the official legal title. Second, improved tenure security could result in the displacement of the original low-income families. The provision of land tenure might result in the increased value of land and thus attract more higher-income households. Third, the legalization of tenure might further encourage others to illegally occupy government or private land.[49]

Government intervention concerning security of tenure in slum and squatter settlements can be roughly divided into three periods. From the 1950s to the middle of the 1960s there was a "period of hostility" when the migrants were generally considered a marginal population illegally occupying public and private land. The second period started with the development of sites-and-services schemes in the early 1970s and led to a policy of upgrading. The security of tenure granted to the participating households in upgrading projects usually led to an increased physical improvement by house owners. The third period is that of "tacit recognition." The degree of recognition of the land tenure in these settlements, of course, varies among countries. Two examples of tacit recognition are Katchi Abadis in Pakistan and irregular settlements in Peru.

LAND TAXATION

Cities in developing countries need effective mechanisms for taxing land in order to recover some of the public money spent on upgrading settlements and providing better infrastructure facilities. McAuslan has identified five criteria for evaluating any forms of taxation: equity, economic efficiency, administrative feasibility, yield in terms of amount of revenue, and political acceptability.[50] Land taxes are generally based on an assessed value of the land derived by one of three criteria: (1) rental values of the land; (2) capital value of land as an underdeveloped site; or (3) capital value of both land and any improvements made on it.[51]

There are variations among countries concerning taxes on land. In Jakarta, for example, a "special tax" based on the length of their road frontage is levied on landholders; this recovers about 60 percent of the costs of roads, bridges, drainage, water, and electricity.[52] In South Korea, the developer acquires and develops serviced plots after land has been designated by the municipal planning agency for development. The serviced plots are then distributed to the original landowners who own enough land to pay for development and infrastructure. The balance of land is sold by the agency to recover development costs.

In India, many cities have reviewed their taxation systems but very few have succeeded in implementing the needed reforms. Property tax rates are usually low and most of the cities have rent-control legislation. Tax rates are fixed on the basis of rents that were determined more than thirty years ago. Therefore, "the tax has no relevance to the present value of properties, the present use, and the potential yield."[53]

LAND TRANSFER

The urban poor's access to land is also affected by land transfer rules and regulations. McAuslan has identified four forms of the state's involvement in private market land transactions: (1) playing a neutral role by, among other things, resolving disputes between parties; (2) playing a more active role by providing for the registration of land ownership; (3) providing credit to buyers through housing banks; and (4) playing a regulatory role by "laying down the terms and conditions on which transfers may take place" or "keeping for itself the right to allow or refuse any particular land transfer."[54]

Increasingly, developing countries are abandoning their neutral roles in private market land transactions. In Fiji, for example, the constitution forbids the sale of customary or tribal land to Indo-Fijians. In Tanzania, after independence, privately owned freehold land was converted into a right of occupancy. Some countries have passed laws to limit the amount of land that can be owned by a landowner, as in the examples of India and Sri Lanka discussed earlier.

PUBLIC LAND ACQUISITION

Land acquisition by public authorities is one of the main mechanisms of direct intervention by the government in the land market. During the 1960s, in most market-based economies, land acquisition was considered necessary to ensure the provision of city-level facilities. More recently, the need for land acquisition to provide subsidized serviced plots to the urban poor has been recognized. Another reason for public land acquisition has been the need for the government to control and regulate the price of urban land in order to restrain the increasing cost of land and to ensure access of middle- and low-income groups.

In the cities of most developing countries, the ownership of land is un-evenly distributed. In many cases, a few individuals or agenices own a major portion of urban land, and they control the release of it to the market in such a manner as to maximize their returns. Misra noted that "although a wide variety of regulatory controls through land use controls and taxation have been imposed by almost all city governments in the region, their impact on making the land market free from the speculative and restrictive controls of a few land bankers has been insignificant."[55] It, therefore, becomes nec-essary for the government to directly intervene in the land market by ac-quiring and subsequently releasing a significant quantum of land. Another reason for the acquisition of land is "to ensure that benefits that accrue to land development are spread as wide as possible and reach a majority of the community."[56]

Many methods have been used in the developing world for the public acquisition of privately owned land. The relative significance of each of these depends upon the local situation, but each has been used successfully to increase the access to land for housing, basic services, and infrastructure. The main methods are:

1. land acquisition through voluntary bargain and sale;
2. public acquisition of leasehold interests;
3. acquisition through barter or exchange;
4. acquisition through public-private ventures such as land readjustment and land sharing;
5. selected regulations that facilitate land acquisition, such as freezing land use and value;
6. acquisition through confiscation and nationalization; and
7. acquisition through gift or deduction.[57]

The main advantage of land acquisition through voluntary sale is that it reduces administrative cost and minimizes land conflicts. Yet, many factors constrain the use of this technique in developing countries. Urban land is usually controlled by powerful private interests and is held for speculative purposes. Because alternative investment opportunities are not as attractive as land speculation, private landowners usually do not respond to the gov-ernment request for sale. Other factors that constrain land acquisition through voluntary sale are that land owners are usually more interested in a private sale because of higher profits; public procurement procedures are often complicated and "public agencies in developing countries surround themselves with rules and practices that have the effect of discouraging or complicating the sale of land";[58] and it is usually difficult to easily determine the price of land.

The public acquisition of leasehold interests has several advantages. Land can be acquired at a lower cost and citizens might be more willing to sell their land through this method. Where the government needs land for a short term, this technique might be the most appropriate. This approach is most widely used in the islands of the South Pacific such as Fiji and Papua New Guinea.

In free enterprise economies, the "compulsory acquisition of land is generally regarded as one of the government's most extreme powers, to be exercised only for specific purposes and in accordance with procedures which given land owners maximum opportunity to object."[59] The need to protect the rights and interests of landowners and, consequently, a complexity of procedures lead to long delays in land acquisition. In India, for example, urban development authorities are faced with long delays in the compulsory purchase of land because landowners challenge their use of powers in the courts.

If the publicly acquired land is not used efficiently and fairly, it can create more resentment among the poor. In the case of Delhi Development Authority, for example, more than 20,000 hectares were taken over in accordance with the city's Master Plan. The authority bought, developed, and sold the land predominantly for upper-income housing. "Through the 1960s, 50 percent of the land went to the high-income groups and 11 percent to the poor. But these are averages which conceal a catastrophic decline in the amount allocated to the poor: from 55 percent in 1961–62 to 2 percent in 1970–71."[60]

There are several incentives that governments could provide to encourage landowners to sell land to the government. These include: adding a part or all of the tax payable on the sale amount to the price of land to be paid to the landowner; providing developed lots of equal value to the landowner; utilizing private sector developers to serve as government agents for large-scale acquisition of land; and providing employment opportunities to a member of the landowner's family to facilitate negotiations. Landowners could be encouraged to organize their own association through which negotiations for the sale of land to the government could take place.

In Malaysia the government is empowered to acquire land for public purposes, utility, residential, commercial, or industrial use. The purchase price paid to the owners is determined on the basis of specified criteria. Recently the focus of the government policy shifted to privatization, and now public authorities are not acquiring much land under powers of compulsory purchase.

LAND BANKING

Land banking implies the reservation of land for future urban use. The main purposes of land banking are to occupy land most suited for the intended purpose, control development through landownership, and facilitate project implementation by avoiding land acquisition delays.

Land can be banked in several ways.[61] First, regulatory approaches could be employed. These include zoning where land is classified for low-cost housing or zoning where development is permitted only on the condition that a specified percentage of land is provided for low-cost housing. Second, land reservation for public purposes could be employed through "official mapping." The government could identify the land it wants to reserve, prepare a map of the designated land, and record it as a legal document. Third, a specified portion of the existing government-controlled land could be allocated for low-cost housing and the ownership of the land could be transferred to land banks for shelter projects. Fourth, direct purchase is a common, though expensive, mechanism to acquire land for shelter projects. Because the land costs are rapidly increasing, the capacity of governments to provide housing for the poor is correspondingly decreasing.

The success of land banking depends upon timely acquisition of land by the public authority. The government authorities "should be able to acquire the potential land before the speculative private developers do so or at least the intent of the authority to acquire land is made known and a ban on its transaction is enforced."[62]

The case of Singapore shows that land banking can facilitate urban development and improve the access of the poor to urban land. However, as Misra noted, effective land banking requires "highly efficient technical and managerial skills on the part of government to understand the intricacies of the market mechanisms, to acquire, develop, and dispose lands with a high degree of competence. Further, the government authorities must have adequate legal powers for land banking and means of raising enough investible finance."[63]

Public agencies could initiate joint ventures with private landowners in pooling land for urban development as an alternative to compulsory or negotiated land acquisition methods. This could be done through land readjustment schemes, such as are used in Japan and South Korea.

LAND POOLING

Land pooling is a form of land acquisition in which "a public authority acquires an area with many plots and many owners, consolidates and develops the holding, and eventually reallocates land in demarcated and serviced plots to its former owners in proportion to their original holdings."[64]

The landowners and the concerned authorities share the cost. Land pooling and readjustment has many problems, however, some of which Doebele has pointed out:

It is administratively complex and is most suitable only in countries in which private rights to land are fully recognized. In urban areas where there is already a great deal of public ownership of developable land, it is not necessary. In other cities where planning regulations are weak and where private developers have provided inadequate and badly planned infrastructure services to gain access to urban fringe land it may be too late to apply land readjustment techniques. Finally, such techniques also depend on good cadastral and registration systems and therefore cannot be used in countries where these are still lacking.[65]

"Land readjustment schemes" have been widely and successfully used in Japan and South Korea. However none of the other countries in Asia have attempted to implement these. Even in Korea the use of this technique has declined during the last few years. It has been argued that such schemes did not keep prices down nor discourage speculation; that the administrative procedures in land readjustment were found to be time-consuming; and that large areas of vacant land are increasingly becoming scarce.

ALTERNATIVE MECHANISMS TO FACILITATE ACCESS

The problems facing the urban land market and access to it by the poor are complex. There is no single solution to the problem. A series of mechanisms and approaches are needed to facilitate the accessibility of the urban poor to land for shelter and services.

Angel and Chirathamkijkul have proposed a strategy for slum reconstruction through sharing as an alternative to eviction.[66] The method is aimed at rehousing slum dwellers on the land occupied by them. Five main elements of slum reconstruction identified under this method are:

1. Land sharing. This means that part of the area of the slum is cleared for development of commercial properties while the slum dwellers are rehoused on the remaining part.
2. Densification. Slum reconstruction through land sharing will require an increase in residential densities.
3. Rebuilding. In many cases, densification will necessitate demolition of existing structures and eventual rebuilding at higher densities.
4. Community participation. Effective implementation of slum reconstruction will also require active participation of all segments of the community in all stages of planning and management, particularly in the processes of allocating plots, demolishing structures, and constructing houses.
5. Cost recovery. Commercial properties in the reconstructed slums could be sold to generate enough funds to pay for part of the cost of land and housing. Such

a source of funds is needed because of the inability of the urban poor to fully pay for the costs.

Doebele has identified eight "new directions" that could be utilized to make land accessible for shelter and services:

1. Urbanization as a wealth producing process. Land prices are increasing significantly, and municipalities and other institutions could utilize such increases in capital values as a source of funds for installing public services.

2. Land readjustment. If the government is to provide new services or extend services to new areas, every benefiting landowner could be asked to provide a fraction of his land, which could be sold by the government to pay for the cost of installing services and facilities.

3. Advance acquisition of development rights. It has been argued that land rights are cheaper to acquire than full titles. Examples of this type can be found in the United Kingdom.

4. The government as a land assembler. The government could assemble large parcels of land through expropriation for projects that are considered in the public interest.

5. Increasing transportation access to fringe land. Appropriately planned transportation investments could open new areas for urban development.

6. Provision of low-income housing as a condition for development permits. The granting of permits for middle- and high-income groups could be made conditional on the construction of a specified number or percentage of low-income homes.

7. More complex patterns of private-private and private-public cooperation in land and housing development.

8. Reemphasis on employment, health, and education as part of housing programs.[67]

Baross argued that the traditional land supply system for the urban poor is breaking down and that new ways should be found to secure land for low-income housing. He has proposed "collective articulation" as an alternative mechanism to increase access to land.

The concept of collective articulation is not merely a tenure form of collective ownership. Rather it is a reformulation of how low-income families can cope with and overcome the obstacles of exclusion from the emerging commercial and administrative land allocation practices. It is termed "collective" because it requires the organization of low-income families in pursuing house actions. The grouping of people offers new opportunities for resource generation, bargaining power, and support of professionals in dealing with the diminishing possibilities of obtaining land on an individual basis.[68]

There are many areas in which government action on land for housing the urban poor is needed.[69] To begin with, there is a need to improve the supply of land for the poor by the formal and informal sectors. This requires, among other things, regulating and providing incentives for the informal subdivision, identifying appropriate standards of land subdivision, and introducing cooperative development schemes. Because unnecessary destruction of the existing informal settlements should be prevented, campaigns to secure land tenure, legitimize the use of land through legislation, and disallow demolition without replacement should be organized.

The existing land settlements should be improved. Governments could link the grant of tenure to infrastructural improvements, encourage community participation in slum improvement, and integrate poor settlements into large-scale redevelopment schemes.

The government's role in increasing the supply of land for the urban poor is crucial; it could appropriate vacant public land, initiate land pooling and readjustment schemes, encourage cross-subsidies in land development projects, or promote cooperation between the public and private sectors to increase the supply of developed land.

Financing the development of land is an important issue in improving the access of the poor to land for housing. This could be accomplished through (1) acquiring land without major subsidies; (2) establishing savings and loans schemes; (3) improving the recovery of loans from the beneficiaries; (4) establishing cooperatives for collectively owning land that can be used as collateral for increased access to credit; (5) taxing development gains on vacant lands; and (6) providing credit for land development.

NOTES

1. There is a growing literature on this subject. Among others, see Angel et al. *Land for Housing the Poor*; Hardoy and Satterthwaite, *Shelter: Need and Response*; Michael G. Kitay, *Land Acquisition in Developing Countries: Policies and Procedures of the Public Sector* (Boston: Oelgeschlager Gun and Hain, 1985); and HABITAT, *Survey of Slums and Squatter Settlements*.

2. Madhu Sarin, "The Rich, the Poor, and the Land Question," in Angel et al., *Land for Housing the Poor*, p. 239.

3. Hardoy and Satterthwaite, *Shelter: Need and Response*, pp. 226–38.

4. Ibid.

5. Paul Baross, "The Articulation of Land Supply for Popular Settlements in Third World Cities," Angel et al., *Land for Housing the Poor*, pp. 180–220.

6. Ibid., p. 181.

7. Ibid.

8. Ibid., p. 197.

9. HABITAT, *Survey of Slums and Squatter Settlements*, p. 42.

10. Ibid., p. 55.

11. Dilip K. Roy, "The Supply of Land for the Slums of Calcutta," in Angel et al., *Land for Housing the Poor*, pp. 98–109.

12. Ibid.

13. Ibid.

14. Emiel A. Wegelin and Chantana Chamond, "Home Improvement, Housing Finance and Security of Tenure in Bangkok Slums," in Angel et al., *Land for Housing the Poor*, p. 77.

15. Ibid.

16. Ibid.

17. Ibid.

18. Peter M. Ward, "Land for Housing the Poor: How Can Planners Contribute?" in Angel et al., *Land for Housing the Poor*, p. 37.

19. Ibid.

20. Utkatu Naiker, "Land for Housing Low Income Workers in the Context of Commercialization of Land Supply in Fiji," in Angel et al., *Land for Housing the Poor*, p. 316.

21. Ibid.

22. On the Katchi Abadis in Pakistan, see, among others, Ahsan, "Provision of Services to the Urban Poor," Schooral, van der Linden, and Yap, *Between Basti Dwellers and Bureaucrats*.

23. See Marga Institute, "Housing in Sri Lanka," *Marga Research Studies*, Vol. 6, Colombo, Marga Institute, 1976.

24. See Peter Ward, "Self-help Housing in Mexico City," *Town Planning Review* 49:1 (1978).

25. See Wegelin and Chamond, "Home Improvement," pp. 75–97.

26. Ibid.

27. Laquian, *Basic Housing*, pp. 57–67.

28. HABITAT, *Survey of Slums and Squatter Settlements*, p. 43.

29. Ibid.

30. Economic Commission for Asia and the Pacific (ESCAP), *Land Policies in Human Settlements* (New York: United Nations, 1985), p. 30.

31. Ibid., p. 31.

32. Patrick McAuslan, *Urban Land and Shelter for the Poor* (London: Earthscan, 1985), p. 66.

33. Ibid., p. 67.

34. Hardoy and Satterthwaite, *Shelter: Need and Response*, pp. 235–37.

35. John P. Lea, "Customary Land Tenure and Urban Housing Land: Partnership and Participation in Developing Societies," Angel et al., *Land for Housing the Poor*, pp. 54–74.

36. Hardoy and Satterthwaite, *Shelter: Need and Response*, p. 227.

37. Ibid., p. 227.

38. Ibid., pp. 235–36.

39. ESCAP, *Land Policies*, p. 34.

40. Hardoy and Satterthwaite, *Shelter: Need and Response*, p. 230.

41. Ibid.

42. McAuslan, *Urban Land and Shelter*.

43. Ibid., p. 23.

44. William A. Doebele, "The Provision of Land for the Urban Poor: Concepts, Instruments and Prospects," in Angel et al., *Land for Housing the Poor*, pp. 348–74.

45. Shlomo Angel, "Land Tenure for the Urban Poor," in Angel et al., *Land for Housing the Poor*, pp. 110–43.

46. Shahid Saleem, "Land Management in the Katchi Abadis of Karachi," in Angel et al., *Land for Housing the Poor*, pp. 144–55.

47. Ibid.

48. Angel, "Land Tenure," pp. 128–32.

49. Ibid.

50. ESCAP, *Land Policies*, p. 98.

51. Ibid.

52. McAuslan, *Urban Land and Shelter*, p. 102.

53. ESCAP, *Land Policies*, p. 36.

54. Ibid., p. 32.

55. Bijay Misra, "Guidelines on Public Land Acquisition Methods and Procedures in Asia" (Nairobi: United Nations Centre for Human Settlements, 1985, mimeo).

56. Ibid., p. 8.

57. For a more detailed discussion of advantages and disadvantages of each of these, see Kitay, *Land Acquisition in Developing Countries*, pp. 13–38.

58. Ibid., p. 15.

59. McAuslan, *Urban Land and Shelter*, p. 91.

60. Ibid., p. 88.

61. Robert S. De Voy and Chawalit Rodrongruang, "Basic Land Banking Concepts and their Application to Low Cost Housing in Thailand," in Angel et al., *Land for Housing the Poor*, pp. 412–29.

62. Misra, "Guidelines on Public Land Acquisition Methods," p. 34.

63. Ibid.

64. McAuslan, *Urban Land and Shelter*, p. 89. For more detailed analysis, see M. Honjo and T. Inoue, eds., *Urban Development Policies and Land Management: Japan and Asia* (Nagoya: Nagoya City, 1984).

65. Doebele, "Provision of Land for the Urban Poor," p. 367.

66. Shlomo Angel and Thipparat Chirathamkijkul, "Slum Reconstruction: Land Sharing as an Alternative to Eviction in Bangkok," Angel et al., *Land for Housing the Poor*, pp. 430–60.

67. Doebele, "Provision of Land for the Urban Poor," pp. 348–74. Also see William A. Doebele, "Concept of Urban Land Tenure," in Harold B. Dunkerley, ed., *Urban and Land Policy: Issues and Opportunities* (New York: Oxford University Press, 1983).

68. Baross, "Articulation of Land Supply," p. 206.

69. Angel et al., *Land for Housing the Poor*, pp. 528–56.

8

POLICY AND PROGRAM
IMPACTS

It was in the 1970s that, with the assistance of international agencies, most upgrading and sites-and-services projects were initiated in developing countries. Though the period of implementation for most projects has been less than a decade, enough experience has been accumulated in Asia, Africa, and Latin America to justify a critical examination of the performance and impact of government policies, programs, and projects. Future financial and administrative commitments by governments and lending agencies to sites-and-services and upgrading projects would obviously be determined by results of the on-going policies and programs. A pertinent question being raised by planners and practitioners, therefore, is how well have self-help policies and upgrading projects worked in meeting the urban service needs of the poor?

The purpose of this chapter is to examine the impact of public policies and programs dealing with urban shelter and services for the poor. Policies and programs are assessed in terms of physical achievements, accessibility to target populations, adequacy of service coverage for the poor, improvement to dwelling units, impact on employment and income generation, use of private and informal sectors in the service delivery, integration of services, replicability, and other impacts on urban areas. While it is difficult to give weight to the above dimensions of policy and program impacts, access to public services for the urban poor is assumed to be the most critical aspect.

PHYSICAL ACHIEVEMENTS

The impact of shelter projects in terms of achieving physical objectives has been significant. The Hyderabad Urban Community Development Project, for example, was expanded in 1976 to cover about three hundred slums with a population of about 300,000 people. The performance of the project has been impressive. Twenty-three wells were dug or renovated and eighteen community halls were built. Other achievements of the project included the construction of 13,000 houses on a self-help basis, the granting of more than a thousand small and larger loans to enable cycle rickshaw drivers to purchase their own rickshaws, and organization of vocational training to residents.[1]

The Integrated Social Services Project in Bongchun-dong, Seoul was extended in 1984 to cover more households. In 1983, the project provided a package of relief services, initiated activities to foster self-reliance among communities, and provided training to community leaders and residents of selected settlements.[2] Relief services that were provided included subsistence allowances, public works projects, house heating, and improvement of sewerage systems and public lavatories. Self-reliance activities included vocational training, job placement, the establishment of credit unions, the provision of pre-school and maternal health facilities, and job placement. Training was provided to Saemaul leaders, women's club leaders, members of community development committees, and housemaids.

Phase I of the Lahore Walled City Project was completed in 1984, and all targets laid down for this phase were achieved as scheduled.[3] The tasks accomplished during this period included the provision of 9,200 meters of water mains, the replacement of 2,700 water pipes, the provision of 18,500 meters of sewerage pipe, 20,500 square meters of street repaving and the provision of street lighting covering an area of about 20 hectares. The Lahore Development Authority (LDA) was given the main responsibility of implementing the project. The semiautonomous status of the authority facilitated, among other things, the timely implementation of the project's various activities.

Physical targets have also been achieved in the case of the Lahore Katchi Abadis Project. Ahsan reported that targets for the training of councillors and the members of development committees have been exceeded; the plan of action for community development has been prepared; construction work for community halls in seven Katchi Abadis was being completed in late 1984; and seven mother and child health (MCH) centers have already been provided. Other outcomes of the project include the provision of dustbin drums and trolleys for garbage removal, the construction of soakpit latrines, the establishment of industrial homes for income-generating activities; and the formation of monitoring boards to establish community-level information systems.[4] Though almost all of the project activities have been completed, the duration of the project had to be extended because residents were reluctant to provide rooms for MCH centers and community homes.

In their evaluation of World Bank-assisted shelter programs in four countries, Keare and Parris reported that their physical objectives have largely been achieved.[5] In the case of the El Salvador project, for example, by the middle of 1980, 4,348 dwelling units had been completed, and 3,540 of these were already occupied, even though some delays were caused by problems in the acquisition of land. Almost all of the project participants received loans for materials. Other project achievements included the installation of four storm drains and the completion of eight footpaths. There were, however, shortfalls in the provision of schools, clinics, and community centers. The performance of the First Lusaka Upgrading and Sites-and-Services Project in Zambia in achieving physical targets was impressive. By early 1981, 98 percent of the required infrastructure had been completed; about twenty thousand families (two thousand more than target) had been served by standpipes, roads, and security lighting; and 7,775 plots in overspill areas and 3,660 in sites-and-services areas had been developed. As in the case of the El Salvador project, there were small shortfalls caused primarily by delays in acquiring land.

The two projects studied in Kenya showed variations in their physical outcomes. Kayila reported that in the case of the Dandora Community Development Project, at the end of phase I only ten plots remained incomplete.[6] Despite an increase in cost during phase II, only about 12 percent of the allottees were in arrears with their payments. Nine out of ten households in the area had access to piped water. Other physical outcomes of the project included the provision of dwelling units to about thirteen thousand persons during the first phase, the provision of schools and health clinics, the completion of additional rooms by allottees within the eighteen-month period, and the establishment of building groups to pool community resources. The delays in meeting some of the physical targets were caused by controversy concerning the applicability of existing building by-laws and Public Health Act rules and conflicts between local political councillors and officials of the Housing Development Department.

The implementation of the Chaani Sites-and-Services Project, however, was delayed. By the end of 1984, allocation certificates had not been issued to any beneficiary, though plots were being surveyed and demarcated. Despite lowering of standards, the cost of construction materials was found to be too high for the project participants. The provision of piped water to the area was also delayed. About 90 percent of the project beneficiaries showed their dissatisfaction with the implementation progress of the project.[7]

The Senegal Sites-and-Services Project had ambitious physical and policy objectives, but several problems hindered their timely implementation.[8] The design standards adopted by the government were too high for the project participants, and delayed provision of services "made the sites uninhabitable for a lengthy period.[9] Due to inflation, the cost of building materials increased. Finally, distance from the city center impeded the process of "progressive development" of houses.

Though no comparable data are available, the aforementioned examples seem to suggest that, contrary to the common belief, the achievement of physical targets in shelter projects has been relatively more impressive than in the case of most development projects planned and implemented through the government's administrative machinery. It should be pointed out, however, that most shelter projects analyzed were provided with intensive administrative inputs and technical support through bilateral and multilateral assistance. Whether the pace of achieving physical targets can be sustained after some of these projects are replicated on the national scale remains to be seen.

ACCESSIBILITY TO TARGET POPULATIONS

The welfare of the urban poor depends upon the extent to which they are able to gain access to public services such as water, health, education, and transportation. Access to these services would enable them to participate effectively in the production of goods and services that are valued in the market. The reality of the situation in cities of the developing world, however, shows that access to these services is exceedingly biased in favor of higher-income groups and that this "tends to reinforce the disadvantages under which the poor usually live."[10] The demand for public services exceeds their supply due to institutional and financial constraints, and this shortage condition necessitates some form of "rationing." As Hassan pointed out, "under these conditions those in a position to exercise political and economic control tend to be the first in obtaining services and the poor are either excluded from obtaining these services or at least can have only minimal access to them."[11] Chapter 2 has highlighted the magnitude of the urban service deficiencies for residents of low-income settlements and the types of biases against access of the urban poor to public services.

A recurring problem with public housing programs during the 1950s and 1960s was that most "low-cost" public housing units remained too expensive for the vast majority of the urban poor. Thus, in nearly all Asian countries, public housing tended to drive out slum dwellers and instead benefited the middle-income families who could afford the rents. Sites-and-services, upgrading, and self-help service improvement policies of the 1970s and 1980s were designed to make urban services affordable to the poor by introducing them incrementally, at standards that kept cost low, or by having community groups contribute labor, money, or materials. The rationale of shelter policies and programs was that the conventional modes of service delivery through housing authorities and private sector institutions did not meet the service needs of the poor, and therefore, target group-oriented shelter projects were needed.

Experience in Asian cities suggests that service extension or provision is affordable by the poor only when there is a large element of self-help and local maintenance involved. Government services for which there are user charges, tax increases, or cost recovery requirements still tend to drive up the cost beyond the reach of a large number of poor residents. Annual rents for public tenements in Madras, for example, have continued to rise over the past decade from Rs.8,000, to over Rs.18,000. More than half of the slum households in Madras earn less and Rs.24,000 a year and only 14 percent earn more than Rs.36,000, which means that a significant number of slum dwellers either cannot afford public tenements or must pay a very large portion of their income for basic housing and utilities.[12]

The affordability of sites-and-services and slum-upgrading schemes has depended a great deal on how they have been carried out. Public housing re-habilitation programs in Seoul, for example, have not only failed to improve the living conditions of many of the city's poor, but have forced them from their neighborhoods or made them more dependent on public assistance to repay housing rehabilitation loans. "Most slum dwellers could not afford to pay the minimum price for the purchase of house units constructed by the renewal project nor can they pay the monthly subscription fee for the main-tenance of the apartment," Whang found.[13] The disruption caused by the demolition of slum dwellings and the construction of new homes and apart-ments discouraged self-help improvements in many of Seoul's squatter areas and imposed a financial burden that few slum dwellers could bear.

Similiar conclusions can be drawn from the experience with low-cost public housing and sites-and-services schemes in Kuala Lumpur. Few of the squatters were rehoused in low-cost public housing because the rents were too high, and many of the sites-and-services schemes had high vacancy rates because squatters could not afford the improved plots. Slum dwellers' in-come was simply too low to support the publicly provided improvements. Only in the on-site, self-help upgrading programs (such as Nadi) in which local resources were used to improve services gradually, did improvements remain affordable.[14]

Even in Indonesia's Kampung Improvement Programme, where service improvements in poor neighborhoods were financed primarily by national, provincial, or local governments, the poorest families rarely received the benefits. Service improvements have usually raised the property taxes of landowners and thus, either directly or indirectly, the living costs of the poor, driving them out of the kampungs where services had been upgraded. KIP has been modified by lowering the standards of service provision and scheduling the improvements incrementally to make the program more af-fordable for the poor. But analysts contend that much still must be done to lower costs for the poorest families.[15]

In Pakistan, several projects have been initiated to provide services to the poor. Most of these are in Karachi and Lahore, the largest cities in the country. Yet, these have not resulted in significant increases in accessibility of urban services to the poor. The number of middle- and upper-income groups in the urban areas is increasing rapidly, leading to an increase in their requirements for urban services. "Any expansion, therefore, in urban social services is designated to cover their growing needs and only the excess is for incremental provision to the urban poor which may not be substantial."[16] A major constraint on the accessibility of shelter projects to the urban poor is the escalating cost of construction. The average case of a modest two-room house with a built-in area of 500 square feet has been calculated to Rs.60,000 two-thirds of which can be financed by the Housing Building Finance Corporation. Ahmad noted that "Assuming 20 percent of monthly income can be spent on loan servicing, only a family with an income of over Rs.2,500 per month will afford this house. This leaves about 65 percent of the households in Pakistan out of the official housing market and unable to find a shelter for themselves."[17]

A decline in the accessibility of the urban poor to housing is also found in India. Income level and, consequently, capacity and willingness to pay for getting a house on a long-term hire-purchase basis are extremely low, while enormous increases have taken place in urban land values and construction costs. Mahotra noted that

despite the central government subsidy, very little of the kind of houses which could be within the means of the urban poor were built. Wide differences between market value of developed land and the value at which it is made available to the urban poor in order to improve their access to housing has often led the beneficiaries to inflate their incomes with a view to become eligible. They have therefore either strong temptations to encash the subsidy through transfers or they are unable to pay back.[18]

The available evidence from sites-and-services projects in India suggests that where such projects are located near the workplace, the accessibility to the target populations increases; these projects can meet the needs of the upper-income strata of the urban poor; the necessity to generate cross-subsidies compels public agencies to make other use of the high-value land and thus choose the low-cost land on the periphery for shelter projects; and where attempts have been made to supplement the self-help activities of beneficiaries and to overcome the problems of initial socioeconomic and cultural dislocation, sites-and-services projects have improved the accessibility of shelter and services to the poor.[19]

The evaluation by Keare and Parris of the four World Bank-assisted shelter projects in terms of accessibility to target populations shows mixed results. The projects were found to be "broadly successful in their targeting."[20] The principal finding of their evaluation with respect to accessibility, however, is that "in both sites-and-services and upgrading projects, the participating populations span a wide range of incomes and tend to be more representative of medium income groups than that of the poorest urban households."[21] Table 8.1 summarizes evidence across projects in El Salvador, Zambia, and

Table 8.1
Urban Shelter Program
(in percent)

National Urban Income Percentile	Sites and Services				Upgrading	
	El Salvador		Zambia			
	Sonsonate (1977)	Santa Ana (1976)	Lilanda (1980)	Matero (1978)	Philippines (1979)	Zambia (1976)
(a) 0 - 20	6	11	28	18	27	38
(b) 21 - 40	38	32	26	38	24	22
(c) upper 60	56	57	46	44	49	40
(d) 41 - 60	37	38	16	14	23	17
(e) greater than 60	19	19	30	30	26	23
TOTAL	100	100	100	100	100	100

Source: Douglas H. Keare and Scott Parris, "Evaluation of Shelter Programs for the Urban Poor: Principal Findings," World Bank Staff Working Paper Number 547, Washington D.C., 1982, Table 4.

the Philippines and presents the percentage of beneficiary households falling within the specific quintiles of the national urban income distribution. We find that approximately half of the beneficiary households belong to upper 60 percent which leads to the conclusions that medium-income households are representative of beneficiary population.[22] The project in Zambia is an exception because it serves the poorest segments of Lusaka's population. Another finding emerging from the table is that, as compared to sites and services, upgrading projects reach a larger percentage of the poorest households, though the extent of the difference between the two is less than what was expected by project designers.

Evidence suggests that the location of a site-and-service project affects its accessibility to target populations. Where a project is located far away from the center of employment opportunities, the project participants might not be from the poorest families. The Rangsit Sites-and-Services Project in Thailand, for example, was located on land that is about two hours by bus from the central part of Bangkok. The project was meant for families with incomes less than $75 a month. By the middle of 1980, more than half of the households in the project area had income that was above the planned maximum.[23]

The accessibility of shelter projects to the target population is determined by a large number of social, economic, political, administrative, or cultural factors and, thus, varies from one project to another. In Chapter 9, an attempt will be made to identify critical factors affecting policy and program implementation and the access of the poor to shelter projects.

HOUSING IMPROVEMENTS

To varying degrees, upgrading and sites-and-services projects have led to improvement in housing in low-income settlements. These improvements have resulted from direct investments by the concerned government or quasi-government agencies as well as from investment of the community's own resources.

Upgrading and sites-and-services projects have led to the provision of services such as water, sewerage, and sanitary toilets, which have had a direct impact on the quality of housing in poor urban settlements. In the case of Olaleye-Iponri Slum Upgrading Project in Nigeria, for example, the siting of public and private toilets and the opening up of an earth drain had a "dramatic impact" on improving living conditions in the area, and on mobilizing community resources for slum upgrading.[24]

The Environmental Health and Community Development Project in Colombo covered about three hundred slums. About 90 percent of the 228 slums surveyed had received assistance under the project for upgrading common amenities. The project led to the construction or rehabilitation of 1,280 toilets, 566 bathrooms, and 789 standpipes.[25]

In Salvador, the World Bank-assisted project ranks higher than nonproject locations in terms of "satisfaction with lot size, living area, housing materials, and overall quality of construction."[26] In the Philippines, some degree of improvement was observed in terms of housing characteristics such as floors, walls, foundation, lot size, number of floors, and water-sealed toilets. In their evaluation of the project in Tondo, Keare and Parris reported that "overall housing quality in Tondo has increased from 60 to 85 percent; or in monetary terms, the absolute increase in housing value following re-blocking ranges from P 6,200 to almost P 8,000 (approximately U.S. $800 to $1,000). Within a short period the project has stimulated housing investments that have in turn raised dwelling quality and value by a substantial magnitude."[27]

The level of housing investment also increased in the case of the shelter project in Zambia. Most of the houses had walls constructed of concrete blocks and roofs made of asbestos cement. Over 90 percent of the area residents were found to be satisfied with their plots; and an overwhelming majority believed the quality of their housing was good.[28]

While, in general, the shelter projects have led to an increase in the investment by residents themselves to improve their houses, the amount of increased investment has not been uniformally high. In the case of Baldia Township, a squatter settlement in Karachi with about two hundred thousand inhabitants, an evaluation survey shows "that, although the residents invest a significant amount of money to improve their housing situation, a relation between the upgrading programme and the magnitude of home improvement has not been very clear."[29] One of the main reasons for this is that, although the planning for the project had been going on since 1977, actual implementation started in 1980. Even before the planning phase, the perceived and de facto security of tenure by residents was quite high. Thus, the initiation of the project and granting of leases did not immediately affect the amount of investment by residents.

Experience suggests that there are several factors that affect the extent of residents' investment in housing improvements.[30] First, where there are too many rigid regulations or administrative procedures, the bureaucratic tangles dampen the enthusiasm of the households involved to invest. Such discouraging controls may include building approvals, requirements related to supplying of building materials, or inaction on resolving security of tenure. Second, it may be that families are able to invest large amounts of cash savings. Third, some families may have their own, different investment plans, more suitable to their situations. "Investment capacity varies from family to family, not only in terms of how much each one can invest over a long period, but also in terms of where they can invest."[31]

One of the consequences of shelter projects is that improvements in housing have benefited landowners and owner-occupied households more than renter households. With the provision of infrastructure and basic urban services in poor settlements, rents have inevitably increased. The poorest renter families either have to pay increased rents or are forced to leave the settlement. A study on tenancy in the upgraded squatter settlement in Karachi, Pakistan, concluded that

the legalization and upgrading policy encourages price increase which worsens the position of tenants.... Everyone living in Baldia Township benefits from the improvement of the basic infrastructure. However, the construction of facilities in houses is not so profitable for tenants ... [who] have to pay their landlords an unreasonable amount of money for the usage of such facilities.[32]

Use of Informal Service Sector

Sites-and-services, upgrading, and self-help service improvement policies were based on the notion that community participation was essential to the success of the programs, and that poor communities should take an active role in helping themselves provide for their basic needs. Thus, the policies, pursued in developing countries sought some degree of participation by the intended beneficiaries and by informal sector service providers. The results, however, have been mixed.

In the Philippines, as in other Asian countries, the failure during the 1950s and 1960s to deal with the needs of the urban poor made slum dwellers suspicious of—and sometimes hostile to—government-sponsored programs during the 1970s and 1980s. In order to carry out sites-and-services and upgrading schemes, therefore, the government had to develop a "people centered approach," that focused initially on changing "the attitudes of cynicism, skepticism, and suspicion among the residents," through intensive community relations and information campaigns to explain projects and elicit community support.[33] In upgrading and sites-and-services projects that required physical restructuring and "reblocking" in slum neighborhoods, the government made these activities the responsibility of residents. By giving them responsibility for reblocking decisions their participation was elicited and their antagonism was reduced. As a result, slum residents maintained some control over the physical adjustments that were made in their communities when services, facilities, or infrastructure were upgraded.

Attempts to involve the informal sector in service provision and to create small businesses and other employment opportunities in slum areas were less successful. "Apart from the difficulties of identifying viable business projects, the need that the proponents have entrepreneurial know-how, posed serious difficulties," analysts found.[34] Because of the lack of entrepreneurial experience in slum communities, loans for small business fell into arrears and costs were never fully recovered.

In Pakistan, much of the participation in urban services delivery programs is indirect, through representation of poor districts on local governing bodies or on the directorates of local development authorities.[35] In some cities, slum dwellers have formed their own community organizations, and in larger cities (such as Lahore) they have formed federations such as the Katchi Abadi League, to bring political pressures on local and national officials. In other cities, slum dwellers make their influence felt through informal political channels, especially through powerful political families or local leaders of the major political parties. Some government agencies that are engaged in urban development and service extension programs attempt to identify local leaders and elicit their participation in individual projects.

Informal sector participation in service delivery has been encouraged by some governments, as has been the involvement of nongovernmental organizations. But as Ahmed pointed out, "one major problem has been the uneven quality of service rendered by the NGOs which attract, besides genuine social workers, all categories of people seeking political and social opportunities and taking advantage of the financial support from the government."[36] Governments have, therefore, begun rating the voluntary organizations and allocating resources on the basis of performance.

More direct forms of participation have occurred in pilot projects such as the Orangi service upgrading program in Karachi. Orangi, the largest slum in Pakistan, lacked even basic sanitation and sewerage services. The Orangi Pilot Project (OPP), therefore, focused on sewage disposal and sanitation as well as on women's health and education services and provision of women's work centers. The project has been successful in establishing "lane organizations" through which self-help activities were carried out and in mobilizing local labor, money, and materials to construct water, sanitation, or other facilities. Technical assistance was provided by government agencies, nongovernment organizations, and volunteer social workers, engineers, and architects. "Beneficiary participation is ensured by the OPP through continuous meetings to motivate people to take care of their own sanitation programme," Ahmed reported.[37] "Once the lane organizations are created, the beneficiaries are not only the participants but also the planners, executors, and directors of the work. Full responsibility for constructing sanitation works lies with the residents."[38] The OPP provided technical supervision and extended services needed to complement those carried out under self-help activities or that could not be provided by the community. Monetary contributions from the community were controlled by lane managers.

Despite the above limitations, the role of the informal sector, particularly in housing finance, has been significant. It has been estimated that 60 to 80 percent of actual shelter provision has been accomplished by the informal finance sector.[39] Housing agencies have become increasingly involved in the provision of sites-and-services and upgrading projects that involve user-financed, user-constructed houses. A report by the Asian Development Bank pointed out that "in the process of implementing these projects, governments have come into increasing contact with financing and building practices of the informal sector and have observed its potential. The governments have recognized the need for greater understanding of the sector's approach."[40] Of particular significance are the informal rotating credit systems as such "chit fund" in India, "bisi" in Pakistan, or "chaer game" in Thailand. In addition to individual family and extended family contacts, groups for informal financing have included nongovernmental organizations such as religious and charitable groups, labor and credit unions, or local social and political associations.

EMPLOYMENT AND INCOME GENERATION

It is usually expected that shelter projects would stimulate employment and income generation by, among other things, utilizing hired labor during construction, initiating employment and business components in the project design, and encouraging people to engage in mutual aid and self-help.

Data from some of the World Bank-assisted shelter projects show several positive results concerning employment and income generation. As the case of the Dandora Sites-and-Services Project shows, families have been able to substantially increase their income by subletting space in their new and upgraded accommodations. Housing construction for the shelter project in El Salvador will provide wages income of U.S. $4.2 million and employment of 3,700 person-years. In the Zambia project, 667 person-years of employment and over U.S. $1 million in wages have been generated. About 30 percent of the households in a Philippine project "relied exclusively" upon hired labor and about 49 percent supplemented their own labor with that of paid workers.[41]

Five employment-generation efforts were made in the Philippine project; these included (1) providing jobs for about five hundred fifty residents in the firms selected for construction; (2) granting 230 loans through a small-business loan program; (3) initiating a vocational skill program; (4) initiating a cottage industries program; and (5) encouraging larger-scale commercial/industrial estates. The last three efforts, however, have not been successful.[42]

Some of the fears about shelter projects are that the participating family's expenditure might rise due to increased cost of housing construction as well as higher service charges and that shelter projects might bring about a decline in family income due to possible disruption in employment. Studies, however, have shown that participation in shelter projects does not necessarily adversely affect income flows; that expenditures for food among participants are not significantly different than those of nonparticipants; and that total income of participant families usually increases because relatives or friends of the families contribute cash gifts or transfer payments before construction.[43]

It is commonly believed that sites-and-services projects disrupt employment in the informal sector because relocation dislocates hawkers and ven-
dors. The case of the Dandora Sites-and-Services Project in Nairobi,
however, shows that informal selling and, to an extent, "illegal" economic
activities somehow continued even though the project was relocated. Informal sector activities also continued in the Tondo area in the Philippines.[44]
Yet, formal initiatives through shelter projects to improve employment in
basic housing sites have been less successful than expected, perhaps due to
"the difficulties involved in trying to put vitality into the informal sector by
formal means."[45]

UNICEF's basic services strategy is aimed at improving services in ways
that build skills and raise incomes of the residents, especially women, of
poor urban settlements. In Guayaquil, Ecuador, the UNICEF project provides special training to some mothers who staff day-care centers; this, in
turn, enables other mothers to work. Furthermore, it assists in training
neighborhood residents as auxiliary health personnel for primary health
clinics and helps to train others in sanitation, nutrition, child care, family
planning, and first-aid practices. In Addis Abada, the UNICEF project supported small-scale poultry farming. In Mexico city, UNICEF projects led to
the training of selected slum residents to be paraprofessional teachers in
nursery and day-care centers that the community was building on a self-
help basis.[46]

In the case of the Lahore Katchi Abadis project, UNICEF assisted in the
training of women and the establishment of vocational training centers to
improve employment opportunities for poor women. In the case of the
Environmental Health and Community Development Project in Colombo,
residents were hired as "health wardens" to work under the supervision of
professional preventative and curative health personnel to disseminate information about improving health and sanitation practices in the slums.

Replicability

The ability of governments to replicate service improvement programs in
poor communities depends heavily on their ability to recover some or all
of the costs of service extension. Their limited ability to extend services to
the urban poor through general revenues has meant that the costs recovered
from services in some communities must be used to finance those in others.

Experience with recovering the cost of urban services through user
charges, taxation, or other means has been mixed, and as a result, replication
has been limited. In Pakistan, the government has found it difficult to recover
costs for the services provided in slum and squatter communities, even
though some of the residents are not poor. Cost recovery through the sale
of improved plots by urban development authorities, for example, has been
limited by their "break-even policy" used to keep the price of redeveloped

land within the means of the poor. In some cities, officials divert the proceeds of land auctions to subsidize services in richer neighborhoods. Underpricing usually leads to land speculation, hence, the profits accrue to speculators rather than to the development authorities.[47]

To the extent that service improvements through self-help activities—in which residents of a community provide labor, materials, or other contributions—lower the costs of service extension or delivery for municipal governments, such schemes as Organi in Pakistan and the Nadi Programme in Malaysia may be successful examples of cost recovery. While they do not generate revenues directly, they free resources for use in other service improvement projects.

In Indonesia, local governments have been able to recover some of the costs of providing services through the KIP program by charging for water, sewerage, or other services and by increasing property taxes. However, the revenue recovered represents only a small portion of the total costs of providing services through KIP.[48]

In the Philippines, the government has insisted on cost recovery for slum-upgrading and sites-and-services projects. However, it has attempted at the same time to make the projects affordable to the poor, and often the two requirements have come into conflict. Keeping projects affordable and still recovering costs has been especially difficult during periods of high inflation. Cost recovery hs been impeded by the rising prices of materials and equipment, forcing the government to lower the standards of services provided to poor communities or to require slum dwellers to pay a larger percentage of their household incomes for service improvements.[49]

Despite the above constraints on cost recovery, shelter projects have demonstrated that low-cost houses can be built and made accessible to the vast majority of the urban poor. In some countires, the demonstration effort has been significant. In Zambia, for example, upgrading through progressive development has been incorporated into the Third National Development Plan. In Pakistan, the Sixth Five-Year Development Plan has recognized the need for alternative strategies and approaches to provide shelter and services to the urban poor. De facto security of tenure has been granted to residents of most squatter settlements. The success of the experimental Tondo project in the Philippines has improved the chances of replicabilty of such projects on a national scale.

The Dandora Sites-and-Services Project in Kenya has had a visible impact on low-income housing and urban development policies and programs in the country and "it has by its presence removed some of the stated and unstated fears about large scale sites-and-services projects at the policy level."[50]

Integration of Services

The self-help, upgrading, and sites-and-services programs of the 1970s and 1980s have gone much further than slum clearance and public housing schemes in integrating services for poor families. By their very nature, sites-and-services projects bring a diversity of essential infrastructure and social services into a community. Upgrading schemes such as those carried out in the Philippines and Indonesia have sought to integrate services incrementally. The Philippines has attempted to integrate employment opportunities into service provisions projects more aggressively than most other countries. Deliberate efforts to integrate services have characterized self-help programs sponsored by UNICEF in Malaysia, Indonesia, and the Republic of Korea, as well as in the Orangi and Baldia slum-improvement projects in Pakistan.

In all of these countries, however, the difficulty of coordinating the activities of the public bureaucracies has been an obstacle to delivering services to poor communities in a more integrated fashion.

PERFORMANCE AND IMPACT OF THE SELECTED PROJECTS

Table 8.2 presents the performance and impact of selected projects. We find that with the exception of the Channi project in Kenya, all the projects had either a moderate or high level of physical achievement, indicating that with adequate political support, shelter and services projects can be effectively carried out by concerned government agencies. In the case of most projects, the accessibility of services and facilities to targeted populations has been moderate. In none of the selected projects has the achievement in improvement in housing been high, though in some cases the information available is inadequate.

In none of the projects has the use of the informal service sector been high. It has been moderate in Nadi, Integrated Social Services, Lahore Katchi Abadis, Environmental Health and Community Development, Dandora, and Hyderabad projects. In most of the projects, the impact on employment has been low. The Hyderabad project indicates a high potential for replicability, and those with moderate potential for replicability are the Lahore Katchi Abadis, Environmental Health and Community Development, Dandora, and Oleleye-Iponri, projects. The performance in terms of integration of services is high for two, moderate for four, and low for one of the selected projects.

Table 8.2
Performance and Impact of Selected Projects

Impact	Nadi	Lahore Walled City	Integrated Social Services	Lahore Katchi Abadis	Environmental Health & Community Development	Dandora	Chaani	Olaleye-Iponri	Block Grants	Hyderabad
Physical Achievement	M	H	H	M	H	H	L	M	M	H
Accessibility to target populations	H	M*	H	H	H	M	M	M	M	H
Housing Improvements	O	M	O	M	M	M*	O	O	L*	M
Use of informal service sector	M	L	M	M	M*	M	L	L	O	M
Employment and income	H	L*	M	L	L*	M	L	L	L	M
Replicability	L	L	L	M	M	M	O	M	O	H
Integration of services	M	H	L	M	M	M	O	O	M	H

Key: H = high; M = moderate; L = low; O = not known.

*Based on partial information.

Source: Compiled by the author.

NOTES

1. William J. Cousins and Catherine Goyder, "Hyderabad Urban Community Development Project," (Nagoya: United Nations Centre for Regional Development, 1985, mimeo.), p. 210.

2. Whang, "Management of Integrated Social Services for the Poor," pp. 14–18.

3. Ahmed, "Lahore Walled City Upgrading Project," pp. 6–12.

4. Ahsan, "Provision of Services to the Urban Poor," pp. 17–18.

5. Keare and Parris, "Evaluation of Shelter Programmes for the Urban Poor," pp. 1–12.

6. Kayila, "Improving Urban Settlement for the Poor," pp. 6–7.

7. Ibid., p. 2.

8. Keare and Parris, "Evaluation of Shelter Programmes for the Urban Poor," p. 11.

9. Ibid.

10. Riaz Hassan, "Socio-economic Constraints on Access to Public Services for the Urban Poor" (Nagoya: UNCRD, 1985), p. 6.

11. Ibid.

12. In-Joung Whang, "Policy Issues in Managing Urban Services for the Poor: The Case of Squatter Improvement in Seoul, Korea" (Nagoya: UNCRD, 1985, mimeo.), pp. 18–22.

13. Ibid., p. 26.

14. Shafruddin Hashim, "Policy Issues in Urban Services for the Urban Poor in a Plural Society: The Case of Malaysia" (Nagoya: UNCRD, 1985), pp. 16–18.

15. Sugijanto Soegijoko,"Urban Services in Indonesia: Policy Issues in Managing the Delivery for the Poor" (Nagoya: UNCRD, 1985), pp. 54–55.

16. Ahmed, "Managing Urban Development," p. 41.

17. Ibid., pp. 17–18.

18. D. D. Malhotra, *Managing Urban Development: Policy Issues in Urban Services for the Poor* (New Delhi: The Indian Institute of Public Administration, 1985), pp.132–133.

19. Ibid., pp. 136–37.

20. Keare and Parris, "Evaluation of Shelter Programmes for the Urban Poor," p. 12.

21. Ibid.

22. Ibid., p. 17.

23. M. J. Rodell, "Sites and Services and Low-Income Housing," in Skinner and Rodell, *People, Poverty and Shelter*, p. 35.

24. Makinwa-Adebusoye, "Upgrading Olaley-Iponri Slum," pp. 25–26.

25. Tilakaratna, Hettiges and Karunaratna, "Environmental Health and Community Development Project," p. 154.

26. Keare and Parris, "Evaluation of Shelter Programmes for the Urban Poor," p. 23.

27. Ibid., p. 29.

28. Ibid.

29. Peter Nietied, *The Third Baldia Upgrading Evaluation Survey* (Amsterdam: Free University, 1984), p. 43.

30. Rodell, "Sites and Services," pp. 21–52.

31. Ibid., p. 31.

32. E. A.Wahab, *The Tenant Market of Baldia Township* (Amsterdam: Free University, 1984), p. 34.

33. Einsiedel and Molina, "Policy Issues in Urban Services to the Poor," p. 34. This section of the chapter borrows heavily from Dennis A. Rondinelli and G. Shabbir Cheema, "Urban Service Policies in Metropolitan Areas: Meeting the Needs of the Urban Poor in Asia," *Regional Development Dialogue* 6:2 (1985), 170–90.

34. Von Einsiedel and Molina, "Policy Issues in Urban Services to the Poor," p. 38.

35. Ahmed, "Lahore Walled City Upgrading Project," pp. 28–31.

36. Ibid., p. 27.

37. Ibid., p. 67.

38. Ibid.

39. Asian Development Bank, *Regional Seminar on Financing Low-Income Housing* (Manila: ADB, 1983), p. 18.

40. Ibid., p. 18.

41. Keare and Parris, "Evaluation of Shelter Programmes for the Urban Poor," p. 38.

42. Ibid., p. 40.

43. Laquian, *Basic Housing*, p. 135.

44. Ibid., p. 137.

45. Ibid.

46. UNICEF, *Urban Basic Sevices: Reaching Children and Women of the Urban Poor* (New York: UNICEF, 1982).

47. Ahmed, "Policy Issues in Urban Services for the Poor," (Nagoya: UNCRD, 1985, mimeo), pp. 38–41.

48. Soegijoko, "Urban Services in Indonesia," pp. 57–58.

49. Von Einsiedel and Molina, "Policy Issues in Urban Services to the Poor," pp. 32–33.

50. T. S. Chana, "Nairobi: Dandora and Other Projects," in Payne, *Low Income Housing in the Developing World*, p. 33.
rvices in Indonesia," pp. 57–58.

49. Von Einsiedel and Molina, "Policy Issues in Urban Services to the Poor," pp. 32–33.

50. T. S. Chana, "Nairobi: Dandora and Other Projects," in Payne, *Low Income Housing in the Developing World*, p. 33.

9

FACTORS INFLUENCING IMPLEMENTATION

The success of urban shelter policies and projects has varied among countries and, in most cases, among projects within the same country. Experience shows that a large number of social, political, economic, and administrative factors influence policy and program implementation. These factors can be examined within five broad categories listed in Chapter 1: capabilities and resources of implementing agencies; beneficiary organization and participation; interorganizational relationships; national policies for upgrading low-income settlements; and environmental factors.

CAPABILITIES OF IMPLEMENTING AGENCIES

The success of shelter policies and projects depends partly upon the extent to which agencies and officials at national, regional, or local levels have developed their abilities to effectively perform the planning, decision-making, and management functions that are formally granted to them. These agencies should have an adequate ability to identify development problems and opportunities in cooperation with local communities; identify or create possible solutions to development problems; and make decisions and resolve conflicts. They should also be able to mobilize resources from the government as well as communities and manage development programs and projects. Of particular importance in the case of shelter projects is the ability of government agencies and officials to have rapport with program beneficiaries and work effectively with the several groups that may exist within a community.

Experience shows that the technical expertise of the implementing agencies' personnel is a necessary but not sufficient condition for implementing shelter policies and programs. In both Dandora and Chaani projects in Kenya, officials of the implementing agencies had the required technical ability. However, there were significant variations between the two projects as to the role of the concerned agencies in encouraging community organization and self-help. The Community Development Division of the Housing and Development Department (HDD) of the municipality of Nairobi played an active role in the formation of construction groups and in the organization of the activities of project participants for self-help endeavors. In contrast, for the Chaani project in Mombasa, the implementing agency did not take adequate steps to establish rapport with the beneficiaries or to organize them into groups for self-help activities. In his study, Kayila partly attributed the relatively greater success of the Dandora project to the human relations skills of the officials of the HDD in Nairobi and their ability to mobilize project beneficiaries for self-help activities.[1]

Implementation of upgrading and sites-and-services policies and programs requires increased interaction and communication between government officials and residents. Among the activities to be performed by project officials are eliciting the support of community leaders, mobilizing community resources, organizing community development committees, and recovering part of the costs for the upgrading from the residents. The performance of such tasks requires human relations and organizational skills on the part of implementing agencies, as has been shown by the case of Hyderabad Urban Community Development Project.

Innovative leadership within the lead implementing agency is crucial to the success of projects aimed at providing shelter and services to the urban poor. In the case of the Nadi project in Malaysia, the Ministry of Federal Territory under the leadership of its secretary-general encouraged multi-agency activation and coordination of development activities; joint submission of budgetary requests by concerned agencies; and the use of the Organizational Responsibility Chart. The change of leadership within the ministry dampened the enthusiasm of the supporting agencies, who abandoned these innovative procedures and reverted to the established and familiar ways of program operation.

Another example of the impact of innovative leadership is provided by the Orangi Pilot Project (OPP) in Karachi. Orangi is the largest slum in Pakistan, with an estimated population of 800,000 persons. Improvement of the area had been impeded by, among other things, the high cost of constructing a conventional sanitation system, lack of technical know-how among the residents for self-managed upgrading, and inadequate organization among the residents. Funded by nongovernmental sources, the project is directed by Akhtar Hamid Khan, who initiated the famous Comilla Project during the 1960s in East Pakistan (now Bangladesh).[2] Khan introduced several innovative changes to eliminate the barriers to slum upgrading. The lane with twenty to thirty houses was adopted as the unit of local organization. Once households in a lane voluntarily agreed to work collectively to tackle the sewerage problem, the OPP provided technical guidance and cost estimates. Residents of each lane collected money from the households and elected their own managers who maintained accounts of incomes and expenditures. Action research by OPP led to the reduction of the cost of drainage, primarily by eliminating the profit that would have been included in the charges of private contractors. The project also provided for motivating and training women in more sanitary practices and in family educational activities. While several of the above techniques to mobilize communities have also been attempted in other shelter projects in Pakistan, the relatively greater success of the OPP is due partly to the innovate leadership of the director, who had long experience in organizing and motivating people for self-help activities and who had the ability to create trust and confidence among local residents.

Where shelter projects are planned and implemented through government agencies directly, established personnel structures and practices occasionally tend to impede innovation. Low salaries, slow advancement, and low morale evoke a passive attitude on the part of agency personnel. In such situations, field officials or local administrators are reluctant to take initiative in dealing with community problems and to exercise their leadership. Officials, for example, failed to take timely initiative to organize the participants of the Chaani project in Mombasa, and thus affected self-help activities. Where the implementing agency has relatively more flexibility, as was the case with semiautonomous Lahore Development Authority, the achievement of physical targets is facilitated.

Bureaucratic organizations in developing countries find it difficult to recognize the significance of the urban poor or to respond effectively to their needs. This was observed during the initial phases of the Nadi project.[3] Reorienting members of such bureaucratic groups to a posture of support for local poor communities could be assisted by incentives and career rewards associated with a positive response to policies and programs affecting the urban poor, and it will require the farsighted and progressive attitudes of political and administrative leaders. Administrative systems in most developing countries, however, are characterized by, among other things, political intervention in recruitment and promotion, "red tape," and rigid personnel regulations that discourage innovation.[4]

ADEQUACY OF FINANCIAL RESOURCES

The experience in upgrading and sites-and-services projects shows that government financial resources are needed to support and strengthen community self-help activities. Where resources allocated to such projects are too small, their impact on the status of the poor remains marginal. The large, and increasing, size of the poor population in most Asian, African, and Latin American cities makes funding a vital issue. The project-level analysis reveals that although funding for upgrading and sites-and-services projects is increasing (due largely to the international agencies such as the World Bank), the amount available is still extremely limited vis-à-vis the magnitude of the problem. Therefore, these projects have reached only a small percentage of the population.

In the case of the Nadi project, government support was reduced in 1983 from M $10 million to M $5.5 million. Though efforts are being made to mobilize additional funds from nongovernmental sources, it remains to be seen whether these efforts will offset the declining government support for the project. The decline of government support has obviously had a negative effect on the initial enthusiasm about the project of the concerned government agencies. The capital cost of the Katchi Abadis Project was only about Rs.8 million (U.S. $0.5 million). The direct cost of the Environmental Health and Community Development Project in Colombo over a four-year period was about U.S. $1.3 million. Though no comparative data are available, these examples illustrate that the percentage of municipal and national budgets allocated to upgrading and sites-and-services projects are still not significant.

COMMUNITY PARTICIPATION

Community participation is a necessary condition for the success of upgrading, sites-and-services, and self-help housing programs. As discussed in Chapter 5, such participation can lead to the reduction of cost, extension of services to all communities, mobilization of community resources, and the people's identification with the project. Other advantages of community participation are that it is conducive to the identification of the felt needs of the residents, to the use of indigenous knowledge and expertise, to accumulation of local cooperative experience, and to an increased awareness of communal interests on the part of the people.

One of the most critical factors that accounted for the relatively greater success of the Hyderabad Urban Community Development Project was the active involvement of the selected communities in the choice of project locations, choice of beneficiaries, selection of community leaders, and mobilization of community resources. Among other things, the increased participation led to the diversification of community leadership and improvement in the living environment of the people.

Formal and informal mechanisms of community participation in the Nadi Project enabled local leaders to influence the location of services, selection of beneficiaries, and the allocation of community resources. On their part, the project staff could not have carried out development activities without the support of community leaders.

The Environmental Health and Community Development Project in Colombo provides an illustration of the relationship between active community participation and improved health and environmental conditions. A survey was undertaken of (1) communities with a high level of community participation and active community development committees (type A); and (2) communities with a relatively lower level of participation and inactive CDCs (type B). The findings show that in type A communities the amenities provided through the project were in a better state of cleanliness and were better maintained than in type B; that in type A more people were benefiting from the health education program; and that type A communities performed better than type B regarding preventive health care practices such as use of the toilet by children, use of boiled water for drinking, and cleaning of teeth. The survey also showed that reported cases of malnutrition were less than 1 percent in type A communities as compared to more than 5 percent in type B; while infant and child deaths due to water-related diseases were 7 percent in type A, the corresponding figure in type B was 25 percent; preschool attendance was 28 percent in type A as compared to 12 percent in type B; and the project target of one toilet for five households and one standpipe for ten households had been achieved in 40 percent of type A and only 20 percent of type B communities. Since the percentage of households below the poverty line in the two samples and average household income in each of the selected communities was almost identical, the evidence suggests that the higher level of community development performance in type A communities was largely because of the existence of active community development committees and greater interaction between health wardens and the people.[5]

The cases of the Dandora and Chaani projects in Kenya also provide an example of the relationship between community participation and project performance. In Dandora, neighborhood committees under area chiefs were used, and the establishment of building groups was encouraged. In the Chaani project, however, mechanisms for community participation were ineffective.[6] The community participation in the Lahore Katchi Abadis Project resulted in mobilization of local resources, while a lack of formal mechanisms for community involvement in the Lahore Walled City Project impeded mobilization of local support.

INTERORGANIZATIONAL RELATIONSHIPS

Successful implementation of shelter projects requires some degree of coordination among national, regional, and local agencies. To achieve complementarity among levels of administration, viable linkages must be established and maintained. Shelter projects involve diverse activities such as acquiring land, granting security of tenure to illegal occupants of land, providing infrastructure and social welfare facilities, and organizing communities for self-help. These activities obviously require the involvement and cooperation of several types of agencies.

The Environmental Health and Community Development Project in Colombo provides an illustration of the relationship between interagency coordination and the success of upgrading projects. The project was implemented through the existing agencies of the municipal and national governments, particularly the Municipal Health Department (MHD), the Common Amenities Board (CAB) and the Urban Development Authority (UDA). The lack of a clear coordinating structure resulted in many instances of uncoordinated activities during the earlier phase of the project. However, by 1982 a coordinating committee headed by the mayor had been established to resolve interagency coordination probelms. A special unit was established in the CAB and community development councils (CDCs) were created. The CDCs were organized into district development councils (DDCs), which finally were joined into the City Development Council. This structure facilitated both horizontal interagency coordination and direct links with community organizations. Improved coordination led to not only the timely achievement of physical targets but also, complementarily, of various components of the project.

In most developing countries, the rigidity of administrative procedures inhibits cooperation among agencies in implementing upgrading and sites-and-services projects. Departmental loyalties usually impede coordination and cooperation at regional and local levels. Government functionaries from various departments tend to work in isolation, pursuing their own interests and responding to those of their departmental superiors.

The proliferation of government and quasi-governmental agencies designed to undertake specialized tasks has, in some case, led to a lack of coordination and consistency of action by concerned government agencies. In Pakistan, for example, duplication of efforts and delays due to interagency disputes are common features. The concerned agencies are under the administrative control of different federal ministries or provincial departments and are reluctant to take an integrated approach to the provision of services.

Because of the proliferation of implementing agencies at multilevels, intergovernmental relations in the process of urban administration have become more complex. Table 9.1 for example, shows that five types of agencies are involved in the provision of services in the main cities of West Malaysia. The practice in Malaysia indicates that clear demarcation between federal, state, and local areas of jurisdiction is lacking; that despite the existence of formal structures, coordinated provision of services continues to be a problem; and that because of increasing predominance of national ministries and departments, popular involvement and mobilization of community resources have been negatively affected.[7]

Table 9.1

Intergovernmental Involvement in the Provision of Urban Services in Selected Malaysian Cities

Service	Alor Star	Butter- worth	George Town	Ipoh	Kuala Lumpur	Treng- ganu	Kota Bharu	Petal- ing
Transportation	L,N	L,N	L,N	L,N	L,N	N	L,N	N
Water Supply	S	S	S	S	S	S	S	S
Sewage and Drainage	L	L	L	L	L	L	L	L
Public Housing	SS	L,SS	L,SS	L,SS	L,SS,SS	SS	SS	SS
Parks and Recreation	L	L	L	L	L	L	L	L
Health Services	L,S,N	L,S,N	L,S,N	L,S,N	L,N	S,N	S,N	L,N
Education	S,N	S,N	L,S,N	S,N	L,S,N	S,N	S,N	S,N
Markets	L	L	L	L	L	L	L	L
Police	N	N	N	N	N	N	N	N
Fire Protection	N	S	L	N	L,N	N	S	N
Public Sanitation	L	L	L	L	L	L	L	L

Key: L = Local authority; S = State government; N = National government department; NS = National statutory body.

Source: G. Shabbir Cheema, "Administrative Responses to Urbanization in Western Malaysia," Journal of Administrative Overseas 16:4 (October 1977), Table 2.

Such organizational variables as the clarity, conciseness, and simplicity of the structure and procedures created to implement shelter projects; the ability of the implementing agency staff to interact with higher-level authorities; and the degree to which components of the project are integrated affect their outcome. For example, organizationally the Kampung Improvement Programme (KIP) in Indonesia was made the responsibility of the local government. The implementation of the specific activities was to be undertaken by the KIP Unit of the local government.[8] As the focal point for carrying out upgrading activities, the unit played a vital role in mobilizing support for the project and providing necessary information to concerned agencies at national and local levels.

In the case of the Hyderabad Urban Community Development Project, the implementing agency staff played an important role in eliciting the support of concerned officials from the Hyderabad Urban Development Authority, the state government, and concerned ministries and departments at the national level. It was their ability to interact with higher-level authorities, and to inform them about positive effects of the experimental project that eventually led to its expansion and replicability.

When the project design provides for integration among the project components, the outcome is likely to be more positive. In the case of the Lahore Katchi Abadis Project, the availability of selected social services was linked to the provision of physical infrastructure by the concerned government agencies, and this contributed to the overall success of the project. The design of the Environmental Health and Community Development Project in Colombo did not adequately provide for integrated delivery of services during the initial phase of the project, and thus adversely affected its outcome.

Project outcomes are also affected by the clarity of project objectives, the accuracy and frequency of interorganizational communication, and the adequacy of procedures for monitoring and evaluation. As the case of the Lahore Walled City Project indicates, where project objectives are clear and the channels of information are open and active between the concerned implementing agencies, complementarity of actions between the agencies can be ensured. Monitoring and evaluating are equally necessary, particularly to elicit the response of communities to initiatives taken by the project staff. In the case of the Orangi Pilot Project, ongoing evaluation of each activity by the project staff led, in some cases, to the discontinuation of those activities that were unpopular among the residents, leading to greater acceptance of the project by communities.

The government-sponsored upgrading projects in Karachi provide an illustration of the significance of interorganizational relationships in achieving project objectives. The Karachi Metropolitan Corporation (KMC), the Karachi Development Authority, (KDA), the Sind Provincial Government, and the central government were directly or indirectly involved in land acquisition, in the issuance of land titles, in recovery of cost, and in organization of the communities. These agencies, however, did not ensure interagency coordination, identify simplified procedures, and have clarity of program objectives. The result was that, despite the existence of strong political support at the national level for the regularization of land tenure in squatter settlements and the fact that most of the land was owned by the government, land titles could be issued to only a small percentage of the squatters.

NATIONAL POLICIES

The capabilities of implementing agencies and resources allocated for shelter and basic urban services depend upon national policies. Of particular importance are the clarity and consistency of national policies and the content of policies concerning land acquisition, security of land tenure, access to credit for shelter, modes of service provision, cost recovery, and role of the informal sector in service provision.

Clarity and Consistency of Policies

Implementation of upgrading and sites-and-services projects is affected by the clarity and consistency of national policies dealing with urban shelter and services. As discussed in Chapter 3, shelter policies in developing countries have passed through several phases during the past three decades. While in most countries the usefulness of participatory, self-help approaches for the provision of shelter and services has been recognized, clarity and consistency in national policies have been lacking. The government of Malaysia, for example, initially supported upgrading, self-help approaches. However, at the operational level, government policy statements were not followed by adequate concrete actions to encourage and support upgrading projects. The support for the Nadi project was reduced. In Karachi, Pakistan, contradictory policy statements by political leaders during the early part of 1970 concerning the amount to be paid by each squatter for land title led to the failure of the Karachi Municipal Corporation to recover the cost of infrastructure from the residents of certain Katchi Abadis. In Mexico, inadequate attention was given to upgrading approaches before 1970. During 1971–76, however, the government's interest in improving low-income housing and on land issues substantially increased. In Venezuela, a policy shift took place in 1974, and a new strategy for barrio development was initiated that focused on physical improvements in low-income settlements.

Participative, self-help approaches to upgrading require long periods of implementation before their impact can be felt at the national level. Continuity in government support for such approaches thus is essential for their success. Where the government policy responses are ad hoc, accumulation of community experiences and replication of experimental projects is unlikely to take place.

Land Acquisition and Security of Tenure

The rigidity of land acquisition procedures and the complexity of granting security of tenure have led to delays in project implementation. In the case of Lahore Katchi Abadis Project, the construction of community halls could not be completed in time because of the inability of the implementing agency to acquire land. The lengthy acquisition procedures in Bangkok, Bombay, Colombo, and Jakarta have also been an impediment to upgrading projects. As discussed in Chapter 7, many approaches and techniques have been employed to facilitate acquisition of land. Yet, the experience shows that the process of land acquisition continues to delay project implementation.

Granting security of tenure has often been more complex than was anticipated. It would seem that when land is owned by the government, the security of tenure would involve only a policy statement by the concerned authorities, legislation to legalize the status of squatters, and issuance of land leases. Each of these steps could be undertaken by the government without major monetary outlays. In practice, one finds that policy statements by governments are not always consistent, and with a change in government, the content and the focus of public policy concerning upgrading is also likely to change. Legalization of occupancy or issuance of leases has been delayed for several reasons. In some squatter settlements residents have assumed that they had security of tenure because of their long stay in the area and frequent policy statements by national and local political leaders, usually during the election period, concerning regularization of their status. In other cases, residents are reluctant to pay for infrastructure and services to be provided by the government after legalization of residents. When issuance of leases is tied to the payment of physical improvements in the area, residents are lukewarm about receiving titles (as was the case in Karachi). When squatters already have a de facto security of tenure and the portion of the cost to be paid by them for infrastructure improvement is beyond their capacity, they are unlikely to be in any rush to obtain leases. In other cases, because of the involvement of several agencies in the process of regularizing squatter settlements, processing the issuance of leases is delayed or interagency conflicts and the lack of a consistent national policy about upgrading confuse project participants. Last, when there is a high level of perceived security of tenure, residents are reluctant to pay for obtaining leases even when they have the capacity to do so.

Access to Credit

Credit available for shelter and basic urban services through public and private sector institutions has been limited. Because of their illegal occupation of land, squatters cannot use land as collateral to obtain credit from banks. Most owner-occupant slum dwellers are also unable to obtain credit to improve their living environment. Private savings, gifts or donations from relatives or friends, and interhousehold transfers are the main sources of financing for shelter improvement. Thus, whenever a project is initiated by the government, residents tend to look at it as a government subsidy and are reluctant to pay even when they might have the financial capacity to do so.

Modes of Service Delivery

The modes of service provision may range from participatory, self-help to top-down, public sector programs. Both have advantages and limitations. Some services are more efficiently and effectively provided by public agencies. This is usually true to "network-based" services such as piped water, electricity, or sanitary sewerage. However, other services—low-cost housing, for example—may be provided more effectively through community self-help efforts with such government support as the provision of credit to purchase construction materials. The most appropriate mode of service delivery depends upon a complex set of factors, among which are the size of the city, the number of the urban poor, the cohesiveness of urban communities, and the type of service.[9] When bureaucracies view problems inaccurately and promote policies that discriminate against the poor, community self-help may be the only feasible means of increasing the access of the poor to basic services.

An appropriate set of relationships between government and nongovernment organizations at all levels facilitates the implementation of upgrading and sites-and-services projects. Community self-help efforts have rarely been successful without some support and cooperation from public agencies. Similarly, even when services are provided almost entirely by government agencies, the involvement of nongovernmental agencies enables project managers to better understand the needs and desires of the poor.

The Role of the Informal Sector

The informal sector has an important role to play in providing basic urban services to the poor. In situations where services provided through government agencies are beyond the financial capacity of the poor, the informal sector may be the only avenue for them to meet some of their service needs. This would indicate that the government should support the activities of the informal service sector. In India, for example, a wide range of traditional occupations and skills in the informal sector has been an integral part of rural and the urban economy.[10] Government has attempted to protect and promote handicrafts and small-scale industries, to link these with modern secondary and tertiary sectors, and to diversify the range of skills and occupations within the informal sector. Yet, Malhotra has noted that "there are a variety of local laws and regulations which directly or indirectly limit the scope of informal sector activities and their income generating potential. Such local regulations impose restrictions in respect of the places where, and timing during which the activities can be carried on.[11]

ENVIRONMENTAL FACTORS

The implementation of urban shelter and services policies and projects seems to be strongly influenced by the sociopolitical as well as the physical environments in which interactions among the concerned groups take place. The experiences in developing countries examined in this book illustrate some of these environmental factors that affect the management of such programs and projects; the degree of political support at multilevels for shelter projects; international technical and financial assistance; social structures and perceptions of the squatters and slum dwellers; political structures and styles; and resource constraints.

Political Support

One of the most critical factors affecting the implementation of upgrading and sites-and-services projects is the quality of political support at national, regional, and local levels for these projects. Support at multilevels is needed because there are typically latent or manifest conflicts between different groups within the city. Squatters and slum dwellers obviously want improvements in their living environment, though the extent to which they are organized to put pressure from below may vary from one settlement to another. Their interests are in conflict with those of the absentee landowners who might be reluctant or unable to make needed improvements to houses and provide infrastructural facilities. As discussed earlier, bureaucracies usually tend to favor the status quo and are, in many cases, unable to build effective linkages with poor communities. Furthermore, bureaucracies are usually biased in favor of middle- and upper-income urban settlements in the allocation of resources. In the final analysis, the conflict is between growing middle- and high-income groups on the one hand, and squatters and slum dwellers on the other. In situations characterized by the scarcity of resources, the allocations by government agencies are biased in favor of the rich. Yet, policymakers need to give the impression that they are concerned about the plight of the urban poor in order to seek political legitimacy. The policy statements, however, are not changed to operational programs with adequate allocations.

Experience shows that when political support, particularly at the national level, exists for upgrading poor urban settlements, it is possible to improve the living environment of the urban poor despite the above conflicts of interest among various groups. The relationship between the degree of political support and the success of slum-improvement and upgrading projects is demonstrated through several cases. In Pakistan, the national government has since 1978 provided the necessary political support for increased security of tenure and the provision of infrastructure in slums and squatter settlements. Though the implementation of government policies and programs has been impeded partly because of scarcity of resources and inability of implementing agencies to establish viable linkages with poor communities, there are, nevertheless, discernible improvements in the case of selected settlements as well as increased security of tenure among the residents of low-income settlements. Similarly, in the Philippines, the national government encouraged innovative self-help approaches and upgrading strategies that led to some noted improvements in the living environment of the residents of Tondo.

Analysis of upgrading experiences in Colombia, Mexico, and Venezuela by Gilbert and Ward showed the relationship between the degree of political support for self-help approaches at the national level and the actual carrying out of development activities in "irregular" settlements.[12] Indeed, several policy periods in each of these countries could be identified based on changing support at the national level.

Political support at the local level is also crucial to the success of upgrading policies and programs. Communities with strong leadership committed to self-help approaches are more likely to be able to mobilize community resources, establish communication links with senior government officials, and motivate local residents to actively participate in planning and managing self-help activities. When there is a threat to the survival of the settlement, the residents and their leaders tend to be more actively involved in self-help-based shelter projects.

International Assistance

Assistance from international and donor organizations has also been an important factor in program implementation. As discussed in Chapter 2, the World Bank assistance for shelter projects has increased substantially since the early 1970s. UNICEF has been playing an active role in providing assistance for basic social services to the urban poor. Other agencies that have also assisted in shelter projects have included the Asian Development Bank and the U.S. Agency for International Development (USAID).

Financial assistance from the World Bank has led to increased allocation of funds to such projects from concerned governments and has also contributed to increased realization among planners and policymakers of the need for clarity and consistency in national policies. With the increased financial and technical support by the Bank, several cooperating governments have substantially increased their own administrative and financial support for implementing upgrading and sites-and-services projects.

Perhaps the most crucial role of any of these international agencies, particularly in the provision of social services, has been played by UNICEF. Major contributions of UNICEF are its advocacy of the "basic urban services" strategy, its provision of technical assistance to governments in designing and implementing upgrading projects, and its direct involvement in organizing and motivating poor urban communities and providing training to local officials and leaders.

UNICEF provided technical and financial assistance to seven of the ten projects analyzed in this study. The other three projects—Lahore Walled City, Dandora, and Chaani—were funded by the World Bank, although UNICEF input has been provided to some of the World Bank-assisted projects as well.

In 1982 UNICEF had specific programs in forty-three countries benefiting low-income urban populations. Experience shows that UNICEF-assisted programs are having a growing impact on government action. In the case of the Integrated Social Services project in Seoul, UNICEF provided the main link for interagency coordination. It provided 100 percent financial assistance for the Block Grants Project and 70 percent for the Lahore Katchi Abadis Project. In the case of Environmental Health and Community Development Project in Colombo, UNICEF provided a major portion of funding and assisted concerned implementing agencies in training health wardens, establishing community development committees, monitoring and evaluating community development activities, and providing basic amenities such as piped water, sanitary latrines, health education, and preschool education.

Social Structure and Perceptions

Experience shows that there are several other factors that affect the success or failure of upgrading policies and programs. If the residents perceive that there is a threat to the survival of their squatter settlement, they are more likely to act collectively and cooperate with implementing agencies. Where the squatters are more homogeneous, they are more likely to cooperate with implementing agencies in mobilizing community resources and paying a portion of the cost of infrastructure and community facilities. Adequacy of information and training affect the perceptions of communities about the shelter project, and, consequently, the extent of their cooperation with the project staff.

Political Structures and Styles

Upgrading self-help approaches are also affected by political structures and styles. While it is difficult to establish a relationship between a regime type and granting security of tenure to squatters, one trend observed is for military governments or military-backed regimes to take significant steps to provide security of tenure to squatters, as has been the case in Pakistan (during the late 1970s) and Indonesia, respectively. Such regimes have sought to grant security of tenure and provide basic urban services, among other reasons, to gain more political legitimacy. Populist regimes tend to mobilize and politicize the urban poor populations, especially during an election period.

Resource Constraints

Where resources at the national level are scarce, the government allocation for upgrading and sites-and-services projects tends to be limited. Countries with low income levels (such as India, Sri Lanka, or Kenya) are not able to allocate sufficient government funds to provide basic urban services. The situation becomes worse in situations in which, because of scarcity of resources, poor urban settlements are bypassed and major government investments are made to improve infrastructure and services in middle- and high-income settlements.

CRITICAL FACTORS IN PROJECT IMPLEMENTATION

Upgrading and sites-and-services projects analyzed in this book have been implemented in different social, economic, administrative, and political conditions. To varying degrees, each of these projects has elements of success and failure, and Table 9.2 presents a summary of some of the significant factors that affected successes or failures of the projects. Despite differences among the countries, several critical factors, listed follows, seem to have affected program implementation in most cases:

1. the degree of involvement of the local community in planning and managing projects;
2. the extent of political and financial support at the national level for upgrading and self-help approaches;
3. innovative and committed leadership at the agency level;
4. the extent to which the interagency coordination is effective;
5. the acquisition of land for shelter and services;
6. the role of the implementing agency in organizing and motivating communities;
7. flexibility of building standards and codes;
8. the support of local political leaders;
9. the existing community management capacity;
10. the extent of community support for the project;
11. technical and financial support and advocacy by international organizations such as UNICEF.

Table 9.2
Summary of Critical Factors in Implementing Upgrading and Sites-and-Services Projects

Project	Critical Factors
Nadi Project, Kuala Lumpur	Multi-agency committee for coordinating activities of over 20 agencies Communally-based political parties as the main channel for patronage and mobilization in a plural society UNICEF technical assistance and advocacy Generous government financial support during the initial phase The degree of the interest of the Secretary-General of the Ministry of Federal Territory
Lahore Walled City Project	Single agency dominant style of implementation Lack of formal channels for community participation in project activities Financial assistance by the World Bank Semiautonomous nature of the lead implementing agency
Integrated Social Services Project, Seoul	Interagency coordination through workshops and review meetings The role of training and research institutions in mobilizing community resources and support The establishment of Community Development Committee to facilitate community participation The provision of relief services to the disadvantaged groups Technical support of UNICEF
Lahore Katchi Abadis Project	Active community participation in project activities Delays in acquisition of land for community halls and vocational training centers Financial assistance and advocacy by UNICEF Political support for upgrading at national and regional levels Financial and technical support and advocacy by UNICEF
Environmental Health and Community Development Project, Colombo	Active role of Health Wardens in motivating communities The establishment of Community Development Committees to serve as communication link between project staff and residents The creation of formal structure for interagency coordination after initial difficulties The relatively higher level of literacy and awareness among the residents UNICEF technical assistance and advocacy
Dandora Community Development Project	The organization and motivation of project participants by the implementing agency Permitting project participants to sublet some rooms to increase their income

Table 9.2 *continued*

Project	Critical Factors
Dandora (cont'd)	The establishment of neighborhood groups for self-help activities The suitability of the project location Financial assistance by the World Bank Interagency conflict concerning building standards and codes
Chaani Upgrading and Services Project	The lack of an adequate beneficiary organization and participation Delays in land acquisitions and payment of compensation Delays in recruitment of staff and selection of contractors Dissatisfaction of project participants due primarily to delayed issuance of letters of allotment
Olaleye-Iponri Slum Upgrading Project	Support of the local elders and other community leaders The demonstrative effect of initial activities on motivating people Representation of all community groups Political support by the Lagos State Government The delineation of responsibilities of the implementing agencies
Surabaya Block Grants Project	The involvement of too many agencies and layers of government Flexibility of approach adopted in selecting activities for funding The involvement of community leaders in choice of locations and selection of beneficiaries Limited management capacities of community leaders
Hyderabad Urban Community Development Project	The flexibility of approach in order to respond to specific needs of communities Mobilization of community's support and resources for project activities Innovative, well-trained, and committed project staff including community workers Effective horizontal and vertical coordination in mobilizing internal and external resources The establishment of basic linkages in development process such as linking communities with voluntary organizations and financial institutions The construction of self-help houses

Source: Compiled by the author.

NOTES

1. Kayila, "Improving Urban Settlements for the Poor."

2. See, among others, Sami Mustafa, "Orangi Pilot Project: A Case Study in Local Participation and Community Development" (Unpublished manuscript, Karachi, 1984), and Akhtar Hamid Khan, "Special Report on Orangi Project," *Pakistan and Gulf Economist* (Karachi, 11 June 1983).

3. For a more detailed discussion on this issue, see, among others, David C. Korten and Felipe B. Alfonso, eds., *Bureaucracy and the Poor: Closing the Gap* (West Hartford, CT: Kumarian, 1983).

4. For a more detailed analysis, see G. Shabbir Cheema, "Introduction," in G. Shabbir Cheema, ed., *Institutional Dimensions of Regional Development* (Singapore: Maruzen Asia, 1981).

5. Tilakaratna, Hettige, and Karunaratna, "Environmental Health and Community Development Project," pp. 13–20.

6. Kayila, "Improving Urban Settlements for the Poor."

7. For a more detailed discussion on this, see G. Shabbir Cheema, "Administrative Responses to Urbanization in Western Malaysia," *Journal of Administration Overseas* 16:4 (October 1977).

8. Suyono, "Kampung Improvement Programme: An Indonesian Experience," in Yeung, *A Place to Live*, pp. 171–84.

9. United Nations Centre for Regional Development, "Expert Group Meeting on Policy Issues in Urban Services for the Poor" (Nagoya: UNCRD, 1985).

10. Malhotra, *Managing Urban Development*, p. 162.

11. Ibid., pp. 163–64.

12. Gilbert and Ward, "Community Participation."

10

CONCLUSIONS AND
IMPLICATIONS FOR ACTION

During the past three decades, the number of the urban poor, and, consequently, deficiencies in urban shelter and services in developing countries,
have increased rapidly. The access of the urban poor to shelter and services
has been constrained by their low income level; by, in some cases illegal,
occupation of land that excludes them from government services, lack of
adequate community participation in delivery systems of municipal governments and semiautonomous development authorities; and by the govern-
ment-imposed building standards and codes that increase cost. Furthermore,
the poor are usually not effectively organized to safeguard their legitimate
interests; political will on the part of policymakers and planners to intervene
on their behalf is weak; and administrative structures and procedures are
usually biased against them.

Governments in developing countries have used four interrelated approaches to provide shelter and services to the urban poor: on-site upgrading, sites-and-services schemes, granting security of tenure to residents of
squatter settlements, and providing subsidized low-income housing. International organizations such as the World Bank and UNICEF have attempted
to supplement government actions by providing financial and technical assistance and advocating participatory self-help approaches. Five phases in
the evolution of public policies concerning urban shelter and services could
be identified: (1) clearance and forced relocation of squatters; (2) low-
income housing schemes followed by slum clearance; (3) the provision of
minimum services for existing slums and squatter settlements; (4) the extension of tenure security and physical upgrading; and (5) the recognition

of the legitimate role of slums and squatter settlements in urban development.

During the last two decades, governments have launched several upgrading and sites-and-services projects. The implementation of ten of these projects has been analyzed in this book. The evolution of the selected projects shows that they were responses to the failure of conventional approaches to meeting urban shelter and services deficiencies. Experience shows that several agencies at various levels are involved in project formulation, allocation of funds, carrying out of project activities, and monitoring and evolution. While implementing agencies have adequate technical skills, their capacity to work effectively with poor urban communities is limited. Mechanisms for interagency coordination to implement shelter projects are weak. In most cases, linkages of implementing agencies with program beneficiaries are based on the top-down approach.

Studies show a variety of modes of community participation in upgrading projects, including identification of community needs, choice of location of services, implementing of agencies and beneficiaries, selection of leaders, control over allocation of project resources, mobilization of community resources, and monitoring and evaluation of projects. In practice, community participation is greater in choice of locations, beneficiaries, and community leaders and minimal in mobilization and allocation of resources and choice of implementing agencies. Factors that have been found to be crucial for community participation include strong local leadership, smallness of the unit, the extent of threat to the survival of the settlement, and the provision of adequate framework by the government for community participation. Other factors are homogeneity of the community, diversified and integrated nature of project activities, information flows and training, and the extent of service deficiencies.

Financing, cost recovery, affordability, and replicability are crucial issues in provision of shelter and services. Though increasing efforts are being made at international, national, and community levels to mobilize resources for upgrading settlements, resources available for such projects are still scarce vis-à-vis the magnitude of the problem. Furthermore, the estimation of affordability levels has been difficult methodologically; the rigidity of building codes and housing standards has increased the cost of shelter and services; and replicability of government-initiated programs has been constrained due largely to cost-recovery problems.

The urban poor have inadequate access to land for shelter and services because the supply of serviced land has not kept pace with rapidly increasing demand and because of the high cost of land in large cities. Where they illegally occupy land, they do not have sufficient security of occupation and are usually not provided with basic services. Governments in developing countries have undertaken, with varying degrees of success, several policy measures to make land more accessible to the urban poor. These have included controlling land use, limiting landownership, granting the security of land occupation and tenure to squatters and slum dwellers, taxing land, regulating land transfer, and acquiring and banking public land. Experience shows, however, that controls on land use and landownership have been extremely difficult to enforce; that the implementation of land acquisition and banking has been delayed; and that granting security of land occupation has been more complex than was anticipated, particularly where it is tied to the recovery of some cost of infrastructure and community facilities.

Preliminary analysis of the efforts of urban shelter policies and programs leads to several conclusions. In most cases the performance of shelter projects in terms of achieving physical objectives has been significant. However, in terms of accessibility to target populations, the results of these policies and projects have been mixed. Usually beneficiaries of government-initiated programs have tended to represent medium-income groups rather than the poorest urban households. Shelter projects have usually led to improvements in housing in low-income settlements because of direct investments by government agencies as well as by the communities. The other effects are that attempts to involve the informal sector in service provision have been less than successful; that these projects have been conducive to employment and income generation; and that replicability of these projects is still constrained by the low level of cost recovery and low implementation capacities.

The implementation and effects of upgrading, sites-and-services, and other self-help approaches has depended upon several factors. Among these are the ability of the implementing agencies to work with poor urban communities; the extent of community participation in project planning and management; and the degree of financial and political support at the national and local levels. The success of these has also depended upon interagency coordination and complementarity of action; clarity and consistency of national policies; degree of government emphasis on land acquisition, security of tenure, access to credit for the poor; assistance of international agencies such as the World Bank and UNICEF; and the modes of service delivery.

IMPROVING THE IMPLEMENTATION OF SHELTER POLICIES

The identification of policy actions needed to provide urban shelter and services in developing countries is difficult because of variations in their administrative and political processes, their socioeconomic structures and because of a lack of adequate comparative data. Yet, experiences and approaches discussed in this book point to several areas in which policy actions are needed to increase the access of the urban poor to shelter and services. Figure 10.1 presents the implementation strategies for this purpose.

Figure 10.1
Implementation Strategies for Urban Shelter Policies and Programs

Performance
and Impact

Interorganizational Relationships

- interagency coordination
- public-private sector cooperation
- clarity and simplicity of procedures

Beneficiary Organization and Participation

- training community leaders
- establishment of community development committees
- participation in need identification, and choice
  of location and beneficiaries
- control over project resources
- participation in monitoring and evaluation

Capabilities and Resources of Implementing Agencies

- technical capabilities and human relation skills
- interaction and communication with residents
- innovative leadership in the agency
- personnel structures and practices
- adequacy of financial resources
- political support for shelter policies
- training urban managers

Contents of Policies

Security of land tenure
Cost recovery
Land acquisition
Identification of the
  urban poor
Use of informal service
  sector
Building codes and
  standards
Access to credit

Granting Security of Land Tenure

Granting security of land occupation and tenure is a prerequisite to the success of any upgrading effort. Past actions by governments—eviction, relocation to new sites, upgrading without titles, community development—have not resolved the issue of land tenure. Though the means of creating security and stability in land occupation will differ among countries, several approaches have been successfully implemented and, therefore, their relevance in different contexts needs to be examined. These include land readjustment, sale of land to squatters through a national mortgage bank, and the provision of dual systems of ownership, that is, community ownership of land and family ownership of dwellings. Other approaches are sites-and-services schemes and the legitimization and improvement of existing squatter settlements through issuance of leases to squatters with or without payments.

Improving Cost Recovery

The recovery of at least a portion of the cost of a shelter project is needed to ensure its replicability and sustainability. Some of the actions that could lead to the improvement of cost recovery include reducing the level of rate of repayment by excluding the cost of land and infrastructure; selecting those project participants who have the required income level and the capacity to pay; and making collection machinery more effective by providing necessary information to participants, identifying sanctions for defaulters and incentives for those who pay regularly, and simplifying collection procedures. Furthermore, communities and their leaders should be actively involved in the process of cost recovery. Also significant is the "political will" on the part of the government to enforce cost-recovery regulations and procedures.

Improving the Supply of Access to and Land for Housing the Poor

There are serious shortages of land in cities of developing countries, particularly for housing the urban poor. Rising land prices and land speculation practices are driving up the cost of urban shelter and services to the point where the poor cannnot afford them. This necessitates intervention in the regulation of land supply and the enforcement of land use planning and controls. The supply of land can be improved through an assessment of the capability of the private sector; regulation of, and the provision of, incentives for informal subdivision; introduction of cost ceilings for land subdivisions; and the introduction of cooperative land development schemes. Other possible measures to improve the supply of land for the urban poor are compulsory acquisition of land by the government, appropriation of public land, and the exchange of privately owned land on the fringe of the city for plots in alternative locations. The government's need to legitimize and improve existing land settlements through granting land tenure and integration of these settlements with processes of urban development; to increase their participation in land development; and to finance the development of land for housing the poor.

Strengthening the Capability of Public Agencies to Implement Projects

Experience shows that in addition to technical skills, personnel of implementing agencies should have adequate human relations skills in order to be able to work effectively with the poor urban communities. Training programs should be designed to reorient government officials and to improve their skills in communicating effectively with urban communities. Innovative leaders in the lead implementing agencies should be identified and they should be provided with incentives and career rewards associated with their positive response to programs affecting the urban poor. Other measures needed to strengthen the capability of implementing agencies include: eliminating rigid personnel regulations that discourage innovation, reducing political intervention in recruitment and promotion, and decentralizing financial authority to the regional and local levels of government and administration.

Identifying the Urban Poor

Effective policies for increasing access to urban shelter and services require the identification of the socioeconomic characteristics of different groups of poor more precisely. Because the urban poor are usually heterogeneous, the successful provision of urban services depends in part on the ability of governments and nongovernmental organizations to tailor programs to the specific needs of such different groups as rural migrants, the employable poor, the handicapped, and seasonal workers.

Promoting Public-Private Cooperation in Service Delivery

In some cases, cooperation between public and voluntary organizations can improve the poor's access to basic services. In order to be most effective, voluntary organizations require cooperation and support of central, municipal, and local government agencies. National and municipal governments should undertake several actions to promote such cooperation. Government community programs should be integrated with activities that are initiated through voluntary organizations. Local human and material resources should be utilized for service improvement. Communities and voluntary groups should be contacted only when concerned agencies can make firm commitments about financial and technical assistance. Other actions needed are training of community leaders and continued maintenance of service provided to communities through government programs.

Increasing Financial Support for Shelter and Services

Because there are many deficiencies in urban shelter and services for the poor in developing countries, the allocation of financial resources from the government needs to be substantially increased. Experience shows that the successful implementation of self-help approaches requires continuous financial assistance from the government. Residents of slums and squatter settlements are characterized, by among other things, low income levels and weak organizational and management capacity. The cost of urban shelter and services has, during the past three decades, increased to a degree that is beyond the affordability levels of the disadvantaged groups. Under such circumstances, some form of subsidy to meet the basic needs of the poor and to supplement voluntary efforts of local communities is inevitable.

Special attention should be given to self-help approaches—sites-and-services, on-site upgrading, basic housing—though which families build and gradually improve their dwelling units as their incomes increase. Public sector institutions can assist communities self-help efforts, by providing low-cost loans to households to enable them to upgrade basic dwellings or to purchase land on which to build their houses and by providing basic infrastructure and utilities that must be extended from an existing network.

Ensuring Community Participation

Several actions are needed to ensure active community involvement in decision making at the local level and in the implementation and benefits of upgrading and sites-and-services programs. These include regular dialogues between government functionaries and the community before the community needs are identified; training concerned government officials in communication skills and participatory approaches; changing planning procedures to facilitate bottom-up planning; and community involvement in the choice of location of services and program beneficiaries. Community participation is facilitated when the government encourages the establishment of community development committees and the training of community leaders; when financial and administrative authority is decentralized and communities are given greater control over allocation of project funds and mobilization of community resources; when communities and their leaders are provided with more information about shelter projects; and when communities are given direct responsibility to carry out at least some of the activities and to monitor and evaluate the results of the project. Finally, governments should provide a conducive national framework for community participation by tolerating conflicts that inevitably result from local organization and encouraging the growth of such local representative institutions as local governments and nongovernmental organizations.

Improving Interagency Coordination

Policies and programs aimed at providing shelter and services to the poor require many organizations with different resources, skills, objectives, and procedures. Their effective implementation, therefore, depends partly upon the effectiveness of interagency coordination. Actions needed to facilitate interagency coordination include creation and maintenance of open systems of communication and exchange of information; delineation of agency responsibilities; standardization of rules and procedures for implementation; and delegation of adequate authority to the coordinating agency. Interagency coordination can also be improved through the use of informal channels, through the establishment of a coordinating committee consisting of representatives of each implementing agency, and through direct involvement of concerned political leaders.

Mobilizing Resources from Communities and the Informal Housing Sector

There is a tremendous potential for mobilization of resources from urban communities and the informal housing sector. Many approaches and strategies have been successfuly utilized and their relevance and applicability should be examined in different contexts. Where feasible, attempts should be made to recover a portion—even though it may be small—of the cost of infrastructure from residents. Programs and projects that have a greater potential for cost recovery and replicability should be given preference. Voluntary savings schemes such as housing lotteries, demand and time deposits, and contractual savings should be encouraged. Formal financial institutions should be flexible in their approaches and methods in order to mobilize resources from informal financing arrangements such as individual family, family contacts, rotating credit systems, savings clubs, religious and charitable groups, labor and credit unions, and local social and political associations. Policy actions needed to encourage private savings through informal channels include ensuring perceived security of tenure, providing access to urban land at an affordable price, initiating flexible payment procedures that accommodate seasonal income fluctuations; and building counseling systems to mobilize community resources. Governments could also attempt to improve recovery of loans from the beneficiaries, to establish cooperatives for collective ownership of land that can be used as collateral for increased access to credit, and to tax development gains on vacant land.

Modifying Building Codes and Standards

Experience shows that in most cases building codes and standards need to be modified to keep shelter projects within the affordability range of the urban poor. Possibilities include reducing plot size, simplifying dwelling designs, and providing cheaper, indigenous materials at subsidized prices. Governments could also lower sanitation standards and allow mixed use of land for housing and commercial activities. These measures would increase housing production, reduce the cost of housing units, and make land use more efficient.

Training Urban Managers

The provision of urban shelter and services also requires adequate training of three groups of urban managers: (1) concerned government leaders and civil servants from the national government, local governments, program management, and field offices; (2) leadership and staff of nongovernmental organizations and nonprofit groups; and (3) formal and informal community leaders. These groups have different roles and functions and the content and the methodology of their training would, therefore, be different. Training of government officials should be aimed at reorienting them to a posture of support to local communities and enhancing their human relations skills to work effectively with the poor communities. Managers from the other two groups should be trained in the processes of planning, implementing, monitoring, and evaluating upgrading projects and other self-help approaches. Government officials and community leaders should have a firm knowledge of urban basic services approaches and of appropriate methods of tools to adapt the approach to the conditions of individual countries.

BIBLIOGRAPHY

Abrams, Charles. *Housing in the Modern World: Man's Struggle for Shelter in the Urbanizing World.* London: Faber & Faber, 1964.

Abueva, J. "Administrative Culture and Behavior and Middle Civil Servants in the Philippines." In *Development Administration in Asia*, edited by Edward W. Weidner. Durham, N.C.: Duke University Press, 1970.

Ahmed, Viqar. "Lahore Walled City Upgrading Project." Nagoya: United Nations Centre for Regional Development, 1984. Mimeo.

———. "Managing Urban Development: Focus on Services for the Poor." Nagoya: UNCRD, 1984. Mimeo.

———. "Policy Issues in Urban Shelter and Services for the Poor." Nagoya: UNCRD, 1985. Mimeo.

Ahsan, Feroza. "Provision of Services to the Urban Poor: A Case Study of Lahore Katchi Abadis." Nagoya: UNCRD, 1984. Mimeo.

Andrews, Frank M., and George W. Phillips. "The Squatters of Lima: Who They Are and What They Want." *Ekistics* 31, no. 183 (February 1974).

Angel, Shlomo et al., eds. *Land for Housing the Poor.* Singapore: Select Books, 1983.

Angel, Shlomo, and Stan Benjamin. "Seventeen Reasons Why the Squatter Problem Can't be Solved." *Ekistics*, 242 (January 1976).

Anthony, Harry A. *The Challenge of Squatter Settlements with Special Reference to the Cities of Latin America.* Vancouver: University of British Columbia Press, 1979.

Aportadera, Arturo D. "Bagong Lipunan Sites and Services Program: the Philippine Experience in Rural Housing and Development." In *A Place to Live: More Effective Low Cost Housing in Asia*, edited by Y. M. Yeung. Ottawa: International Development Research Centre, 1983.

Asian Development Bank. *Financing of Low Income Housing.* Manila: ADB, 1983.

Bamberger, Michael et al. *Evaluation of Sites and Services Projects: The Evidence from El Salvador.* World Bank Staff Working Paper no. 549. Washington, D.C.: World Bank, 1982.

Bamberger, Michael, Bishwapura Sanyal, and Nelson Valverde. *Evaluation of Sites and Services Projects: The Experience from Lusaka, Zambia.* World Bank Staff Working Paper no. 548. Washington, D.C.: World Bank, 1982.

Baross, P. "Four Experiences with Settlement Improvement Policies in Asia." In *People, Poverty and Shelter: Problems of Self-Help Housing in the Third World,* edited by R. J. Skinner and M. J. Rodell. London: Methuen, 1983.

Beier, George, Anthony Churchill, Michael Cohen, and Bertrand Renaud. "The Task Ahead for the Cities of Developing Countries." *World Development* 4, no. 5, 1976.

Bird, Richard. *Intergovernmental Fiscal Relations in Developing Countries.* World Bank Staff Working Paper no. 304. Washington, D.C.: World Bank, 1978.

Breese, Gerald, ed. *The City in the Newly Developing Countries.* Englewood Cliffs, N.J.: Prentice-Hall, 1969.

Bromley, R. "Introduction—The Urban Informal Sector: Why Is It Worth Discussing?" *World Development* 6 (1978).

Bromley, R., ed. "The Urban Informal Sector: Critical Perspectives." *World Development* 6, no. 9/10 (1978).

Bryant, C. "Squatters, Collective Action, and Participation: Learning from Lusaka." *World Development* 8 (1980).

Bryant, C., and Louise White. *Managing Development in the Third World.* Boulder, Colo.: Westview Press, 1982.

Buick, Barbara. *Squatter Settlements in Developing Countries: A Bibliography.* Canberra: The Australian National University Press, 1975.

Burgess, Rod. "Petty Commodity or Dweller Control? A Critique of John Turner's Views on Housing Policy." *World Development* 6, no. 9/10 (1978).

Cheema, G. Shabbir, ed. *Managing Urban Development: Services for the Poor.* Nagoya: UNCRD, 1984.

————. *Reaching the Urban Poor: Project Implementation in Developing Countries.* Boulder, Colo.: Westview Press, 1986.

Cheema, G. Shabbir, and Dennis A. Rondinelli, eds. *Decentralization and Development: Policy Implementation in Developing Countries.* Beverly Hills, Calif: Sage Publications, 1983.

Cohen, Michael A. "The Challenge of Replicability: Towards A New Paradigm for Urban Shelter in Developing Countries." *Regional Development Dialogue* 4, no. 1 (Spring 1983).

————. "Replicating Urban Shelter Programs: Problems and Challenges." In *Urban Services in Developing Countries: Public and Private Roles in Urban Development,* edited by Dennis A. Rondinelli and G. Shabbir Cheema. London: Macmillan Press, forthcoming.

Cornelius, W. A. *Politics and the Migrant Poor in Mexico City.* Stanford: Stanford University Press, 1975.

Cousins, William J., and Catherine Goyder. *Changing Slum Communities.* New Delhi: Manohar, 1979.

Davidson, Forbes, and Geoff Payne, eds. *Urban Projects Manual: A Guide to Preparing Upgrading and New Development Projects Accessible to Low Income Groups.* Liverpool: Liverpool University Press, 1983.

Dietz, Henry A. *Poverty and Problem Solving under Military Rule: The Urban Poor in Lima.* Austin: University of Texas Press, 1980.

Doebele, William A., ed. *Land Readjustment: A Different Approach to Financing Urbanization.* Lexington, Mass.: Lexington Books, 1982.

Drakakis-Smith, D. W. *Urbanization, Housing and the Development Process.* London: Croom Helm, 1981.

Dunkerley, Harold B., ed. *Urban Land Policy: Issues and Opportunities.* New York: Oxford University Press, 1983.

Dwyer, D. J. *People and Housing in Third World Cities: Perspectives on the Problem of Spontaneous Settlements.* New York and London: Longman Group Ltd., 1975.

Economic Commission for Asia and the Pacific (ESCAP). *Land Policies in Human Settlements.* New York: United Nations, 1985.

EsCAP. *See* Economic Commission for Asia and the Pacific.

Feldman, K. "Squatter Migration Dynamics in Davao City, Philippines." *Urban Anthropology* 4 (1975).

Gilbert, Alan, and Josef Gugler. *Cities, Poverty and Development: Urbanization in the Third World.* Oxford: Oxford University Press, 1982.

Gilbert, Alan, and Peter Ward. "Community Action by the Urban Poor: Democratic Involvement, Community Self-help or a Means of Social Control." *World Development* 12, no. 8 (August 1984).

————. "Community Participation in Upgrading Irregular Settlements: The Community Response." *World Development* 12, no. 9 (September 1984).

Goel, H. R. "Indian Experience in Managing Services for the Urban Poor." Paper presented to the International Seminar on Managing Urban Development, Seoul, 20–23 November 1984.

Grimes, Orville F. *Housing for Low Income Urban Families: Economics and Policy in the Developing World.* Baltimore: The Johns Hopkins University Press, 1976.

Grindle, Merilee S., ed. *Politics and Policy Implementation in the Third World.* Princeton, N.J.: Princeton University Press, 1980.

Gunasekera, H. M. "Management of Services for the Poor in the Urban Sector in Fiji." Nagoya: UNCRD, 1984. Mimeo.

HABITAT. *See* United Nations Centre for Human Settlements.

Hardoy, Jorge E., and David Satterthwaite. *Shelter: Need and Response.* Chichester, England: John Wiley, 1981.

Hashim, Shafruddin. "Policy Issues in Urban Services for the Urban Poor in a Plural Society: The Case of Malaysia." Nagoya: UNCRD, 1985. Mimeo.

Hassan, Riaz. "Problems of Access to Public Services for the Urban Poor." *Regional Development Dialogue* 6, no. 2 (1985).

Hollnsteiner, Mary Racelis. "People Power: Community Participation in the Planning of Human Settlements." *Assignment Children* 40. Geneva: UNICEF, 1977.

Honjo, M., ed. *Urbanization and Regional Development.* Singapore: Maruzen Asia, 1981.

Honjo, M., and T. Inoue, eds. *Urban Development Policies and Land Management— Japan and Asia.* Nagoya: Nagoya City, 1984.

Hosaka, Mitsuhiko. "An Overview on Indonesian Urban Service Management." Nagoya: UNCRD, 1984. Mimeo.

Ingle, Marcus D. "Implementing Development Programs: A State of the Art Review." Washington, D.C.: U.S. Agency for International Development, 1979. Mimeo.

Jere, Harrington. "Lusaka: Local Participation in Planning and Decision-making." In *Low-Income Housing in Developing World*, edited by Geoffrey K. Payne. Chichester, England: John Wiley, 1984.

Jimenez, E. *The Economics of Self-Help Housing: Theory and Some Evidence.* World Bank DEDRB, Urban and Regional Report no. 80–16. Washington, D.C.: World Bank, 1980.

Juppenlatz, Morris. *Cities in Transformation: The Urban Squatter Problem in the Developing World.* St. Lucia, Queensland, Australia: University of Queensland Press, 1970.

Kayila, James O. "Improving Urban Settlements for the Poor: Case Studies of Dandora and Chaani Projects in Kenya." Nagoya: UNCRD, 1984. Mimeo.

———. "Managing Urban Development: Kenya's Experience." Nagoya: UNCRD, 1984. Mimeo.

Keare, Douglas H., and Scott Parris. "Evaluation of Shelter Programs for the Urban Poor: Principal Findings." World Bank Staff Working Paper no. 547. Washington, D.C.: World Bank, 1982.

Kent, George. "Community-Based Development Planning." *Third World Planning Review* 3, no. 3 (August 1981).

Kitay, Michael G. *Land Acquisition in Developing Countries: Policies and Procedures of the Public Sector.* Boston: Oelgeschlager Gun and Hain Publishers, 1985.

Knight, Peter T., ed. *Implementing Programmes of Human Development.* World Bank Staff Working Paper no. 403. Washington, D.C.: World Bank, 1980.

Korten, David C., and Filipe B. Alfonso, eds. *Bureaucracy and the Poor: Closing the Gap.* West Hartford, Conn.: Kumarian Press, 1983.

Laquian, Aprodicio A. *Basic Housing: Policies for Urban Sites, Services, and Shelter in Developing Countries.* Ottawa: International Development Research Centre, 1983.

Lea, John P., and John M. Courtney. *Cities in Conflict: Studies in Planning and Management of Asian Cities.* Washington, D.C.: World Bank, 1985.

Lee, Michael. "Myth of Affordability." *Third World Planning Review* 7, no. 2 (May 1985).

Lim, Hong Hai. "Country Review for Malaysia." Nagoya: UNCRD, 1984. Mimeo.

———. "Nadi Integrated Social Services Programme, Kuala Lumpur." Nagoya: UNCRD, 1984. Mimeo.

Linn, Johannes F. *Policies for Efficient and Equitable Growth of Cities in Developing Countries.* World Bank Staff Working Paper no. 342. Washington, D.C.: World Bank, 1979.

Lloyd, P. *Slums of Hope? Shanty Towns of the Third World.* New York: Penguin, 1979.

Majumdar, T. K. "The Urban Poor and Social Change: A Study of Squatter Settlements in Delhi." In *The Indian City: Poverty, Ecology and Urban Development*, edited by A. de Souza. New Delhi: Manohar, 1978.

Makinwa-Adebusoye, Paulina. "Upgrading Olayeye-Iponri Slum in Lagos Metropolitan Area." Nagoya: UNCRD, 1984. Mimeo.

———. "Urban Poverty in Benin City, Nigeria: Interim Report." Nagoya: UNCRD, 1984. Mimeo.

Malhotra, D. D. *Managing Urban Development: Policy Issues in Urban Services for the Poor.* New Delhi: The Indian Institute of Public Administration, 1985.

Mangin, W. "Latin American Squatter Settlements: A Problem and a Solution." *Latin American Research Review* 2 (1967).

Marga Institute. "Housing in Sri Lanka." *Marga Research Studies* 6 Colombo: Marga Institute, 1976.

Marris, P. "The Meaning of Slums and Patterns of Change." *International Journal of Urban and Regional Research* 3 (1979).

Mazmanian, Daniel A., and Paul A. Sabatier, eds. *Effective Policy Implementation.* Lexington, Mass.: Lexington Books, 1981.

McAuslan, Patrick. *Urban Land and Shelter for the Poor.* London: Earthscan, 1985.

Minerbi, Luciano. "Beneficiary Organizations and Mobilization of Local Resources for the Delivery of Urban Services to the Poor." Nagoya: UNCRD, 1985. Mimeo.

Misra, Bijay. "Guidelines on Public Land Acquisition Methods and Procedures in Asia." Nairobi: United Nations Centre for Human Settlements, 1985. Mimeo.

Misra, R. P., and G. Shabbir Cheema. "Group Action and Popular Participation." In *Local Level Planning and Development*, edited by R. P. Misra. New Delhi: Sterling, 1985.

Montgomery, John D., ed. "Services for the Urban Poor: Issues in Implemention, Access and Participation." *Regional Development Dialogue* 6, no. 2 (January 1986).

———. "When Local Participation Helps." *Journal of Policy Analysis and Management* 3, no. 1 (1983).

———. "The Informal Service Sector as an Administrative Resource." Nagoya: UNCRD, 1985. Mimeo.

Montgomery, John D., Harold D. Lasswell and Joel S. Migdal, eds. *Patterns of Policy: Comparative and Longitudinal Studies of Population Events.* New Brunswick, N.J.: Transaction Books, 1979.

Moser, Caroline. "Evaluating Community Participation Projects." London: Development Planning Unit Working Paper no. 14. 1983. Mimeo.

Nakamura, Robert T., and Frank Smallwood. *The Politics of Policy Implementation.* New York: St. Martin's Press, 1980.

Nawawi, Mohammad A. "Political Participation, Basic Services and the Urban Poor in Developing Countries." In *Managing Urban Development:Services for the Poor*, edited by G. Shabbir Cheema. Nagoya: UNCRD, 1984.

Nelson, Joan A. *Access to Power: Politics and the Urban Poor in Developing Nations.* Princeton: Princeton University Press, 1979.

Nietied, Peter. *The Third Baldia Upgrading Evaluation Survey.* Amsterdam: Free University, 1984.

Oberland, H. Peter, ed. *Improving Human Settlements: Up with People.* Vancouver: University of British Columbia Press, 1976.

Pasteur, David. *The Management of Squatter Upgrading.* Westmead, England: Saxon House, 1979.

Payne, Geoffrey K., ed. *Low-Income Housing in the Developing World: The Role of Sites and Services and Settlement Upgrading.* Chichester, England: John Wiley, 1984.

———. *Urban Housing in the Third World.* Boston: Routledge & Kegan Paul, 1977.

Pearse, Andrew, and Matias Stiefel. *Debater's Comments on Inquiry in Participation: A Research Approach.* Geneva: United Nations Research Institute for Social Development, 1980.

Peattie, L. R. "Housing Policy in Developing Countries: Two Puzzles." *World Development* 7 (1979).

———. "Some Second Thoughts on Sites and Services." *Habitat International* 6, no. 1/2.

———. *The View From the Barrio.* Ann Arbor: University of Michigan Press, 1968.

Perlman, J. *The Myth of Marginality: Urban Poverty and Politics in Rio de Janeiro.* Berkeley: University of California Press, 1976.

———. "Strategies for Squatter Settlements: The State of Art as of 1977." In United Nations Centre for Human Settlements (HABITAT), *The Residential Circumstances of the Urban Poor in Developing Countries.* New York: Praeger, 1981.

Prakash, Ved. "Affordability and Cost Recovery: Selected Urban Services for the Poor." Nagoya: UNCRD, 1985. Mimeo.

———. "Financing Urban Development in Developing Countries." UNCRD Working Papers no. 82–86. Nagoya, Japan: UNCRD, 1982.

———. *Fiscal Policy and Resource Mobilization for Urban Development in Asia.* Manila: The Asian Development Bank, 1977.

Pressman, Jeffrey L., and Aaron Wildavsky. *Implementation.* Berkeley: University of California Press, 1973.

Redclift, M. R. "Squatter Settlements in Latin American Cities: the Response from Government." *Journal of Development Studies* 10 (1973).

Renaud, Bernard. *National Urbanization Policies in Developing Countries.* London: Oxford University Press, 1982.

———. *National Urbanization Policies in Developing Countries.* World Bank Staff Working Paper no. 347. Washington, D.C.: World Bank, 1971.

Report of the Expert Group Meeting on Policy Issues in Urban Services for the Poor, Nagoya, Japan, 13–17 August 1985.

Richards, P. J., and A. M. Thomson, eds. *Basic Needs and the Urban Poor.* London: Croom Helm, 1984.

Riggs, Fred W. *Administration in Developing Countries: The Theory of Prismatic Society.* Boston: Houghton Mifflin, 1964.

Rivkin, Malcolm D. "Some Perspectives on Urban Land Use Regulations and Control." In *Urban Land Policy Issues and Opportunities.* World Bank Staff Working Paper no. 283. Washington, D.C.: World Bank, 1978.

Rondinelli, Dennis A. "Projects as Instruments for Development Administration: A Qualified Defence and Suggestions for Improvement." *Public Administration and Development* 3, no. 4 (1983).

―――. *Secondary Cities in Developing Countries: Policies for Diffusing Urbanization*. Beverly Hills, Calif.: Sage Publications, 1983.

Rondinelli, Dennis A., and G. Shabbir Cheema. "Urban Service Policies in Metropolitan Areas: Meeting the Needs of the Urban Poor in Asia." *Regional Development Dialogue* 6, no. 2 (1985).

Rondinelli, Dennis A., and G. Shabbir Cheema, eds. *Urban Services in Developing Countries: Public and Private Roles in Urban Development*. London and New York: Macmillan, forthcoming.

Sada, P. O. "Residential Land-Use in Lagos: An Inquiry into the Relevance of Traditional Models." *African Urban Notes* 7 (1972).

Salinas, Willy Bezold, and Falvio Moreno Jimenez. "Integrated Basic Services for Lima's 'Young Towns.'" *Assignment Children 57/58*. Geneva: UNICEF, 1982.

Sarin, Madhu. *Slum and Squatter Settlements in the ESCAP Region*. Bangkok: Economic and Social Commission for Asia and the Pacific, 1980.

Sazanami, H., ed. *Metropolitan Planning and Management*. Tokyo:Japan Society for the Promotion of Science, 1982.

Schoorl, J. W., J. J. van der Linden, and K. S. Yap, eds. *Between Basti Dwellers and Bureaucrats: Lessons in Squatter Settlement Upgrading in Karachi*. Oxford: Pergamon, 1983.

Sembrano, M. A. et al. *Case Studies on Development of Slums, Squatter and Rural Settlements: The Philippines*. Quezon City: Ateneo de Manila University, Institute of Philippine Culture, 1977.

Shubert, Clarence. "Providing Urban Basic Services: A Comparative Analysis." Nagoya: UNCRD, 1984. Mimeo.

Skinner, R. J. and M. J. Rodell, eds. *People, Poverty and Shelter: Problems of Self-Help Housing in the Third World*. London: Methuen, 1983.

Smith, Thomas B. "The Policy Implementation Process." *Policy Sciences* 4 (1973).

Sugijanto, Soegijoke. "Managing the Delivery of Urban Services for the Poor in Indonesia: Case Study of KIP in Bandung." *Regional Development Dialogue* 6, no. 2. Nagoya: UNCRD, 1986.

Swan, Peter et al. *Management of Sites and Services Housing Schemes: The Asian Experience*. Chichester, England: John Wiley, 1983.

Tarigan, T., Soedarjo and Suakat Sacheh. "Block Grants Project in Surabaya." Nagoya: UNCRD, 1984. Mimeo.

Thornley, Jennifer R., and J. Brian McLoughlin. *Aspects of Urban Management*. Paris: Organization for Economic Cooperation and Development, 1974.

Tilakaratna, S., S. Hettige, and Wilfred Karunaratna. "Environmental Health and Community Development Project: A Case Study in the Slums and Shanties of Colombo." Colombo: UNCRD, 1985. Mimeo.

Turner, Alan, ed. *The Cities of the Poor: Settlement Planning in Developing Countries*. London: Croom Helm, 1980.

UNICEF. *See* United Nations Children's Fund.

United Nations. *Popular Participation in Decision-Making for Development*. New York: New York: United Nations, 1976.

―――. *Report of HABITAT United Nations Conference on Human Settlements*. New York: United Nations, 1976.

———. *Urban Slums and Squatter Settlements in the Third World.* New York: United Nations Centre for Housing, Building and Planning, 1975.

United Nations Centre for Human Settlements (HABITAT). *Community Participation in the Execution of Low-Income Housing Projects.* Nairobi: HABITAT, 1983.

———. *Human Settlement Finance and Management.* Nairobi: HABITAT, 1980.

———. *Human Settlement Policies and Institutions: Issues, Options, Trends and Guidelines.* Nairobi: HABITAT, 1984.

———. *Human Settlement Policy: Issues in the ESCAP Region.* Nairobi: HABITAT, 1984.

———. *Land for Human Settlements.* Nairobi: HABITAT, 1984.

———. *The Residential Circumstances of the Urban Poor in Developing Countries.* New York: Praeger, 1981.

———. *Small-Scale Building Materials: Production in the Context of the Informal Economy.* Nairobi: HABITAT, 1984.

———. *Survey of Slum and Squatter Settlements.* Dublin: Tycooly International, 1982.

United Nations, Department of Economic and Social Affairs. *Administrative Aspects of Urbanization.* New York: United Nations, 1970.

United Nations, Department of International Economic and Social Affairs. *Patterns of Urban and Rural Population Growth.* New York: United Nations, 1980.

United Nations Children's Fund (UNICEF). *Reaching Children and Women of the Urban Poor.* UNICEF Occasional Papers Series no. 3. New York: UNICEF, 1984.

———. *Report of the Community Participation Workshop.* New Delhi: UNICEF, 1981.

———. *Social Planning with the Urban Poor: New Government Strategies.* Geneva: UNICEF, 1982.

———. *Urban Basic Services: Reaching Children and Women of the Urban Poor.* New York: UNICEF, 1982.

United States Agency for International Development. *Annual Report Fiscal Year 1984.* Washington, D.C.: USAID, December 1984.

Van Meter, Donald, and Carl E. Van Horn. "The Policy Implementation Process: A Conceptual Framework." *Administration and Society* 6, no. 4 (February 1975).

Von Einsiedel, Nathaniel, and Michael L. Molina. "Policy Issues in Urban Services to the Poor: The Case of Metro-Manila." Nagoya: UNCRD, 1985.

Wahab, E. A. *The Tenant Market of Baldia Township.* Urban Research Working Paper. Amsterdam: Free University Press, 1984.

Walsh, Annemarie H. *The Urban Challenge to Government: An International Comparison of Thirteen Cities.* New York: Praeger, 1969.

Ward, Peter. "Self-help Housing in Mexico City." *Town Planning Review* 49, no. 1 (1978).

Weiner, M. *The Politics of Scarcity.* Chicago: University of Chicago Press, 1962.

Whang, In-Joung. "Management of Integrated Social Services for the Urban Poor: The Case of Bongchun-Dong, Seoul." Nagoya: UNCRD, 1984. Mimeo.

———. "Managing Public Services for the Urban Poor in Korea." Nagoya: UNCRD, 1984. Mimeo.

————. "Policy Issues in Managing Urban Services for the Poor: The Case of Squatter Improvement in Seoul, Korea." Nagoya: UNCRD, 1985. Mimeo.

White, Alastair. "Squatter Settlements, Politics and Class Conflict." University of Glasgow, Institute of Latin American Studies Occasional Papers no. 17. Glasgow: University of Glasgow, 1975.

————. "Why Community Participation: A Discussion of the Arguments." In *Assignment Children 59/60*. Geneva: UNICEF, 1982.

Williams, Walter, and Richard Elmore, eds. *Social Program Implementation*. New York: Academic Press, 1976.

World Bank. *Learning by Doing: World Bank Lending for Urban Development*. Washington, D.C.: World Bank, 1983.

————. *Shelter: Poverty and Basic Needs Series*. Washington, D.C.: World Bank, 1980.

————. *Urbanization*. Sector Working Papers. Washington, D.C.: World Bank, 1972.

————. *World Development Report 1980*. Washington, D.C.: World Bank, 1980.

Yap, Kioe-Sheng. *Leases, Land and Local Leaders: An Analysis of a Squatter Settlement Upgrading Programme in Karachi*. Amsterdam: Institute for Geographical Studies, Free University, 1982.

Yeh, S.H.K. and A. A. Laquian, eds. *Housing Asia's Millions: Problems, Policies, and Prospects for Low-Cost Housing in Southeast Asia*. Ottawa, Ontario: International Development Research Centre, 1979.

Yeung, Y. M., ed. *A Place to Live: More Effective Low-Cost Housing in Asia*. Ottawa: International Development Research Centre, 1983.

INDEX

abandoned properties, 135
Abrams, Charles, 33
absentee landowner, 115, 186
action research, 177
active involvement, defined, 80
ADB. *see* Asian Development Bank
administrative responses, types of, 72
adult literacy, 51
affordability: defined, 117; factors to gauge, 117; steps in assessing, 120–121
agencies, coordination role of, 65
Ahmed, Viqar, 89, 162, 167
aided self-help, concept of, 35
Alliance for Progress, 42
allottees, 68
Andres Perez, Carlos, 94
Angel, Shlomo, 35, 147, 152
architects, roles of, 64
artesian well, 123
Arumbakkam Project in Madras, India, 113, 127
Asian Development Bank, (ADB), 112, 167

Bagong Lipunan Community Association, 39

Bagong Lipunan Sites and Services (BLISS) program, 39
barangay, 95
barrio development, 93
Barrio Urbanization and Servicing, Department of, 93
bayanihan, 129
beneficiary organization, participation and, 10–11
benefits: participation in, 80; types of, 80
Benjamin, Stan, 35
bottom-up planning, 103
break-even policy, 169
building code concerns: density, 123; dwelling size and design, 122; materials, 122; mixed use, 123; plot size, 122; sanitation, 122–123
building codes, 121–123
building materials standards, 122
building standards, modification of, 201
Burgess, Rod, 34
Bustee welfare development committees, 87

Canadian International Development Agency (CIDA), 43

capital market, U. S., 113
Ceiling on Housing Property Law
    (1973), 144
centers of employment, land and, 134
Chaani Upgrading and Services Project
    (Kenya), 51, 68, 112, 159, 179
Cohen, Michael, 36, 130
collection procedures, effectiveness of,
    126
collective articulation, concept of, 153
Comilla Project (Bangladesh), 176
Common Amenities Board (CAB), 66,
    180
communal land laws, 136
communal participation, defined, 85
communal toilet, 123
communities: mobilization of resources
    from, 200–201; socioeconomic char-
    acteristics of, 84
community, heterogeneous, 96
Community Action, Department of, 93
community development committees
    (CDCs), 66, 88, 89, 90, 92, 99
community leaders, training of, 103,
    106
community organizers (COs), 87
community participation, 4, 79–106;
    constraints impeding, 84–85; de-
    fined, 81; ensuring, 199–200; factors
    conducive to, 95–102; implementa-
    tion and, 178–179; modes and
    forms of, 85–87; theory and practice
    of, 79; in urban shelter policies, 4
community resources, mobilization of,
    82–83, 103
competitive user's organization, 93
construction: through contractor, 129;
    through self-help, 129
cooperatives, establishment of, 4
cost recovery, 3; constraints on, 170;
    direct method, 124; enforcement of,
    128; factors determining, 124–126;
    improvement of, 197; indirect meth-
    ods, 124; performance of shelter
    projects and, 127; through sale of
    improved plots, 169; three methods
    of, 123–124
cost reduction, 82; role of state in, 72

Council of Elders, 90
Cousins, William J., 70, 87, 99
credit access, 184; implementation and,
    184
credit unions, as funding source, 114
crown land, 139

Dandora Community Development
    Project (Kenya), 51, 68, 92, 112,
    121, 123, 159, 168, 169, 170, 179
decentralization, 103 decision making,
    participation in, 80
Delhi Development Authority, 150
direct payment, cost recovery and, 123
diversification of projects, community
    participation and, 100-101
Dong Housing Renewal Club, 89
donor organizations, 187
dwelling size and design standards, 122

Economic Commission for Asia and
    the Pacific (ESCAP), 12
Einsiedel, Nathaniel, 102
emergency housing, defined, 26
eminent domain, 115
employment centers, municipal govern-
    ments and, 74
engineers, role of, 64
entrepreneurial experience, lack of in
    slum communities, 166
environmental degradation, 5
environmental factors, implementation
    and, 186–189
Environmental Health and Commu-
    nity Development Project (Col-
    ombo), 50–51, 64, 66, 68, 89, 95,
    101, 112, 164, 169, 179, 180, 182,
    188
equity-oriented programs, 79
evaluation, participation in, 80
expertise, increase in, 83

Federal District Constitution, 93
Federal Programme for Skill Develop-
    ment, 39
financial resources: adequacy of, 177–
    178; implementation and, 177–178
financing: long-term, 116; role of state

in, 72; schematic approach, 116; systemic approach, 116

flexibility of approach, community participation and, 98–99

freehold land, 139

funds: allocation of, 58; sources of, 111

Gilbert, Allan, 44, 86, 93, 94

Goel, H. R., 39

gotong royong, 129

government attitude, community participation and, 98

government bureaucracy, paternalistic attitude of, 85

government land, distribution of, 115

Goyder, Catherine, 70

HABITAT, 27

Habitat Conference (Vancouver), 133

Hassan, Riaz, 160

health, municipal governments and, 74

health wardens, 67, 68, 169

Herrera-Campins, 94

homogeneity of community, community participation and, 99

hostility, period of, 147

house construction, methods of, 127

household composition, as criterion in assessing affordability, 120

household life styles, 120

house improvement, income's positive relation to, 141

House-maid Self-Help Club, 8, 9

housing activities, citizen participation in, 86

Housing and Development Department (HDD), 176

Housing Guarantee Loans program, 43

housing lotteries, 114

Housing by People, 33

housing policy: self-helping, 34; viable, 33

housing problems, in Third World, 34

housing shortages, 22

housing standards, 121–123

Hyderabad Urban Community Development Project, 52–53, 63, 69, 71, 87, 98, 99, 100, 101, 111, 157, 176, 178, 181, 182

identification, with project, 83

implementation: compliance approach to, 7; defined, 7; factors influencing, 8, 10–11, 175–189; participation in, 80; political approach to, 7; role of state in, 72

implementing agencies, 10; capabilities of, 57–76, 175–177

income: as criterion in assessing affordability, 117–119; difficulties in estimating, 118; irregular sources of, 118; sources of in poor urban settlements, 118

income targeting, 121

individual participation, defined, 85

infant and child mortality, 50

informal sector: implementation and, 185; mobilization of resources from, 200–201; role of, 185; use of, 166

information flows, community participation and, 101

inner city slums, defined, 26

institutional credit, unavailability to urban poor, 115

Integrated Social Services Project (Seoul), 49–5O, 58, 63, 66, 89, 99, 158

integration of projects, community participation and, 10O–101

interagency coordination, 64–67; improvement of, 20O

international assistance, implementation and, 187–188

International Development Association (IBA), 128

interorganizational relationships, 8; factors influencing effectiveness of, 8; implementation and, 179–182

Junta, 93

jute lines, 137

Kampung Improvement Program (KIP), Indonesia, 40, 111, 123, 127, 137, 161, 170, 181

Karachi Development Authority
(KDA), 182
Karachi Municipal Corporation
(KMC), 128, 146, 182, 183
Katchi Abadi League, 167
Katchi Abadis projects, 50, 58, 64, 65,
70, 88, 97, 101, 102, 158, 169, 178,
179, 182, 183, 188
kelurahan, 95
Khan, Akhtar Hamid, 176
knowledge, increase in, 83
Korea Institute for Population and
Health, 63
Korea Institute for Research in Behav-
ioral Science, 63

Labor Development Authority (LDA),
50, 65, 69, 88, 158, 177
labor unions, as funding source, 114
Lahore Katchi Abadis Project, 50
Lahore Municipal Corporation, 65, 69,
71
Lahore Urban Development Programme, 49
Lahore Walled City Project, 49, 58,
68, 88, 98, 102, 112, 158, 179
laissez-faire policies, defined, 38
land: acquisition of by urban poor, 2–
3; as hedge against inflation, 134;
and houses, mixed use of, 123; illegal alienation of, 139; illegal occupation of, 28; pooling, 151–152;
transfer, 148; use controls, 133,
141–144; use patterns, 141
land access: improvement of, 197;
mechanisms for, 136–140
land acquisition: implementation and,
183–184; voluntary sale and, 149
land banking, 151
land market, intervention of public authorities in, 135
land occupation, patterns of, 136
land organizations, 167
landowners, as beneficiaries of shelter
projects, 165
land ownership: limits, 144–145; regulation by law, 144–145
land shortage, 134–136

land supply: articulation of, 135; processes of, 135
land taxation, 147–148; criteria used
in, 148
land tenure, 136; implications of, 145;
municipal governments and, 74; security of, 145–147
land tenure patterns, colonialism's effect on, 145
Land Use Decree, 143
Law on the Reform of Ownership of
Urban Land, 144–145
lead agencies: multilevel responsibilities
and, 58, 63; technical and managerial skills, 63–64
leadership: formal, 96; informal, 96
leases, long-term, 137, 141
legal refugee colonies, 137
Lim, Hong Hai, 63
local experiences, accumulation of, 84
long-term financing, 116
low-income housing, financing, 114
low-income level, 27
Lusaka Squatter Upgrading and Sites
and Services Project (Zambia), 92,
159
Lyari Slum Improvement Project in Karachi, Pakistan, 128

Mahotra, D. D., 162, 185
Malaysian Chinese Association (MCA),
69, 71
Malaysian Indian Congress (MlC), 69,
71
malnutrition, diseases linked to, 21
marginal land, 135
market groups, 92
masses, defined, 80
maximum housing standards, arguments against, 122
military-backed regimes, 188
Ministry of Federal Territory, 65, 71,
176
Molina, Michael L., 108
Mombosa project (Kenya), 123
Montgomery, John D., 74, 76
mortality, infant and child, 50

mother and child health (MJCH) centers, 158
municipal governments, loss of function of, 10
Municipal Health Department (MHD), 180
mutual aid, defined, 128

Nadi Integrated Social Services Project (Kuala Lumpur), 44, 48–49, 63, 65, 69, 71, 72, 87, 96, 111, 170
Nairobi City Council, 51
National Family Planning Board, 48–49
national policies: clarity and consistency of, 183; implementation and, 182–185
National Vocational Training Project, 39
native land, 139
Nawawi, Mohammed A., 85
needs, felt, identification of, 83
needs assessment, role of state in, 72
non-government organizations (NGOS), 37

off-site infrastructure, recovery costs of, 116
Olaleye-Iponri Slum Upgrading Project (Lagos), 52, 66, 72, 164
on-site infrastructure, recovery costs of, 116
Orangi Pilot Project (OPP), 167, 176
organizational participation, defined, 86
organizational responsibility chart, 65, 176
ownership, modern concept of, 136

panchayat raj, 129
participation: communal, 85; concept of, 79–81; defined, 80; diversification of community leadership and, 178; four types of, 80; individual, 85; organizational, 86; relational, 85–86
passive involvement, defined, 80

past collective actions, community participation and, 100
patron-client relationships, 93
perceptions, implementation and, 188
pit latrines, 123
planning, role of state in, 72
plot size standards, 122
policy evolution, stages in, 40–41
policy implementation, study of, 6–8
policy issues, 2–5
policymakers: lack of administrative will in, 29; lack of political will in, 29
policy and programs: evolution of, 33–53; impacts, 157–171
political associations, as funding source, 114
political structures, implementation and, 188
political support: implementation and, 186–187; projects and, 70-72
poor, exploitation of by rich, 81
poor urban settlements: characteristics of, 24–27; typologies of, 24–27
popular government, private sector and, 34
popular participation: defined, 80; four levels of, 81
Prakash, Ved, 111, 125
privately owned land, distribution of, 115
private ownership rights, vs. public control over land, 143
private savings, through informal channels, 114–115
private sector, popular government and, 34
program, defined, 6
program beneficiaries, linkage between government agencies and, 67
project(s): commitment to, 83; defined, 6; lack of agency coordination in, 65, 66, 67; single-purpose, 100
project activities, control and supervision of by community, 103
project beneficiaries, criteria for, 103
project implementation: community

participation in, 126; critical factors
in, 189
project personnel, weaknesses of, 63
property taxes, rise of as result of service improvements, 161
public agencies, strengthening capability of, 198
public education, demand for, 22
public funds, allocation of, 3
Public Health Act rules, 159
public housing rehabilitation programs, 161
public land acquisition, 148–150
public land reserves, 144
public safety, municipal governments and, 74
public sector shelter strategy, critical elements of, 114
public services, minimal access to by poor, 160

quality control, role of state in, 72

Rangsit Sites-and-Services Project (Thailand), 164
rapid urbanization, 10, 15, 21; consequences of, 1
recoverable costs, 112
relational participation, defined, 85–86
relational skills, lack of, 64
religious organizations, 92; as funding source, 114
relocation, 34
replicability, 130, 169–170; projects indicating high potential for, 171
research institutions, role played by, 58
resource constraints, implementation and, 189
resource contribution, 80
resource mobilization, 3; at international level, 113; at local level, 114; at national level, 113–114
restrictive policies, defined, 38
Rondinelli, Dennis, 7
Rural Community Development Programme, 63
Rural Urban Committee, 52

Sang Kancil Project (Kuala Lumpur), 71, 111
Sang Kancil Project (Kuola Lumpur), 39, 48
sanitation: municipal governments and, 74; standards, 122–123
Secretariat of Popular Promotion, 93
security of tenure, 133, 140, 170, 187; granting of, 197; implementation and, 183–184
selected projects, evolution of, 44–53
self-help: aided, 35; defined, 128; House-maid Club, 89; lane organizations, 167; mutual, 129
self-reliance, encouragement of, 99
Senegal Sites-and-Services Project, 159
service deficiencies, community participation and, 102
service delivery: modes of, 185; promotion of public-private cooperation in, 198–199
service-delivery systems, 28
services, extension of to all communities, 82
shack towns, government created, 25
shanty towns, 24
shelter: percentage of income spent for, 119; supply and demand of, 120
shelter package, cost of, 119–120
shelter policies, improving implementation of, 195, 197–201
shelter projects: accessibility to target populations and, 160–164; affordability of, 117; collection procedures and, 126; cost of land and, 126; dissatisfaction with, 159; employment and income generation in, 168–171; housing improvements and, 164–168; incompleted, 159; increasing financial support for, 199; physical achievements, 157–160; project implementation and, 126; selection of participants and, 126
significance of shelter, recognition of, 41–44
similar perceptions of needs, community participation and, 100
sites-and-services projects, 111–113

Skinner, R. J., 94
slum dwellers, increasing number of, 2
slums, defined, 27
Slum Upgrading Project, 66
smallness of unit, community participation and, 95–96
social associations, as funding source,
114
social structure, implementation and,
188
Social Welfare Centre, 63
sociopolitical hierarchies, internal, 84
spending patterns, as criterion in assessing affordability, 120
squatters, increasing number of, 2
squatter settlements, 24; defined, 27;
heterogeneous, 102
squatter settlement strategies: legalization and, 34; on-site upgrading and,
34
Squatter Upgrading Project (Lusaka,
Zambia), 101
standards, role of state in determination of, 72
strong leadership, community participation and, 96–97
subletting, 123
subsidies, minimization of, 116
Sungnam New Town Development
program, 89
supportive policies, defined, 38
Surabaya Block Grants Project (Indonesia), 52, 69, 90, 98
surcharge, cost recovery and, 123
survival threat, community participation and, 97

tacit recognition, 147
Tamil Nadu Housing Board, 113
tax revenues, cost recovery and, 124
technical expertise, of implementing
agencies, 176
temporary occupation licenses (TDL),
136
Third World, 110, 144; housing, 35;
housing problems, 34
Third World cities, 22, 142

Town and Country Planning Act
(1971), 142
transportation, municipal governments
and, 74
Turner, John, 33, 34, 86, 140

unemployment, 5
UNICEF-assisted activities, 67
United Malay National Organization
(UMNO), 69, 71
United Nations Centre for Human Set-
tlements (UNCHS), 12, 114
United Nations Centre for Regional
Development (UNCRD), 11, 12, 44,
86
United Nations Children's Fund (UNI-
CEF), 12, 36, 43, 44, 50, 51, 52, 58,
64, 66, 86, 89, 90, 97, 111, 112,
130, 169, 171, 187, 193, 195
United Nations Conference on Human
Settlements (1976), 35, 43
United States Agency for International
Development (USAID), 43, 113,
187; housing objectives of, 113
unsanitary neighborhoods, diseases
linked to, 21
upgrading projects, 111–113
urban, defined, 15
Urban Basics Services Approach, principles of, 36
urban community participation experiences: examples from Africa, 90–92;
examples for Asia, 87–90; examples
from Latin America, 93–95
Urban Development Authority (UDA),
64, 66, 180
Urban Development Committee, 66
urban growth, 16–19; future, 18–19;
large cities vs. small cities, 17; past
trends, 16–17
urbanization, and national planning,
110
urbanization patterns, future, 18
Urban Land Ceiling and Regulation
Act (1976), 144
urban land reform zone, 142
urban managers, training of, 201
urban migration: pull factors contrib-

uting to, 17; push factors contributing to, 17
urban poor, 15–29; characteristics of,
  21; childhood mortality and, 21;
  constraints on access of the, 27–29;
  fertility rates and, 21; identification
  of, 198; increase in, 193; median age
  and, 21; weak organization of, 29
urban population, rapid growth in, 1
urban poverty, 5; growing incidence
  of, 2; incidence of, 19, 21
urban projects, professional administrators and, 10
Urban Renewal Committee, 66
urban service deficiencies, governments
  and, 1
urban services: deficiencies in, 1, 21–
  22; optimal distribution of responsibilities for, 74, 76; public management styles for, 72, 74; standards
  for, 28–29
urban settlement, defined, 15
urban shelter policies: community participation in, 4; implementation of,
  6–8
urban shelter and services, increase in
  demand for, 5
urban transport, future requirements
  for, 22

Vila El Salvador (Lima), 83, 94, 100,
  159
Village Development Committee, 68

Ward, Peter, 86, 93, 94
Ward Development Committee, 92
Water and Power Development Authority (WAPDA), 65, 69
Water and Sanitation Authority, 65
water storage system, 123
water supply: demand for, 22; expansion of facilities, 37
Whang, In-Joung, 89–161
women's association, 92
World Bank, 12, 16, 19, 36, 42, 43,
  51, 58, 110, 111, 112, 117, 122,
  124, 127, 129, 130, 178, 187, 193,
  195; lending programs, 113
World Bank-assisted shelter programs,
  158, 168
World Bank loan, 113
World Bank Studies, 2

Yusof, Khairuddin, 65

Zambian United National Independence Party, 127
Zone One Tondo Organization
  (ZOTO), 146
zoning, effective use of, 142

ABOUT THE AUTHOR

G. SHABBIR CHEEMA is Development Administration Planner, United Nations Centre for Regional Development, Nagoya, Japan. He received his Ph.D. from the University of Hawaii and has taught at Government College, Pakistan, the University of Hawaii, and Universiti Sains Malaysia. His areas of interest include comparative public policy, regional and urban development planning, rural development, and community participation. He has undertaken field research in the People's Republic of China, Malaysia, and Pakistan. Dr. Cheema has coordinated numerous cross-national, comparative research projects on management aspects of rural, regional, and urban development and provided advisory services to governments in several developing countries. He has been consultant to the Asian Development Bank, United Nations Development Programme, and the Food and Agriculture Organization. He has published numerous articles in professional journals and books dealing with international development policy and urban and regional development planning. Dr. Cheema is also the author, co-author, or editor of twelve books and monographs on development policy, planning, and administration.